On Austrian Soil

On Austrian Soil

Teaching Those I Was Taught to Hate

Sondra Perl

State University of New York Press

The cover photo shows the Hungarian Monument to the Holocaust erected in
1964 at the Mauthausen Memorial Site at the Mauthausen Concentration Camp
on the outskirts of Linz, Austria.

Cover photo by Gert Fessler, used by permission.

Published by
State University of New York Press, Albany

For information, address the State University of New York Press,
90 State Street, Suite 700, Albany, NY 12207

Production by Judith Block
Marketing by Fran Keneston

Library of Congress Cataloging-in-Publication Data

Perl Sondra.
    On Austrian soil : teaching those I was taught to hate / Sondra Perl.
      p. cm.
    Includes bibliographical references.
    ISBN 0-7914-6389-3 (hardcover) — ISBN 0-7914-6390-7 (pbk.)
    1. Perl, Sondra—Relations with Austrian students.   2. Jews, American—
Austria—Innsbruck—Biography.   3. College teachers—United States—
Biography.   4. Jewish college teachers—Austria—Innsbruck—Biography.
5. Teaching—Case studies.   6. English language—Rhetoric—Study and
teaching.   7. Composition (Language arts)—Study and teaching (Higher)
8. Holocaust, Jewish (1939–1945)   9. Intercultural communication.
10. Students—Austria—Attitudes.   I. Title.

DS135.A93P497 2005
943.6'424004924073—dc22   2004007554

10 9 8 7 6 5 4 3 2 1

For Sara, Josh, Sam, and Cara
May you carry this legacy lightly

The author wishes to thank the following people and publishers for permission to reprint copyrighted material:

Thomas Lux for "The Voice You Hear When You Read Silently" published by *The New Yorker*, July 14, 1997. Reprinted by permission of Thomas Lux.

Cara Fessler for permission to print her photographs of Innsbruck buildings and monuments taken in 2002.

Yale University Press for four lines from Charlotte Delbo, Rosette C. Lamont, translator, from *Auschwitz and After*, 1995, p. 12. Reprinted by permission of Yale University Press.

The Rabbinical Assembly for the selection by Rabbi Cyrus Adler from *Sabbath and Festival Prayer Book*, 1946, p. 304. Reprinted by permission of the Rabbinical Assembly.

The Stadtarchiv/Stadtmuseum for two photographs of Innsbruck from *Innsbruck 1938–1945*. Reprinted by permission of the Stadtarchiv/Stadtmuseum, Innsbruck, Austria.

Portions of chapters 1 and 2 originally appeared as "Facing the Other: The Emergence of Ethics and Selfhood in a Cross-Cultural Writing Classroom" from *Narration as Knowledge: Tales of the Teaching Life*, edited by Joseph Trimmer, 1997. (Heinemann-Boynton/Cook, a subsidiary of Reed Elsevier Inc., Portsmouth, NH, 1997.) Copyright held by Sondra Perl.

The image of the Holocaust is *with us*—a memory which haunts, a sounding board for all subsequent evil—in the back of the mind . . . for all of us now living: we, the inheritors.

Terrence Des Pres, Treblinka, viii

ﻫ

We need to look closely at the border where our empathy ends; there our potential for cruelty begins.

Anne Roiphe, A Season for Healing, 21

Contents

Author's Note on Names and Language

The two families whose lives are intertwined in this book, Margret Fessler's and mine, are represented here by their real names. So, too, are Horst Schreiber, the Austrian historian; Susan Weil, the American professor at The City College of The City University of New York, who coordinated the master of arts program in New York; and Tanja Westfall, an American participant in the program, who also served as course coordinator in Innsbruck. Out of respect for privacy, I have changed the names and altered the descriptions of the other teachers who studied with me in Innsbruck. I have also changed the names of other faculty members from CUNY who are mentioned in passing.

The conversations included in this book all occurred. In order to recount them, I relied, often, on a journal I kept, but more often on memory, at best a faulty instrument. I have attempted to be faithful to what I understood at the time and what I still, years later, consider to be the intent and the emotional tone of each encounter, but I, like any writer of memoir, am neither omniscient nor free of bias. Any misrepresentations are my own. The written work of the Austrian teachers makes visible their remarkable facility with English. Aside from minor matters of punctuation, their letters, e-mail correspondence, and other writing, while excerpted, remain unedited.

Introduction:
The Road to Dialogue

It is 1996 when I stand, for the first time, on Austrian soil. My reaction to this simple act surprises me. Placing my feet on earth that carries the imprint of memory causes me to ask: Who am I? What has formed me? And what will happen when I find myself teaching those I have been taught to hate? For sitting before me in a classroom, I suspect, will be teachers whose parents cheered Hitler.

Will these teachers be any different from their parents, I wonder. If I tell them I am Jewish, will it affect how we work together? And more to the point, do I want to tell them? For despite a liberal upbringing, I carry within me a deep-seated prejudice: Austrians and Germans are evil. Underneath their culture and politics lies a capacity for cruelty unsurpassed in the world.

The setting for this story is the University of Innsbruck; the students, Austrian teachers of English enrolled in a master's degree program sponsored by The City University of New York. But *On Austrian Soil* is not just a teaching story. The walls of the classroom cannot contain it. For each time I return to Innsbruck, my questions become larger, the issues more challenging. My students, teachers themselves, come face-to-face with the question of their responsibility not only to the past but also to the future. I come face-to-face with my relationship to Judaism.

ે**ﻌ**

Until these trips, my life was neatly divided. For over twenty-five years, I taught writing and literature at The City University with little concern for religion. I saw myself as an agnostic, assimilated American Jew for even longer. In Austria, neither position would suffice. Standing on what had once been Nazi-occupied territory forced me to look hard at long-held assumptions, to confront divisions that would no longer hold—divisions in my own life, divisions among people.

I do not imagine that I would be telling these stories if I had not been a teacher in Austria. If I had traveled as a tourist I would have been content to hold on to my hatred. But then, I never would have traveled as a tourist to Austria. Born several years after the end of the Second World War, I absorbed what was in the air around me: American Jews must boycott German products; Germans are wicked; it could happen again. As far as I was concerned, Austrians were no different. Wasn't Hitler, after all, an Austrian?

As a Jew, I had no desire to challenge my childhood prejudice. But as a teacher, I could not do otherwise. For in my classroom I do my best to enact the values I hold dear: everyone in the class is welcome; everyone's story matters. I see my task, as teacher, to listen and to teach my students to do the same. I expect all of us to treat each person's work, each person's words, with respect.

But my years inside classrooms did not prepare me for the experience of teaching people I had been taught to hate. Nor had I ever needed to examine an equally unsettling sentiment: my ambivalence towards Judaism. Never before had I needed to ask what it meant for me to speak openly as a Jew. In Austria, I discovered that I had no choice.

≥●

The lessons I learned in Austria accompany me now as I stand on American soil. They are with me in my classroom in New York, when I teach those whose histories, backgrounds, ages, ethnicities, and religions differ from mine. They are with me every time I hear about a new slaughter, another terrorist attack, another suicide bombing. I am reminded then that hatred is rooted deeply in the soil that we call our own and in the families and cultures to which we give our allegiance; that prejudice is perpetuated by the stories we repeat to our children and whom they come to perceive as their age-old, lifelong enemies.

I hope this book will foster a public dialogue on what it means for the victims and perpetrators of atrocities—and for their families—

to speak, listen, and, most of all, write together of the agonizing legacies passed down to them. *On Austrian Soil* offers one example of what is possible when the inheritors of hatred turn towards one another in dialogue. It shows what it means in practice, both within and outside the classroom, to enact an ethics of education. It offers a pedagogy of hope.

When I first traveled to Austria, I did so as a teacher. But while there I also became a student. One of the lessons I learned is that a writing classroom offers those willing to grapple with unsettling issues a new place to stand, a place where prejudice can wither and empathy can be nourished. There is no teacher's guide for this journey: the road to dialogue is rocky and full of pitfalls. But it beckons me as no other ever has.

1

A Simple Invitation

When the phone rings one January morning in 1996, I have no inkling that the invitation I am about to accept will be the beginning of an odyssey. I hear only a voice at the other end of the line proposing a compelling piece of work.

Dr. Susan Weil, who coordinates a cross-cultural literacy program at The City College of The City University of New York, is inviting me to spend a few weeks in the summer teaching in Austria. There are eleven students, Susan tells me, two Americans and nine Austrians. All but one are practicing teachers of English. All are enrolled in a master's degree program in language and literacy at City College. But while the teachers receive their degrees from The City College of The City University of New York, they never actually attend classes in the States. The two- to three-week intensive courses are taught in Austria—in this case, Innsbruck—by City University faculty.

Quickly I take stock of my life. I am an English professor whose specialty is the teaching of writing. I've led teacher training institutes for over twenty years. Before I had children, I traveled every summer. But for the past twelve years, since the birth of my daughter, Sara, and twin sons, Josh and Sam, I've stayed close to home. The trip I make most frequently is to the pediatrician's office.

I'm tempted to accept. I have always dreamed of combining teaching with traveling. Working with teachers for whom English is a second language intrigues me. I am certain my husband will understand, and we have a babysitter we trust. I say yes on the spot.

It is only after I put down the phone that doubts begin to creep in. What have I done? It's not the teaching that troubles me; it's the place. For as much as I yearn to travel, Germany is the last place on Earth I want to go. Austria is a close second.

꒰

On June 28, I am sitting in the plane, imagining two and a half weeks without kids, dogs, phone calls, or car pools. Amazing—I have the next nine hours to myself, to read, review my plans for the course, or just sit there and not do a thing.

As I settle back in my seat, my attention is drawn to the large screen at the front of the cabin where every few minutes a map charting our progress appears. The major cities are labeled first in German, then in English.

Without warning, I hear the voice of my mother: *We're Jews. If we had been born there instead of here, we would have been herded into cattle cars and sent to the camps.*

Images of the Holocaust come unbidden: photographs of emaciated prisoners in striped pajamas, their agonies clearly visible in their hollow eyes and haggard faces; film clips of Hitler, right arm raised in the *Sieg Heil*; the worn pages of a novel I cherished, Meyer Levin's *Eva*, the story of a Jewish girl who tried to survive by "passing," living in Nazi-occupied Austria under an assumed name, pretending to be Christian. At thirteen, I was gripped by her courage and imagined myself in her place, spending hours in my bedroom practicing the sign of the cross, genuflecting, yearning to be safe—and Gentile, like the popular girls in my junior high school. A question that haunted me then: If I had been born there, would I have survived? A question that haunts me still.

Suddenly, my face feels hot; sweat breaks out on my forehead, gathers in my armpits. I am an adolescent awash in fear, assaulted by language and all it calls up in me. The Holocaust. The gas chambers. Auschwitz. Treblinka. Tears sting my eyes, slide down my cheeks. I don't want to be hated or hunted. I don't want to be counted among the dead or despised. I hate Hitler with all the fury a thirteen-year-old can muster. I hate the Germans. I hate the entire world for allowing this to happen. I want to scream, to stamp my feet in protest, to turn my back on all of it: atrocity, history, Judaism.

Taking long, slow breaths, I tell myself to calm down. Reaching for my bag, I find a tissue, wipe my eyes, and put on my sunglasses.

I glance sideways, hoping no one has noticed. Why have I agreed to teach in Austria?

The answers come quickly: I've been hired to do a job I love. The Holocaust ended over fifty years ago. I'm an adult, not a thirteen-year-old. I miss traveling. Why should I refuse? After all, Austrian teachers shouldn't be different from other teachers.

But then, once again, I hear my mother's voice. *No matter what they say or do, no matter how stunning their accomplishments in art, music, and philosophy, within every German, every Austrian, lies a Nazi in disguise.*

&

On June 29, I arrive at the airport in Innsbruck and am greeted by Tanja Westfall, the coordinator of the Innsbruck courses and one of the two American participants in the course. A bubbly, vivacious woman in her late twenties, with thick, brown hair and a big smile, Tanja has invited me to stay with her in the tiny village of Hatting, a short train ride from the city and the University of Innsbruck, where the courses are to be held.

As I deplane, all I can do is stare, eyes wide open, mouth agape. The snowcapped mountains that rise so steeply seem to protect the order and calm of all that lies below: the churches with their steeples rising above the towns; the towns, almost toy-like in their precision, surrounded by fields in nuanced shades of green, sloping ever higher; on each slope, sturdy wooden houses in brown and ocher; on each house, window boxes overflowing with geraniums. I had no idea Innsbruck was so beautiful. Only later do I realize that for a moment I have forgotten this exquisite land once harbored unspeakable horrors.

After we collect my luggage, Tanja drives us to her flat. While she is making lunch, I unpack and settle in. Joining her in the kitchen, I glance out the window. I notice her neighbor, an old man, working in the garden next door. He is wearing blue overalls and a cap, using a scythe to cut the grass. Raising both arms up above his head, he brings them down swiftly, neatly cutting through the dry yellow weeds; then piling them to one side, he takes a step and begins again. I imagine such a scene has repeated itself for centuries: peasants in the fields, cutting hay, storing it for winter as feed for the animals. A simple world, bucolic, peaceful, timeless.

But suddenly I wonder if he was a Nazi. Maybe he still is. What would he say if he knew a Jew was sleeping in the next house? And then, just as suddenly, I turn from the window.

&

On July 1, the first day of class, Tanja and I arrive early. The room is airy with large windows facing the Inn River. The mountains and their snow peaks rise in the distance. The tables and chairs are arranged in rows with a lectern at the front. I ask Tanja to help me move the furniture. This is not the way I want to begin. We push the lectern into a corner and rearrange the tables into one large square. Then we place twelve chairs around the perimeter. This will be a collaborative endeavor; we will be speaking to and with one another. I will lead the conversation, but I won't dominate it.

Soon the teachers, my students, arrive. We begin formally, with handshakes and introductions. Thomas, the other American student, has a round face, kind eyes, and an arresting dark beard. Hans, fair-haired and portly, is the only other man; his wife, Martina, trim and businesslike, is also in the course. Both appear to be in their forties. Andrea, with curly red hair and bright green eyes, is in her twenties. The youngest member of the group, she has brought some bread and cheese for our first day. The eldest, Hilde, a large, soft-spoken woman in her fifties, has brought bottles of apple juice and club soda to mix the popular *Apfelsaft gespritzt*.

Tanja introduces me to several women with blond hair: Margret, big-boned with a strong, purposeful handshake; Ursula, willowy and graceful, with a shy smile; and Christa whose face causes me to gasp inwardly. With hair the color of straw, clear blue eyes, a perfectly straight nose, and prominent cheekbones, Christa looks to me like a member of Hitler's master race, an Aryan beauty.

The last two to arrive are Astrid, an attractive woman whose long white hair is pulled back in a bun, and Ingrid, thin and birdlike, with sharp eyes behind wire-rimmed glasses. Astrid, in her late forties, has a daughter who plays cello with the Vienna Philharmonic; Ingrid, turning thirty, has two young children at home.

Margret and Andrea, I soon discover, have each already obtained one master's degree and teach in prestigious *Gymnasien*, Austrian high schools for college-bound students. Christa teaches at a private Catholic school for girls. Tanja and Hans both teach at the university. Thomas works in a language immersion program for adults. The others all work in the *Hauptschule* system, roughly equivalent to the vocational tracks in American schools.

I am to teach two graduate courses—one on the teaching of writing, the other on the teaching of literature. Rather than lecture, I invite my students to join me in a range of activities and then to reflect with me on what they are learning. When it comes to reading and writing, I know of no other approach that makes as much sense.

We begin that first night, simply enough, by writing about our experiences with writing. I write along with the group, then invite people to read aloud all or a part of what they have written. I respond to each person's draft by carefully rephrasing what I hear, focusing on the theme of each story. As we go around the room, we hear a range of increasingly sad tales.

Hans, brash and bold, vividly recounts the harsh criticism he received. "I stopped writing," he reveals, smiling ruefully, a shock of blond hair falling over his eyes, "I was so ashamed of my errors."

Margret recalls that at the university "writing was not about our ideas." Her chin juts out as she speaks with some anger: "Your writing had to be perfect, or you felt you were stupid."

Most of these teachers admit that they dislike writing, don't do it very often, and associate it with struggle and pain. The most common denominator: feeling judged and falling short.

"Isn't there another way?" Thomas implores, his dark eyes serious and brooding.

"There is," I promise. "There are ways to make writing come alive so that each person's voice counts. So that teaching is about much more than what students do wrong. We will explore this way of teaching together over the next few weeks. Tonight was just a start, but can you already begin to see what's different here?"

The teachers spontaneously rap their knuckles on the tabletop. I flinch. "Did I say something wrong?"

Hans quickly explains, smiling broadly, "That's our way of saying thanks. It was a great beginning."

On the drive home, Tanja tells me this is high praise.

≀▲

At our second meeting on July 2, everyone is a bit more familiar. Smiles are wider, handshakes and hellos more heartfelt. Christa places a vase of homegrown flowers on the snack table. Andrea, chatty and effervescent, adds a platter of *Speck mit Brot*, explaining to me that thin slices of ham and hardy bread are an Austrian staple; Margret brings a bowl of strawberries. Hilde, once again, mixes *Apfelsaft gespritzt*.

I begin a discussion of one of the texts I had assigned, *A Letter to Teachers* by Vito Perrone, an educator who invites teachers to consider the meaning and purpose of their work. "What do we most want our students to come to understand as a result of their schooling?" Perrone asks.[1] He then articulates a clear and hopeful vision of what is possible in classrooms:

> If we saw the development of active inquirers as a major goal, much that now exists—workbooks and textbooks, predetermined curriculum, reductionism, teaching to tests—would, I believe, begin to fade. Teachers would be free to address the world, to make living in the world a larger part of the curriculum.[2]

It was statements like these that I expected to discuss with the Austrian teachers.

But they are struck by something else Perrone has written, something so obvious to me I have never before stopped to examine it: "Education at its best is first and foremost a moral and intellectual endeavor."[3]

Andrea, her green eyes clouded, is bewildered. "What does this mean?" she asks. "Do you honestly think education is connected to morality?"

I do, I think to myself. But I want to move slowly here. I want to understand why Andrea is asking this question and to discover if her bewilderment is shared by others.

"Do most of you have this question?" I ask, looking around the room, examining their faces. Several people nod.

I suggest that they break into small groups to talk about their responses. But as I move from group to group, I hear: "We all follow the same procedures"; "Teachers here are taught not to speak about what they believe"; "We can't deal with morality in the classroom."

"This is not our way," says Hans, with quiet certainty, crossing his arms on his chest and nodding his head.

"That's right," echoes his wife, Martina. "We have been trained to keep ourselves and our values outside of the curriculum. In the classroom, we must be morally neutral."

The other text I have assigned also challenges the views of these teachers. In *Literature as Exploration*, Louise Rosenblatt claims that teaching involves taking an ethical stance. She writes:

> The teaching of literature inevitably involves the . . . reinforcement of ethical attitudes. It is practically impossible to treat . . . any literary work . . . in a vital manner without confronting some problem of ethics and without speaking out of the context of some social philosophy. A framework of values is essential to any discussion of human life.[4]

Andrea finds the whole issue curious. She is perplexed by Rosenblatt's insistence that a teacher should not "try to pose as a completely objective person" and that "a much more wholesome educational situation is created when the teacher is a really live person" who, when appropriate, can state his or her "attitudes and assumptions . . . frankly and honestly."[5]

"How can one be a whole human being in the classroom?" she wonders aloud, her red curls framing her face. But most of the others seem not to share her curiosity.

I am taken aback that this group of Austrian teachers, at least those who have spoken so far, seem to find a focus on ethics troubling. But only a few have spoken. Most have remained silent.

What did you expect? You are working with the children or grandchildren of Nazis, says my mother's voice. Have you told them you are Jewish? If they knew, would they still rap their knuckles with such enthusiasm?

This is not an issue, I respond. Almost everyone in the room looks younger than I, and I was born after the war. These teachers in front of me are not responsible for what happened.

Well, their parents were alive then, she replies. Your father was a staff sergeant in the U.S. Army. Their parents could easily be my age. What did their parents or even their grandparents do?

But Mother, I answer, I have not come here to accuse them. I have come to teach them.

But then, I ask myself, isn't this precisely the issue? What am I teaching here? Do the moral questions that concern me have a place in this classroom?

At break time, as the teachers snack on cheese and chat in German, I stand back and observe. As a group they appear kind, caring, bright. They have come with the desire to understand new theories and progressive practices in the teaching of writing and literature. This much I can impart to them. And yet there is so much I already feel I can't impart, can't say, can't admit, don't want to face, here or ever. Slowly, I let out a sigh.

≥●

On July 4, I am sitting in Tanja's garden at a wooden table under an apple tree. The homework assignment is to compose a piece of writing that matters; the topic and form are open. I have come outside to work on mine.

The sun feels warm on my back; flies buzz around my head. Annoyed, I swat them away. Once again, I am haunted by thoughts of the Holocaust, of what happened literally on the ground on which I am now walking, living, breathing. I picture the SS, marching through the streets of Innsbruck, hounding the Jews, pulling them from their homes, rounding them up and packing them off in cattle cars. I see blood staining the streets, the blood of those who were too slow or too old, those who tried to hide or dared to resist. I hear the screams of mothers as children are pulled from their arms, the burst of machine gunfire. Tears spring to my eyes as I write:

> What am I doing here
> in the homeland of Hitler's birth?
>
> Why have I come
> across an ocean
> to a land and a language
> I've never wanted to know?
>
> Never would I come here
> to the land where Nazis reigned,
> to the place where your people
> turned my people
> into objects of derision and hate.
>
> Like the numbers
> etched into their forearms
> images are seared in my brain
> of bodies, piled high
> in ditches, of hair
> and teeth, piled high
> in corners.

I see the laboratories
the wombs of young women
filled with concrete
the bodies of babies
flung aside

And the Mengele selection
the preference for twins

Oh
my twins

This thought blots out all others. I am wordless. I cannot go on. I want to go home, to get out of this place, this country. Back to my own people. I'm startled at this. I'm not religious. For most of my life, I have been ambivalent about Judaism, more interested in blending into a Christian world than standing out as a Jew. And yet, here, the Jews have become my people.

ॐ

On July 5, the fourth class meeting, there is turmoil in the classroom. The teachers are finding it excruciatingly difficult to write. No matter how many different methods I show them, when they have to sit down and face the blank page, they freeze.

Ingrid, one of the young teachers from the *Hauptschule* system, precise and pointed in both looks and style, challenges me openly with her frustration. "I just can't do this. Why should I even try? If I want to say something to someone, I can call them up and talk."

Hans, who teaches business courses at the university, concurs, tossing that unruly shock of blond hair out of his eyes. "What is the point of writing if the teacher does not give you a topic? I do not mean to be rude, but to me this activity is a waste of time."

I recognize this phenomenon. American teachers who have written only academic papers often resist invitations to write more creatively. But never before have I seen such deep distress in a group.

We are sitting around our classroom table. "Why do you think this is so hard?" I ask.

Ingrid responds promptly: "Our professors never asked us to be so creative. When we are asked to write in school, we expect to be given assignments with specific requirements."

I am aware that how I respond is crucial. Eleven teachers are watching me.

I say, "It sounds as if many of you are blocked." I can see their bodies relax. "In fact, it sounds to me as if you are describing a kind of paralysis."

I can almost hear the sighs of relief. I have adequately named their dilemma. But while I am speaking, I realize that I am also speaking about myself; they are mirroring my own paralysis.

"Look," I say. "I can answer the question, 'Why write?' But for now, I think it's important to let the question sit. Why don't we break into small groups and see what others have to say. You can either share the work you have brought or talk about why writing was hard for you. You know," I add, "you can be fairly certain that if you are experiencing a problem here, at some point, your students may too."

I have placed myself in a group with three Austrian women: Margret, whose comments in class have impressed me; Christa, whose quiet presence intrigues me; and Martina, who other than supporting Hans, has been reserved. We move our chairs into a corner of the classroom. As they pass out copies of their work, Christa and Margret each comment that neither of them experienced any trouble finding a topic.

Christa agrees to read first. In a quiet voice, she reads aloud the story of her mother's struggle with cancer and her quiet death at home; by the time she finishes, we are there with her, standing around her mother's bed, praying for her release. We all have tears in our eyes.

Margret volunteers to read next. Her piece is not as straightforward, her voice less certain. It takes me a moment to realize that she is using a child's point of view to convey utter helplessness in the face of an abusive father.

Christa comments on the power of Margret's last line—"How can you cross the chasm if the bridge is not there?"

"I feel, what is the word . . . ?" Christa asks pausing, "stranded?"

"Yes," I say, jumping in. "That's exactly the word. I also feel how stranded and lost that child is."

Margret's face, closed until now, relaxes. I see the hint of a smile.

We turn to Martina who has remained remarkably quiet. "I have not been able to write a thing," she admits, the lines around her thin mouth tightening. "I've tried, really, but I am just so tired, and for me the school year is still not yet over. I still have meetings and paperwork to complete. It is not possible for me to do this right now . . ." Her voice trails off.

We listen sympathetically and suggest that she find some way to make her exhaustion the subject of her writing.

"Well, that could work," she says, smiling ruefully, "maybe . . . "

Now it is my turn. I inhale deeply, still not sure what to say. "I have been keeping a journal about my experiences in Austria," I begin, "but I doubt whether I can tell you what I am writing about."

They look at me with surprise. They have no idea, I think, and I have no idea what to say next.

I look at Christa's face, still tear-stained. Then I imagine the stranded child Margret just described. "It's a lot like Margret's chasm," I say. "I don't know if there is a bridge here."

They sit quietly, waiting for me to go on. I know I have to continue, to make some explanation. But what? We are just beginning to build some trust in the group. Will I shatter it if I mention the Holocaust? Do I dare? And yet, if I don't, how can I possibly explain what is happening to me?

I look at each one, and in a halting voice, I finally say, "O.K., I'll tell you what's going on. The more I walk on this land, the more my mind fills with images of the Holocaust. I see it everywhere I turn, every time I see an old person, every time I try to write. But how can I talk about this? I . . . well . . . I don't think I should. This is not why I am here."

Margret straightens her back and looks at me hard, her eyes narrowing. With undisguised vehemence, she exclaims, "How can you *not* talk about this? We never discuss our past, but we must! Of course, you should continue to write, and you must let us hear it."

"You are encouraging me?" I ask, startled.

She nods.

I am speechless. I can barely face what I am feeling. Each time it surfaces I want to push it away. Now this Austrian woman is urging me to make my fears public in a roomful of Austrians?

"I don't know," I respond hesitantly. "I'll try to keep writing. Maybe I'll be able to read some of my work to the three of you, but I'm not sure I can share this with the large group."

"You must try," urges Margret.

"You all agree?" I ask.

"Yes," says Christa.

"Yes," says Martina.

"There is nothing more important you can do here," adds Margret.

ð.

For the rest of the evening, I am in turmoil. I suspect it might be useful for the teachers to learn that I, too, am having a writing block. But I am petrified to raise the issue of the Holocaust with them, scared that they will reject me and my questions, even more scared to face these questions myself.

Several hours later, when the entire group reassembles to reflect together on the night's work, I have made up my mind to speak. It's a risk, I know. But how better to emerge from behind the mask of professor than to reveal what moves inside me? How better to answer Andrea's question about how to be a whole human being in the classroom?

The twelve of us are seated around our large table. My heart pounds as I begin to talk: "Before we write reflections tonight, I want to say something about the paralysis that Ingrid and Hans mentioned earlier today. I, too, have been experiencing it. Every time I try to write, I silence myself."

Not a sound in the room. I have caught their attention.

"I came here to teach," I continue, "but I now realize I also came with questions about what happened here, in Austria, over fifty years ago. I don't expect you to explain the war to me. But I am curious about all of you. How do you cope with the knowledge of what happened here?"

It is so quiet I can hear the clock on the wall ticking.

"For the past few days, I have been plagued by questions about your history. I have felt I cannot ask them, that I cannot write about them, that it is not my place. But I also realize that I am not morally neutral and if I pretend I am—if I act as if these questions are not important to me—then I am contradicting myself, denying theories I have asked you to consider, subverting my own values."

I take a breath. I am greeted by blank stares. I assume that references to war and moral neutrality are sufficient to explain what I am referring to. I cannot bring myself to utter the words "Holocaust" or "Jew."

"You don't need to speak right now," I say. "But if you have a response, I'd like to hear it. I am mentioning this tonight because I want you to see that even a writing teacher can, at times, be blocked. And that one way out of this block is to begin to speak about it. So why don't we all write some reflections, now, on whatever comes to mind about tonight's work."

People pick up their pens. The concentrated quiet in the room tells me that everyone is writing.

I ask for volunteers to read. It is as if no one has heard a word I've said. Astrid, strands of white hair escaping from her bun, excitedly describes what is happening in her writing group. It is so valuable, she says, to see what her peers are writing. Ursula demurely expresses interest in changing topics. Hilde sees a new way to begin.

Margret reads last:

> How can we not address Sondra's questions? How can we avoid talking about the fascism in our land, our country, our blood? How can we not teach our children who they are and be willing to take the beating of the world? We are the generation that must respond. Our parents can't and won't. We must own our dark side.

As Margret looks up, our eyes meet. This night as we leave, there is no knuckle-rapping. Only silence.

ஃ

For July 6, the fifth session, we have an eight-hour class with time to work in both small and large groups. Following this session, we have a four-day break. It would be so much safer to move on, to act as if I hadn't raised anything unusual the night before. But my instincts tell me it would be wrong. I want to name what occurred, to mark it in some way. I also want to see if anyone is feeling unsettled by the personal turn of events I have initiated.

As we gather around the table to go over the day's schedule, I ask for everyone's attention: "I want to begin today by returning to some of the issues we raised last night. I want to take a few minutes to retrace the steps we took." There is no fidgeting, no looking out of the window.

I summarize the events—beginning with Ingrid's and Hans's questions about the purpose of writing and ending with my revelation about my own writer's block. Then I say, "I can't help thinking that we have an unusual opportunity here. We can act as if nothing momentous happened last night, or we can approach the questions I raised with care and respect and see what occurs. We have a chance, I think, to speak across cultures."

As I conclude my talk, people get up and begin the day's work. I do not know whether I have reached them; do not know if they are aware that when I refer to "my questions" I am referring to the Holocaust, to their parents, to their own knowledge and responses. I am still speaking obliquely, wanting to open a dialogue, not shut it down. And I still cannot say the word "Jew" in front of them.

❧

For the literature course, we have been meeting in reading groups, discussing our responses to Toni Morrison's *Sula*, a poignant and powerful novel. Almost everyone seems to be pleased with the experience of keeping a "reading log" or a "response journal." Ingrid comments that this approach encourages students to respond honestly. Hilde, whose vision of classrooms has not dimmed with increasing age, plans to use this approach with her weakest students. With these teachers, I have discovered, it is easy to talk about pedagogy.

But the conversation stalls when I move us into the larger implications of the novel. "It's hard to be born in America," I say slowly, looking at the group, "without absorbing prejudice."

They look at me without commenting. I continue, "The question for many American teachers is what to do about racism. We often use Toni Morrison's work because it helps us address a range of racial issues. But many teachers I know well, particularly white teachers in urban classrooms, also wrestle with their own prejudices, knowing that the roots of racism are deep, that they may have to acknowledge and combat racism in themselves before they can really reach their students."

Do they see the connection? I wonder. Do they understand I am suggesting that Austria is not the only country where a violent, eliminationist racism took hold? I don't know. The teachers nod, smile, even take notes, but they do not respond.

The pace picks up again several hours later when writing groups meet. Now it is obvious that everyone is actively engaged. The talk is lively, even boisterous. One writing group does not return for a scheduled activity. They report later, shocked by their own behavior, that they were so involved with one another's work, they just couldn't stop. I am delighted by their disobedience.

Sitting at our small table, Martina, Margret, and Christa encourage me to read the poem I have been working on. I consent, but I lower my eyes as I recite the lines about Nazis, about "your people" and "my people." My voice quivers as I read.

When I finish, I look up. I see tears in their eyes. "Thank you," says Margret quietly.

One hurdle overcome, I think to myself. I've admitted that I am Jewish. They could not know how hard this was for me. But I notice that I also feel relieved. For now I assume the group will understand why I am asking about the past. After today, I assume, the classroom grapevine will transmit the news: Sondra is a Jew.

ಎ

Several hours later, I am sitting on a stool in a local bar with Tanja, Thomas, Andrea, Martina, and Hans. Drinking beer, enveloped in cigarette smoke, we tell stories of family life. Andrea, a mother of three, asks me about child rearing in New York. "Can you leave your baby in the car while you run into a shop?" she asks, alluding to a common practice in Innsbruck.

"Are you kidding?" I exclaim. I describe my fear of having my kids out of my sight for even a minute when we are in a supermarket or at a playground. "New York is a wonderful, exciting place," I continue, "but as a parent, it is hard not to worry or to imagine threats even when there aren't any."

Then she asks, "Is it safe to visit Chinatown and Harlem and the Jewish quarter?"

I can only smile. "Being aware of personal safety is important in every neighborhood," I respond first. "Chinatown is relatively safe; so is Harlem these days. But in New York, Andrea, there is no Jewish quarter. In New York, being Jewish is so common, it's like, well . . ." I burst out laughing, recalling a quip a British colleague once made, "it's as if everyone is Jewish."

I doubt that the group has any notion of what I am referring to, but everyone joins in laughing. Suddenly, I notice, I feel a greater sense of ease among them. Not bad, I think, making a Jewish joke at the half-way mark.

2

History Becomes Real

uring our four-day break, Margret calls. She and her husband, Gert, are planning to go hiking. Would Tanja and I like to join them? As Tanja relays their invitation, I nod eagerly.

The next day dawns bright and sunny. Waking early, I limber up—leg lifts, sit-ups, a few yoga stretches—then join Tanja for a breakfast of fruit, yogurt, and muesli. Lacing up my hiking boots, I feel my excitement mounting. On the drive into town, we chat amiably. At a parking lot near the university, we find Margret and Gert waiting for us.

Margret introduces me to her husband, a tall, muscular man with piercing blue eyes and white hair, worn long, down to his shoulders. He smiles, reaches out to shake hands, and says, shyly, "My English is not . . . so good."

I smile back, "My German is worse." And with that, we pile into their red van, our backpacks chock full of cheese, bread, water, and chocolate.

We take an hour's drive to south Tyrol, passing through picturesque villages, each with its town square, church, wooden houses, and flower boxes. Tanja, Gert, and Margret converse in German. I am content to look out the window and let them take charge.

Soon we are on the trail. "It should take about two hours to reach the top," Margret remarks. I am eager to begin, to test my muscles against the mountain. I'm impressed at the numbers of people coming and going: children running ahead of their parents, infants in slings, teenagers with orange tank tops, tattoos, and purple-streaked hair, couples walking hand in hand, old folks with hiking sticks and strong muscular legs.

Gert quickly outdistances us. With his long strides and easy gait, he is soon out of sight. Tanja and Margret adjust their pace to mine which, despite my enthusiasm, is slow. I am surprised to find that there are barely any flat stretches. The hike is mostly uphill, the top nowhere in sight.

I need to stop often and catch my breath. I'm embarrassed that I'm holding them up. "Please," I implore Margret, "go ahead and catch up with Gert."

She furrows her brow and smiles. "I can hike with Gert any time. It's you I'd like to walk with today."

The air is warm; the sun, strong. We pause occasionally to drink some water and eat some cheese. As we climb, we chat about novels and films, our lives as teachers, finally our upbringings. Margret, the fourth child out of five, comes from a Catholic family, two girls and three boys. Her Italian mother and Austrian father divorced years ago. Her sister lives on the island of Cyprus; two brothers and their families live nearby in Innsbruck, the other in Linz. She rarely sees her father and his second wife.

My family, I explain, came to America in the early 1900s, my mother's family from Poland, my father's from Russia, their 1912 arrival recorded in ledgers at Ellis Island. I am the eldest of four, two boys and two girls. We all live near each other. My mother, remarried after the death of my father, has eight grandchildren.

Tanja describes the small town in central Wisconsin where she grew up: "My parents, my brother, and I lived on a farm outside of Rudolf—population 492—home to three bars, a bowling alley, and a feed mill," she laughs. We laugh too when she tells us that Christmas mail gets stamped with a red-nosed reindeer.

"I came to Austria when I was twenty-four," Tanja explains. "I had a teaching assistantship from the Fulbright Foundation, and my plan was to stay for one year. But Austria just felt right," she says, "and so I never left. I'm amazed that I've been here for five years already." An adopted child, Tanja adds that she knows nothing about her ancestors.

The trail leads us into a stand of evergreens. The trees tower above us, filtering the sunlight. The air under the canopy is cool, raising goose bumps on my arms. We pause to put on sweaters. As we continue to climb, we become quiet. I focus my attention on each step, lifting first one foot, inhaling deeply, exhaling as I put it down in front of me, then lifting the other. My calf muscles are beginning to ache.

Tanja and Margret move out ahead of me but turn back often to make sure I am O.K. I wave them on. Alone, I find a rhythm that suits me. As I climb higher, my thoughts turn inward. Talk of families brings back the past. Making my way up the slope, I trace another path in my mind: the one laid out for me as a child and then, later, a teen.

I see my first home, a three-family house in the Weequahic section of Newark, New Jersey. I see the front stoop, where neighbors congregated on summer nights, the rain gutters that ran along the sides, the clotheslines strung from back windows, bed sheets flapping in the wind. I recall the soft touch of pussy willows that grew behind the garage, the scent of lilacs in the spring air.

Pausing to catch my breath, I picture the three-room flat I lived in with my parents on the top floor just above my mother's parents. I hear the three short raps of a broomstick that echoed whenever my grandmother wanted something. The sound of Nana's broomstick hitting the ceiling was my signal to run downstairs.

I see the larger apartment we moved to—one floor below my grandparents—when I was four, when my sister, Sheri, was born. Now when Nana needed something, she'd stamp her foot. I recall how much I enjoyed scrambling up and down the back stairs, retrieving a milk bottle, delivering the *Star Ledger*, happy to serve as go-between, the daily link between mother and grandmother.

Continuing to climb, I remember how safe I felt in Newark. Doors were never locked, not even at night, and family was always near. As I emerge into the sunlight, faces come back to me: I see my grandfather, my Poppa, a hardworking, energetic man with a gnarled finger and an easy smile, his lively brothers—Herman, Emil, Sam, the twins, Maxie and Mendy—and his only sister, Minnie, whose big bones, freckled face, and blazing red hair made her stand out. I see my father's mother, my Grandma Rae, a widow, and her brothers and sisters—Izzie, Joe, Nathan, Max, *tante* Becky, *tante* Lena, and the youngest, Miriam, who used the modern English term, aunt. Their father, I knew, had been a rabbi and at one time, as children, they had all huddled together under tables in Siberia.

But in Newark, no one spoke about the past. My family was forward-looking; their future, undeniably American. And while people emigrated from different countries, to my eyes, everyone was alike. In other words, everyone was Jewish. In fact, I realize, pausing again to catch my breath, as a child I assumed the entire world was Jewish. I had never met anyone who wasn't.

I move off the trail, find a place to sit, and pull off my sweater. I take some chocolate and a water bottle from my backpack. I have been hiking for at least three hours. I know that Margret, Tanja, and Gert must have reached the summit, must be eating at the *Gasthof* they told me awaits us above the timberline. But I am incapable of taking another step without first taking another break.

Leaning against a rock, turning my face to the sun, I close my eyes and see our second home, a split-level house in South Orange, New Jersey, a suburb of Newark. At age nine, I knew this move to a home of our own signaled my father's success, his rise from fire alarm salesman to company president, his delight in having emerged from the confines of working-class life.

I knew, too, that I was supposed to be pleased. I had my own room, a swing set, a Shetland sheepdog named Jigsie. I was still sur-rounded by Jews. But these Jews were different. They belonged to country clubs. The mothers wore Bermuda shorts and played golf. The girls knew things I didn't know: where to buy clothes; how to play softball. I didn't think we fit in.

What I did like, I recall, was attending synagogue. Although they never accompanied us, my parents, in a nod to suburban mores, joined Temple Israel, a Reform congregation, and sent Sheri and me to Saturday school. Sitting against a rock in southern Tyrol, I recall how I enjoyed sitting in temple, listening to Hebrew prayers, how the plaintive, pleading tone of the music often brought tears to my eyes.

I open my eyes and squint into the sun. Inhaling deeply, I know I must get up and keep climbing. By now, the others must be worried. I put on my backpack, adjust the weight, rejoin the hikers on the trail. The path is steeper now, the ascent more challenging: mostly rocky with short switchbacks, up and around, up and around. My calves ache with each new step, but I can glimpse the roof of the *Gasthof*, its flag waving in the breeze.

I marvel at the people, still eagerly climbing, passing me by with a nod. I marvel even more at the view: at my feet, wildflowers; below me, forests, dappled in shades of green; below the forests, tiny towns; connect-ing the towns, rivers, curving like snakes; above me, the sun, glinting off the snow peaks; and above the mountains, the clouds, the sky.

Climbing higher, I see our third home, which, like the *Gasthof*, rested on top of a mountain—the South Mountain, in Short Hills, New Jersey—the home that accompanied my father's dizzying ascent to the top of the business world. I recall how delighted my father was with the prominence of our house, how my younger brothers, Richard and Robert, grew up loving it. But, to my thirteen-year-old eyes, "the big house," as we called it, was too big. I felt dwarfed by its enormous rooms and secretly longed for the days when my grandparents were just a stairway away. The big house, with its indoor pool, its sauna, its tennis and handball courts, embarrassed me. It made me stand out when all I wanted to do was fit in.

To me, at thirteen, my father's achievements meant only another move to another suburb—to a different world entirely. The Short Hills I entered in 1960 was a Christian enclave. I remember how strange I found it: there were Jewish kids in school but the popular ones were the Gentiles. The girls had names like Linnie, Ginnie, Jodie, and Chrissie. They wore round-collared blouses fastened with circle pins and went to church on Sunday. They were anything but loud and as different from the suburban Jews of South Orange as I could imagine. I was fascinated by them and longed to be like them.

Hiking up the last stretch, mustering my last ounce of strength, lifting one heavy leg, then the other, I recall how valiantly I tried, cutting my hair to look like theirs, dressing the way they did, even changing my name, telling everyone to call me Sandi. And, for a while, I recall, it worked. I became one of the "Short Hills girls." I was invited to their homes, introduced to their parents. But something wasn't right. Someone's mother would stare at me too long. Someone's brother would joke that Jews had horns. I didn't know what to do with my discomfort, except to pretend it didn't exist.

I look up, wiping sweat from my forehead. The *Gasthof* is close. Just a few more turns. I shoulder my pack and climb on. But I am spent, out of breath, and stop abruptly on the trail.

Three burly men, hiking briskly, nearly run me over. I don't understand their German but their tone is clear. I'm in the way, why don't I move over. What a stupid woman, probably an American.

They are ridiculing me, I think, like the brothers of my Gentile friends. You're right, I think to myself, I'm not fast. I did not grow up hiking the Alps. I'm struggling, and I don't belong here. In fact, I think defensively, had I been born here a generation ago, you would have packed me onto a train, confiscated my belongings, and moved into my house. Hiking your mountains doesn't make me one of you. I'm a fool to think I can come here, put on a pair of hiking boots, and fit in.

I am surprised at this surge of anger. I inhale deeply and fill my lungs with mountain air. I feel the sun beating down on my shoulders, my sweat-soaked T-shirt clinging to my back. Where did that outburst come from? I like to walk and to reflect. But being on my own, hiking on Austrian soil, surrounded for hours by people speaking German must be getting to me.

I look out over the great expanse of mountain and sky. It is so beautiful—above the trees, below the snow. It takes effort, I realize, to climb a mountain; it also takes stretching, I remind myself, to see beyond one's own narrow view. I am close to the top. I can do this.

When I reach the *Gasthof*, I let my backpack slip to the ground as I collapse into a chair. Margret and Tanja huddle close. Gert brings me a glass of water. Slowly, I revive. Over clear broth and hardy bread, I smile wanly and tell them I've had quite a journey.

ે

On July 11, when we return from the break, everyone seems relaxed. Munching on peanuts and chocolate, we recount recent happenings. I describe my struggle to reach the top of the Zillertal. My legs still ache, but I am proud, I admit, to have made it and eager, I confess, to hike again.

A beaming Ingrid bursts into the room. "I read that article you assigned about the move from product to process in the teaching of writing," she exclaims. "The one about the paradigm shift. You know," she says excitedly, "I think I've had one."

We all start to laugh. Her enthusiasm is contagious.

The rhythm of the course is now carrying us along. Drafts are piling up; readings are being completed. There is a purposeful hum.

There is also much less fear. The teachers seem more willing to encounter the uncomfortable experience of not knowing what they will say or write. They are, in addition, forming their own answers to the question, "Why write?" But only two are willing to discuss the questions I'd raised earlier.

Back in our writing group, Martina, who has not yet written a word, confides that my questions leave her feeling helpless. Then she adds, "My family lived in the country. My mother had nine children. The Nazis gave her Hitler's medal of honor for mothers who produce children for the Third Reich. She refused to wear it. All my parents ever said is that it was a terrible time."

It is Margret who responds most fully. In her mid-forties, outspoken and opinionated, Margret chafes at the characteristic silence of Austrian culture. My questions seem, finally, to have given her permission to speak.

"My in-laws," she begins, "were enthusiastic supporters of the Nazis. My father-in-law joined the Nazi party before it was legal to do so. He served in Hitler's army, fighting for six years."

Christa, Martina, and I sit silently, waiting for Margret to continue. But I am instantly on guard.

"My mother-in-law was the leader of a Hitler youth group of Tyrolean girls. She was proud," Margret pauses, "proud that her framed picture hung on the wall of the Reich Chancellery in Berlin."

So it's true, I think. *Their parents were Nazis.*

"We, my husband and I and our daughter, share a house with them. We have done so for years. Most of the time I cannot bear to look at them, to look into their eyes. It pains me," she says, searching my eyes now, "just to see them in the garden, knowing their history."

I nod. *It pains me too.*

"And your husband?" prompts Christa.

"He is as angry about it as I am. But he cannot talk to them. He has never been able to. In the sixties, he and his brother rejected everything their parents stood for. They became radicals, joined the Maoists."

The sons of fascists become communists, I think.

"How did you meet?" I ask.

"At a protest against nuclear power. Over twenty years ago. Gert is ten years older than I am. I was so impressed with him. But as soon as I met her, I could tell his mother didn't like me. She wanted him to marry someone else, someone prettier, and less opinionated." Margret laughs but the sound that emerges is harsh.

"How do you relate to her now?" I ask.

"I rarely talk to her. We all used to argue all the time. But we have learned that it is pointless to condemn them. We get nowhere.

"Now we all live separate lives," she continues. "In our garden there is a tree with a bench around it. We all sit with our backs to the tree, facing out, not looking at each other. We all exist in our own separate worlds. With this immense silence in the middle. It is such a perfect metaphor for my life.

"Only our daughter goes back and forth with ease. This is the hardest part," Margret says, her voice breaking. "How can I teach her to hate her own grandparents? How can she ever understand?" A tear rolls down her cheek. Brushing it away, she becomes quiet.

The four of us sit in silence for a moment, then agree to take a break.

❧

It is a clear day, the sun shining over the Inn River, the snowy peaks glistening in the distance. I decide to go outside, to get a breath of fresh air. As I stand on the bank of the river, looking out over the water and then up at the surrounding mountains, I see my father. Wounded in a freak accident just before his unit was shipped overseas, my father never fought against the Nazis. While his buddies battled on the beaches of Normandy, he remained in America, organizing shows and sports extravaganzas for stateside soldiers, a prelude to the business conventions, replete with company songs and company cheers, he would stage later in life.

As I walk along the riverbank, I see his mother, my Grandma Rae, and our large, extended family in the basement of a *shul* in Irvington, New Jersey, where at least eighty of us would gather to celebrate Passover. I recall how my cousins and I would run wild, hiding under tables, giggling, happy to ignore our grandparents bent over prayer books. My father would laugh, holding a video camera, happily taping the songs, the comic skits, the kids' antics. Oblivious to any religious significance, he viewed family Seders as another great spectacle.

Settling myself on a bench, watching people stroll along the riverbank, I notice a woman with blond hair. She reminds me of my mother whose light hair and blue eyes distinguished her from everyone else in the family. Characteristically sunny, my mother, Ruth, Rivka, Rivkele, greeted each day with a smile. She sang Broadway show tunes in the car and the kitchen. She still does. I see her today, sitting in an Italian restaurant singing along as a piano player croons. Soon he'll ask her to join in. She'll agree, get up, take the microphone in her hand. When she's finished, people will applaud, will think she's a professional, that she's had voice lessons. She hasn't. She was born with a voice so resonant it makes people cry.

Growing up at her side, I learned that the world was a good place, that one must be kind and understanding. That tomorrow will be better than today. That it is good to have hope. Rarely angry, never spiteful, my mother is not temperamentally a hater. But when it came to the Germans, her warmth would turn to ice, her face would freeze, her eyes narrow in disgust. As a child, I knew something had to be radically wrong. These people must be evil to turn my mother to stone.

Her condemnation was confirmed for me as I grew older and discovered photographs of the Holocaust. I pored over them—pictures of wooden barracks, of electrified barbed wire, of starved bodies with shaved heads thrown carelessly into large pits—until I felt sick. At thirteen, I could not grasp how one group of people, Christians no less, could march another group into the gas chambers; could not make sense of a world that reviled Jews, that either rejoiced or looked away when the Jews were gassed. But one thing I knew for sure: Had I been born in the land my grandparents had left, such a fate would likely have been mine.

Imperceptibly, my shock turned to fear, the fear turned to hate, and the hate began to harden. I began to hate the perpetrators—the Germans, the Austrians, the Poles—anyone who participated in the destruction. I began to hate God for allowing it to happen. And, I think, I also began to hate myself.

For I yearned to be like the girls in my junior high school, quiet and cultured, worldly and well traveled. I understood why the families of my Gentile friends did not like Jews. I didn't like them either, or at least what I took to be Jews: those-upwardly mobile, financially successful men and women who wore their wealth too visibly for me.

I recall our dinner conversations in the big house. My father would need to travel to Germany on business. My mother would refuse to accompany him, and I would side with her. *How could a Jew willingly walk into that Nazi hell?* But then his work would take him to Miami Beach. He would fly us all down and put us up in the penthouse of the Fontainebleau Hotel, a sprawling resort on the ocean with outdoor restaurants and an indoor skating rink. As a teenager, I'd look askance at manicured women who never swam and overweight men sporting gold chains.

Walking along the Inn River, letting my eyes rest on the pastel-colored houses that line its far side, I realize that years ago a complicated dynamic entered my inner life: revulsion for the Jew-haters alternated with revulsion for the Jews.

My father has been dead for twenty years, but his twinkling eyes, his boundless enthusiasm, his love of America are still vivid to me. What would he say now if he saw his daughter struggling with ghosts in an Austrian town?

If he were alive, could I explain to him that I loved the world of immigrant Jews he wished to escape? That his financial success, however well deserved, was also a cause of conflict for me? That in order to be accepted in the Short Hills of my youth, I felt I needed to blend in? That like Eva, the protagonist of my childhood fears and dreams, I, too, felt compelled to remake myself in the image of my Christian schoolmates?

à

Back in class, it is writing time. People are working quietly on their drafts. I sit down at a table in the corner and look out at the group. I no longer see Austrians. I see individuals who are becoming my friends. I start another poem:

> For protection, I have hated you.
> All of you. There was
> no distinction to make.
>
> Germans? They're all Nazis
> I said. Austrians. The same.
>
> But now, I have come among you.
> You have given me room
> to speak. Now
> I see you with your passion
> and your pain.
>
> Your humanity
> becomes visible to me.

In our final small group meeting of the day, we take a break from responding to drafts to talk about our families. Margret, Martina, and I discover that all three of us have adolescent daughters.

I ask Margret when her daughter was born.

"In 1984," she responds. "She just turned twelve."

"Mine too," I smile. "What month?"

"April."

"Mine too. What day?"

"The 24th," Margret answers.

"April 24th?" I ask, incredulous.

She nods.

"But that's my daughter's birthday, too!" I respond.

We both grin.

"What's your daughter's name?" she asks.

"Sara," I respond. "What's yours?"

"Cara."

We start to giggle. We barely know each other, may never see one another again, but right now, we feel a closeness beyond anything we can put into words.

"Amazing," I say.

"Amazing," she nods, looking back, her eyes smiling.

ða

On July 13, our final day, expectations are high, the mood is light. We need to add another table for the array of food: wine, cheese, homemade soufflés, tomatoes from Ursula's garden, basil from Hilde's.

We have reached the end of many hours of hard work. Much of our time this night will be spent in celebration: reading finished work aloud; appreciating what it took for each of us to get to this point; planning for the future; and reflecting together, one last time, on what we have all learned.

Tonight, too, we will see the presentations by the reading groups. In addition to working on our writing, we have also been reading and responding to "young adult" novels. I have asked each small group to create a presentation that brings the book to life. This light-hearted but serious assignment is designed to show that writing is not the only way to demonstrate an understanding of a text and to experience how other forms of expression—music, art, drama—bring other kinds of intelligence into play.

The presentations are at once silly, serious, and wonderful. Ursula, Hilde, and Astrid are touchingly sweet as cats from Beverly Cleary's *Socks*. Hans and Thomas as American toughs with switchblades, slicked-back hair, and cigarettes dangling from their lips make the violence of S. E. Hinton's *The Outsiders* palpable. Christa, Andrea, Ingrid, and Martina enter in checked lumberjack shirts and baseball caps worn backwards and perform a rap song with the words from Judy Blume's *Then Again, Maybe I Won't*, made even funnier by their accents: "Maybe I vill, maybe I von't."

Margret and Tanja enact a scene from Roald Dahl's *Matilda*. Tanja in schoolgirl garb plays the irrepressible Matilda; Margret, wearing a black leather jacket and shiny black boots, her hair pulled tightly into a bun, plays the vicious headmistress, "the Trunchbull." When she enters, brandishing a whip and berating Matilda for her stupidity, I blanch. Her voice is chilling. My friend resembles a guard in a concentration camp. It is all I can do to contain myself.

Margret succeeds in capturing the wanton cruelty of a certain kind of teacher, dramatizes the abuse of power prevalent in so many classrooms. At the end, when she puts down her whip, we go wild with applause.

The final event of the evening is the "readaround," a more serious time when each person is given an opportunity to read a piece of writing to the group. Rather than discuss each piece after each reading, we listen attentively, clap, and move on.

Hilde has written about a woman who wakes up to find herself in a hospital bed, partially paralyzed after a car accident. Thomas gives a science fiction rendering of a woman intent on destroying the lives of the men she loves. Ursula describes a trip through France. Tanja reads a story of adoption. Ingrid has us in stitches as she reads her piece on the pleasures of organic gardening, punctuated by the pain of dealing with proliferating slugs.

When Margret reads her work, we become quiet. I can hear the tension in her voice. It is reflected in our faces, mirrored in the postures of our bodies. We sit spellbound as she evokes, in a poem entitled "Innocence," the remorse her unrepentant Nazi father-in-law has never expressed:

> *We didn't mean to*
> *brand your arms*
>
> *We didn't mean to*
> *rip off your clothes*
>
> *We didn't mean to*
> *make you crawl on your knees*

We didn't mean to
select you on the ramp

We didn't mean to
send you to the gas

We didn't mean to
hurt anyone on our march to Norway

We didn't mean to
load a cross on our offspring's shoulders

We didn't mean to
cut off the human bond

We don't mean to
Say, "Forgive us."

We were wrong the same!

When she finishes reading, I let out a long, deep breath. I catch her eye and nod. She smiles back. It looks like a smile of relief.

Then Martina clears her throat. She has something she'd like to read. It is a letter to Louise Rosenblatt, a rewrite of an earlier assignment. She begins slowly, her voice shaking:

Dear Mrs. Rosenblatt,

You originally wrote your book *Literature as Exploration* in 1938, one of the darkest years of Austrian history. While you were writing, enlightened by cultural pluralism, terrible things happened here from the "occupation" to *Reichskristallnacht*. And so many Austrians—Jewish Austrians—who wrote the best literature, were in danger, not allowed to publish, and had to leave the country. Or worse. Please, Mrs. Rosenblatt, may I express to you my deepest regret for all of the atrocities?

Yours sincerely,

Martina

I am astonished. For the past two weeks, Martina has been unable to write, has offered excuse after excuse. And now this. I knew Rosenblatt's book was first published in 1938. But I hadn't thought about that because I was eager to focus on the relevance of her message to our lives today.

Nineteen thirty-eight was the year of the *Anschluss*, when Austrians welcomed Hitler with open arms, when those Jews who were lucky or had the means were still able to flee. It took Martina's observation and her imaginative reaching out across time and space to remind me again how the land we inhabit alters the way we read and write.

Sitting there, impressed with all that these teachers have done, grateful to have come among them, I sense once again how much I have changed. I have brought another poem with me, not sure whether I will read it aloud:

> *What pain has lain*
> *dormant*
> *inside me?*
>
> *This is not my*
> *history.*
> *I was not born*
> *here. But the souls*
> *of six million*
> *still haunt,*
> *still call.*
>
> *What is this hatred,*
> *born here*
> *nurtured here,*
> *turned hysterical?*
> *So overwhelming,*
> *so encompassing,*
> *it annihilates the other?*
>
> *Can I find this hatred*
> *in myself?*
> *Or is the higher ground*
> *of victim*
> *preferable?*

I decide not to read it. It is too raw, it raises too many unsettling questions, questions I'm not ready to face. Instead I read a piece I have written to my daughter who is homesick during her first experience at sleep-away camp. I try to reassure her, explaining that each of us comes up against our own fears, our own demons, whenever we venture into the unknown. As I read I wonder: To whom am I really writing, Sara or myself?

When the readaround is over, we take a break and chat quietly for a few minutes. I feel the pride in the room. We are amazed by what we have just heard, by the sheer power of writing, the talent we have witnessed, the courage our colleagues have displayed—most in a second language.

With one hour remaining, I announce that there is still enough time to write final reflections. Then as we move around the room to read, it is clear that the question, "Why write?" has been answered. Now, for most, the question is, "How can I offer this experience to my students?"

No one is more adamant about the value of a learner-centered classroom than Margret, who reads to us her reflection on teaching:

> I want to support my students in resisting all those leaders who seek to turn their minds into copies of their own, unquestioningly taking what they are offered. A mind that asks questions, reflects, and dares to speak out for all the values once acknowledged to be worthy . . . will be the goal I set for the students in my classroom. Is this utopian? . . . I don't know. But considering our tradition, I have come to ask the following question: Are there any mistakes a teacher could make that are worse than teaching young people to march joyfully into an atrocious war?

I feel tears welling up; sense within me a mix of relief, gratitude, even joy. This time, when everyone raps knuckles, I do the same.

ۆ

On July 16, on the plane home, I think about the courses, the teachers, the little bit of German I now understand, the exhilarating and exhausting hikes up to the snow peaks, my family waiting for me in New York. I recall the scene at the airport that morning. As Tanja and I arrived, we were surprised by Martina, Hans, and Margret, who had formed an impromptu goodbye party. Just before I entered passport control, Margret handed me a package with a letter inside:

> I was so eager to bring to words what had been brooding in my heart for such a long time . . . This experience of reading each other's words and of responding to each other had its climax in a feeling of revelation. If you, Sondra, hadn't been so courageous to ask your careful questions, I would never have been able to answer them. When I eventually realized you were Jewish, it hit me right in my heart and my brain: you are kin to all those people who suffered inconceivably by atrocities committed by my people. History became real and present. I could hardly bear it. I had nothing to offer. An apology would just have been a token weighing so little that the scales of justice would not have moved an inch. Yet with you I have learned that some people are willing to look closer even if it seems impossible to bear doing so. Thus others get the chance to learn.

As I relax into my seat and follow the westward progress of the plane on the screen in front of me, I think about all that has happened. I came here just to teach. It was such a simple invitation.

3

Interlude: Fall-Winter 1996-1997

ack in New York, familiar rhythms reassert themselves. On weekdays, I drive my children to school, walk my dogs in the park, and immerse myself in reading, writing, and teaching. On weekends, my husband, Arthur, and I go out to dinner, see a film, visit with family and friends, or, more often than not, order pizza and watch a video with our children.

Everything seems the same. But everything has changed. Austria does not recede into the background. Memories of Margret and what we said to one another become more vivid. As I recount my experiences in Innsbruck, I realize how deeply I have been touched.

It's not just that Margret and I gave birth to our daughters on the same day or even that mine is the granddaughter of Jews and hers the granddaughter of Nazis; it's not just that my hesitant questions gave Margret an opportunity to speak about her pain or that her heartfelt response shattered my lifelong stereotype. Something else also happened.

In Margret, I saw a mirror image of myself: someone I might have been had circumstances been different. She carried the same shock, the same disgust and fear, the same revulsion. Yet, without my questions she would never have voiced her pain; without her words, I would never have known that my pain was shared by someone I had been taught to hate.

I also realize something else. For most of my life I have been embarrassed to admit that I am Jewish. At thirteen, I learned to play down Judaism and to ignore anti-Semitic remarks. I learned, essentially, how to pass. Even worse, I secretly shared the world's disdain. All I permitted myself to see in the Jews around me was their ostentatious behavior, and inwardly I recoiled. I did not want to be associated with a people so loud, so garish.

In Innsbruck, though, I could not pretend a distance I no longer felt. I was no longer able to say, "I choose not to identify as a Jew." This realization so startles me, it takes my breath away. I feel I am standing on the edge of a precipice and do not know what will happen once I take the next step.

ع٠

I am surrounded by words. My journal, my classroom notes and folders, the teachers' drafts and revisions all lie scattered on the floor. Each time I examine them, I become immersed in the issues of last summer. What does it mean to teach? In what ways is teaching an ethical act? How can one be a full human being in the classroom?

I am struggling with these questions because I need to prepare a talk. The Carnegie Foundation for the Advancement of Teaching has selected me as the 1996 New York State Professor of the Year. This award, created by the late Ernest Boyer, is designed to bring greater prominence to teaching, to make public the idea that what counts at universities, along with publication and scholarship, is a commitment to excellence in the classroom.

Throughout the fall, I am asked to speak about teaching, first to reporters, then on local television. In the spring I am scheduled to speak at the Graduate Center of The City University, where I am a member of the doctoral faculty. Wrestling with what to say, not sure, at first, what approach to take, it dawns on me that in a program designed to celebrate my award, nothing would be more fitting than to take my audience inside that Innsbruck classroom, to tell the story of what happened there.

While I am writing, Tanja calls and raises the possibility of my returning to work with the group in February. We would focus on research methods, and I would show the teachers how to document their own work in classrooms. At first, I am hesitant. Austria seems so far away. I am not eager to leave my family again.

As I continue to work on my talk, however, other arguments assert themselves. My first course focused on the teaching of reading and writing. But in one of those surprising turns that can occur in a classroom, it also became an inquiry into the values that underlie teaching. What better way to determine the impact of this work than to help the teachers document the changes they are now making in their classrooms?

I spend several months drafting my talk. I call it "Facing the Other" and, as I work on it, Innsbruck begins to take on a life of its own. As I sit at the computer, the teachers' faces seem to float across the screen. Their words echo in my ears. I realize I want to see them again; I do not want what happened among us to end so abruptly. Most of all I want to see Margret again, to discover if we can continue to pursue together the issues of history and hatred that speak so deeply to both of us. But what finally convinces me to return are the letters and e-mail I begin receiving from the group.

Tanja reports on a meeting with the teachers, telling me "how meaningful" my work with them had become, "how eagerly" they await my decision about coming back. "Please say yes," she writes, "for all of our sakes!"

Then Ingrid writes to say:

> [I hope you will be] our definite teacher for the February course . . . You know how much I questioned the necessity of writing. All the more have I been fascinated by it ever since . . . Having learned to appreciate the benefits of a reading and writing workshop, I want to share them with my students. This will be especially exciting as, at least in my part of Austria, I do not know any school where similar work has been done . . .

I have not forgotten Ingrid's initial resistance to writing. How gratifying it is to hear how fully she now embraces it.

Adding to the chorus is Margret's irresistible excitement:

> You should see me in my English classes! I have started a Writing Project!! Adventure live! I start my classes with what I call 'aware-ness training' . . . So far they have reacted positively—even the 'tough' guys! . . . It may sound exaggerating but I have changed my way of teaching . . . If only you could be my mentor and guide me through this expedition!

The following week Tanja sends another note, reporting that the teachers are becoming more "learner-centered." What does this mean? I wonder. Could they possibly be enacting their own versions of what it means for teachers to be full human beings in their classrooms? I can only know, I realize, if I return to teach them again.

 је.

In the fall, Margret and I begin a regular correspondence. She writes to me about her work in her classroom; I respond with enthusiasm. We are, after all, two teachers content to "talk shop." Then, little by little, we introduce each other to our families. We tell stories of family life, discuss children's needs and husbands' interests. It is as if we are preparing the ground. Neither one of us knows yet how to raise the larger issues.

Margret's letters are polite, even a bit formal. I am, after all, her American professor. An experienced teacher in her mid-forties, she is still my Austrian student. How do we find the right tone? It is impossible not to wonder whether each of us is expecting too much, or whether we have built this friendship into something more than it is. Nonetheless, I find myself reading her letters with pleasure. It is clear to me that we connect not only as teachers but also as women. In December, she writes:

> Thank you for your letter. I was really excited when I got it, because I had tiny doubts once in a while whether you shared my feelings about our work and our mutual understanding...Deciding to return [to Innsbruck] must have been difficult. There's your work and most of all your family—I know from my own experience that I try to be "sensible" and spend the free time I have with Gert and Cara, just being here and doing all the things a "proper" housewife and mother would do. And still, at the back of my head and heart, there's this urge to engage in things that seem to offer new territory to me. This was exactly the situation before enrolling in the M.A. program. Gert has learned to sense whether a thing is important for me . . .
>
> I'm really enthusiastic about the fact that you'll come back in February. It's like waiting for relatives and looking forward to what they'll bring along. Honestly, it gives me more strength to go on with my project, because what I've learned so far is that circumstances in my school are so difficult that only a small number of my students will profit right away from the work we do. For the others it's like opening a small window through which they do not yet dare to look . . . Maybe one day they'll think of

the work we've done together, and it will become meaningful for them. . . .

Today is a wonderful Sunday morning. Gert got up early and went on a ski tour. We already have lots of snow. I'm staying at home, as Cara has to videotape a detective story for her English classes. This means that the house will be buzzing with girls who seem to be interested in boys only . . . I can hardly stand watching these things going on. It took me a long time and some therapy to reverse the lessons I learned in my childhood and adolescence, namely, that a woman's life is only worth living if men take notice of her. So when watching Cara's friends, I have difficulties in accepting that their behavior could just be "normal" for puberty.

Now Cara has popped in asking me whether I could join her for breakfast. It's the second Advent Sunday. Do you celebrate that? Honestly, I've got no idea at all how you celebrate Christmas and the time before. I would very much like to, though.

Advent Sunday? Do Jews celebrate Christmas? Margret's questions make me smile. It occurs to me that I may be the first Jewish person she has ever met.

I write back in January:

> . . . You asked about the holidays. In general, I would say that Jews do not celebrate Christmas. Some Jews—a minority, I think—do buy Christmas trees. But my friends would not do that. We are not Orthodox, not even very observant, but we do see ourselves as Jewish.
>
> This doesn't make Christmas any easier though. Christmas decorations light up the houses, holiday songs can be heard in the stores, men dressed as Santa Claus stand outside asking shoppers to make donations to various charities. I have always felt excluded from the festivities, and yet it is hard to imagine celebrating a holiday that is, by definition, Christian.
>
> Christmas is especially hard on Jewish children. Just a few weeks ago, Josh, one of my 9-year-old twins, asked, "Why can't we have a Christmas tree?" And last year, Sam, his brother, asked, "Why are we the minority?" They don't understand why something so appealing—and so pervasive—can't also belong to them. Since the Jewish holiday of Hanukkah occurs at the same time of year, we try to make our celebration equally joyous. But it is hard when on TV, in the stores, and on the streets, the children are bombarded by the signs and symbols of Christmas.

My relationship to Judaism is also complex. When I was 13, we moved to a suburb that had very few Jews. In that town, I learned how to downplay being Jewish. It was clear to me that the Christians in my town had prejudices about Jews, and I so wanted to fit in that I avoided conversations about religion. I thought I could continue this avoidance last summer, but as you know, to do so in Austria felt wrong to me.

I have often wondered, if I hadn't said anything, would anyone in the group have known I was Jewish? Did anyone think I went too far? Did I upset anyone?

I still remember how deeply it touched me when you were talking about your in-laws. Has your writing had an impact on your relationship with them? . . . I know it may be risky for us to continue what we started, but I think we still have so much to say and to learn from each other, don't you?

It takes at least one week for letters to travel between New York and Innsbruck. I know that Margret will not have time to answer mine before I arrive. She can't know that being so open about my religion is hard for me. She can't know that ever since our encounter last summer, I have been asking myself what it means to me, an assimilated Jew, an American professor of English, so able to help others turn their lives into texts, to come face-to-face with the meaning of my own.

While my letter is traveling to Innsbruck, another short note from Margret is traveling to me. It arrives just before I leave. She has arranged to meet my plane on Saturday morning. We'll have lunch, then she'll drive me to Tanja's where I will room for the week. She concludes, "Seeing you again is like Christmas for me, and having met you at all is one of the greatest gifts I've ever received."

Straightening my desk, I notice the final draft of my talk, "Facing the Other." It occurs to me that I ought to show it to Margret. It is her story too. I place it in my bag. At this moment I could never imagine that this act will change the direction of the course we are about to begin.

4

A Second Course, a Second Inquiry

In February 1997, seven months after my first trip to Innsbruck, I arrive at the airport in the morning. As I leave the customs area, I see Margret, waving, accompanied by Gert and their daughter, Cara. Suddenly I feel shy.

Margret's obvious delight calms my fears. She hugs me and takes my arm, Gert shakes my hand, Cara smiles. Soon we are in their red van, driving through Innsbruck and then up into the surrounding hills. It becomes steeper and steeper. Houses perch on slopes. Sheep graze on the hillsides. I catch my breath on a sharp curve. "How do you manage to drive these roads in winter?" I ask.

"In heavy snow," Margret says, laughing, "we don't."

A few more hairpin turns and we reach their home in a secluded spot overlooking the city. I follow her along a narrow wooden walkway to her front entrance. The house is built on several levels. I stop to take in the view. Margret points out the Golden Dome, the famous Innsbruck landmark, in the middle of the Old Town. I'm captivated by everything I see. But I am also on guard. Where are the Nazis? I wonder. Later Margret explains that her in-laws live in a separate section of the house with a separate entrance.

Inside, I manage to relax. Her home has a strikingly familiar feel. It is not unlike mine with its modern construction, its light wood floors, and its large glass doors that open onto a wooden deck outside. Margret takes me on a brief tour. Her kitchen, smaller than suburban kitchens in America, gleams with its dark marble counters and gray Formica cabinets. Her living room, with black leather couches and overstuffed pillows, is elegant and spare. A high-powered telescope stands in one corner; Gert, she tells me, likes to look at the stars. Her office makes me smile. Small and book-lined from floor to ceiling, it, too, reminds me of my own. But what I like best is the warm and natural feeling that her house evokes. It is light and airy, with sunlight streaming through the windows, and views of snowcapped mountains rising steeply in the distance.

Margret suggests we hike up to a nearby *Gasthof* for lunch. I readily agree, wanting to see more of the local landscape, knowing that once the course starts, there won't be any time for hiking. Gert and Cara decide to accompany us. Neither of them speaks much English, and I have picked up only a smattering of German, so we communicate primarily with eyes and hands. Lunch, *Knoedelsuppe*, one large dumpling in broth, is punctuated with gestures and smiles and the occasional translation offered by Margret. After coffee and a moment to relax in the unusually warm winter sun, we hike home. Margret makes tea and serves it in the living room.

"I'm really glad to be back," I say, settling myself comfortably on the couch.

Margret nods. "I'm glad too. Last summer before your course started, when Professor Soloway was here working with us on designing research projects, we were all very unhappy."

I had heard some of this history before and was aware that the teachers lobbied for me to return because they already knew we were compatible in terms of style and approaches to classroom research.

"Regarding research methods, there really is a difference of opinion at City College," I explain. "The professor you had last summer is obviously in the more traditional camp. You know," I say, moving closer to what I sense we really want to talk about, "I've never met Beth Soloway, but my guess is that she is Jewish."

"Really? Why do you say that?" Margret says, her voice rising.

"Well, her name for one. You can often identify Jewish names. But I would only really be able to tell if I met her."

Margret's eyes widen in disbelief. "What do you mean?" she exclaims. "You can tell by looking at someone whether or not that person is Jewish?"

"Well, not always," I say, slowly. "But often. Take Susan, the coordinator of the M.A. program, for instance. Her last name, Weil, is Jewish, but I only needed one look to know that she is not. She doesn't have a Jewish face."

"But how is that possible?" Margret stammers, losing her composure. "What is it that identifies someone as Jewish?" I can almost hear the doubt beginning to swell inside her. How can I say such things?

We are sipping chamomile tea in oversized salmon-colored cups. Through the glass deck doors, I can see the mountains rising in the distance above the timberline. I look out, then back at Margret. "I don't know how to explain this," I say deliberately. "There's a way of talking and acting. I mean, can't you tell the difference between the French and the Germans?"

"Well, yes," she says skeptically. "But then there's language and culture."

"I know it may be artificial, but for a minute, try to put aside the difference in language," I say. "Think about the way people move. Think about how they express themselves in their bodies, what their faces look like. Don't you think there are characteristic differences between different groups of people? Say, for example, between Italians and Swedes?"

Margret frowns. She is troubled, shocked even. But I am too: shocked at what I am saying and surprised at how tangled my thoughts are becoming. Am I suggesting that people can be lumped together by the size of their noses or the color of their skin? Surely, I am not saying that. But then, what? Aren't these differences merely superficial? Aren't all people basically alike?

And more to the point: What is it that makes someone recognizably Jewish? As Jews assimilate, outward signs such as *tefillin* and head coverings disappear. But still, at least in the States, I can usually identify a Jew at a glance. In fact, I do it all the time. I lean forward, pick up my teacup, and try again, but find myself going off in another direction.

"There is something more about being Jewish than the religious part," I explain. "Most of my friends identify with being Jewish by their connection to Jewish culture and Jewish life. But on the whole we lead quite secular lives."

"You mentioned this in your last letter," Margret muses.

"Yes. You can be born into a Jewish family, you can know your heritage is Jewish, but you can still have little or no connection to the religion. In fact, for many years, I struggled with the question of whether I should even pass on Judaism to my kids. If being Jewish means bringing the world's hatred upon you, why would one choose it, especially for one's children?"

"But did you really think you had a choice?" Margret asks.

I go on to explain that when Arthur and I were younger, we thought it possible to explore many different cultures and to live among many different people, feeling some allegiance to each one. But as we became older, we concluded that openness to everything also meant commitment to nothing. We began to think that denying one's heritage is shortsighted—if not dishonest.

"For us," I explain, "exploring one's roots won out. And I have to admit that there is something in Judaism that speaks to me even if I can't say what it is."

"Do your children know about the Holocaust?" Margret asks, quietly.

I move uneasily on the couch and look out at the darkening sky. "Well," I sigh, "in one sense, of course. They know the name Hitler. They have heard of concentration camps. But do they really know? It is difficult to decide how much to tell them. I have tried not to instill in them the same hatred my mother instilled in me, and so, perhaps, I have done too little."

"I know," Margret says, her eyes growing dark. "I struggle with this question all the time. How much to tell Cara."

"What does Cara know about her grandparents?"

"What can she know?" Margret responds. "They love her; she loves them. They love when she visits them. She brings light into their lives. I know I must tell her someday, but how can I? Do I have a right to cast a shadow on their relationship? I fear it will open such a huge gap."

I nod. "That's a hard question. You must find it so uncomfortable, living with them, seeing both sides."

"I do," she says, her voice low. She is looking directly at me. "It is painful for me to watch the old man in his garden, knowing what he harbors in his heart."

"Do you think he feels remorse?" I ask, looking back.

"Not really. For years, he and his cronies would go out on April twentieth to celebrate Hitler's birthday. I honestly think they all wish for the old days."

Once again, our eyes meet. We sigh. I should feel outraged. Somewhere in this house is a man who wishes Hitler had won the war. Maybe I should get up and leave. But what would such a gesture accomplish?

I hold her gaze but say nothing. It's getting late. The room has become chilly.

Finally, I ask, "How much do you think the group is aware of what is going on between us? Of the questions we share about the past?"

"Not much," Margret responds. "They think the war has got nothing to do with them. Most prefer not to see themselves playing any role in history."

"But do you think they would be willing to talk more about their sense of the past?" I probe.

"It's hard to say. There was so little response last time. Why should this time be any different?"

I nod, shrugging my shoulders. "I guess you're right. And this time," I tell her, "we are not in a course where people have the option of writing about anything they want. By the time I leave next week, I must be sure everyone has a clear research question and a way to proceed."

"Well," she responds, "I don't think you should act as if the only important questions are the ones we bring about research. And anyway, do you really think we can separate our research questions from who we are as people?"

❧

A little while later, as Margret is driving me to Tanja's where I will be staying for the week, she says haltingly, "Sondra, you are the first Jewish person I have ever known. Ever since we met, I have wondered what I would have done . . . how I would have acted if we had been friends during the war."

She looks at me quickly and then back at the road. I think I see tears glistening in the corners of her eyes.

"How can you know?" I ask quietly. "Would you have risked your life and the life of your family to save mine? Would I have done the same had our roles been reversed?"

In some ways, I think, our questions, spoken gently as we drive through picturesque Austrian towns, are melodramatic. It is 1997. We are living in modern, democratic countries. We are safe. We cannot with any certainty know how we would have behaved. There is no need to ask ourselves these questions. And yet, I know, we must.

On Sunday, our group reconvenes in the same room we used the previous summer. Only this time instead of newness and uncertainty we come together with the excitement of seeing old friends. Smiling, exclaiming, we shake hands, hug, kiss on both cheeks. Everyone has returned except Ursula who is in the hospital with pneumonia.

Before we begin to work, Hans wants to make an announcement. He has been in touch with the faculty at City College and has heard about my Carnegie Award. We cannot begin, he declares, without an appropriate celebration. Martina joins him in pouring champagne into cut-glass goblets, and everyone gathers round to congratulate me. Embarrassed, I blush, my delight obvious.

After we seat ourselves around the familiar large square table, I ask each person to take some time and tell us what has happened since July. "What questions have emerged? What are you thinking about in terms of research topics?"

Andrea, again first to volunteer, tells us that she is excited about the changes she sees in her *Gymnasium* students when they begin to use writing as a way of learning. She wonders if this is an appropriate topic for research. Thomas, his dark brows knitting together as he speaks, explains that he works with adults who have problems learning English. He wants some guidance.

Christa, whose fine features and fair hair still make me think of Aryan beauty, mentions several possibilities. The one that excites her the most revolves around sixteen young girls who have voluntarily begun to work in a reading and writing club.

Sharp-eyed Ingrid, wire-rimmed glasses perched on her head, has brought along some writing her fourth-form students have done in response to their reading of Roald Dahl's novel *Matilda*. "There is so much going on, but my colleagues seem to see only what is missing. I would like to see what you see."

And Astrid, white hair pulled back tightly, voices concern over how her students will fare with the teachers at the next level. "How can I prove that the new methods I have adopted since last summer really work?" she wants to know.

I notice myself nodding and smiling, so pleased to have returned.

ಿ♪

Later that night, curled up on my bed at Tanja's, I write in my journal:

> Our work from last summer's writing groups is carrying over. I like how everyone listened carefully. It's powerful to build from the base we've already established.

Unbeknownst to me, Margret also decides to keep a journal, to record what is happening in the course and between the two of us. Later in the week, we agree to share our writing and hand each other envelopes with handwritten entries tucked inside either at the beginning or end of each class.

On the first night she writes:

> It has been a hard day's work to generate these first research questions. I thought there was too much "proving" in the questions, and it was tough for me to find the right words to help generate meaningful questions. And in between, I watched you and thought about where you were and your desire to learn about what bothers you so much. Will we be able to find a balance between being nurtured—and encountering each other? . . .
>
> I have just talked to Gert about what I am writing. He seemed to be sad, and he told me that he envied us—you and me—because he understands so little when we talk. He told me that he really wishes he had the language to talk to you the way I am able to. He feels like he's not being authentic if I am the one who does the talking. He said he would never be able to express to you in his words what he wants to say . . . I was so startled to realize he can talk to you as little as he can to his father or his mother. . . .
>
> I am thinking of my Cara now, and I would so much wish to carry all the burden for her—whatever it takes to enable her to go on living without having to realize one day that she is despised for what other generations have done or not done. And I am so angry with all those people who shun responsibility, who ignore the past and make me and my child carry a heavier burden than we should.
>
> I do not know who I would have been sixty years ago. I can't say that I would have been a heroine and would have helped your people to survive. What I am certain of is that I would not have volunteered or cheered, and if I had not had the

courage to speak out loud and clearly, I would have been haunted by my cowardice until the day I died.

I started to talk to Cara last night. I felt so helpless, but I am a lot better off than you. How can you teach your daughter about the past without teaching her to condemn us all? How can I teach my daughter about the past without putting the burden on her shoulders and still teach her empathy with you and your people? Can empathy be taught?

There are so many questions in my head. Yesterday you said that when you saw Susan you knew that she was not Jewish. You also said that had you seen Beth Soloway, you would have known if she were Jewish. But what does that mean? How can you tell if a man or a woman is Jewish? I could never detect the difference between a Roman Catholic and a Protestant. You seem to be suggesting that I am totally mistaken to believe that being Jewish is sharing a religion and nothing else. Could that really be so? . . .

I am sitting here realizing how fortunate I am having gotten to know you. If only we could talk more! . . . Time is so precious. I don't want to waste a minute.

I won't read these words for another two days, but when I do, I will not be surprised and will write back immediately. From the moment we sat drinking tea in her living room, I sensed that Margret and I would surpass the intimacy we discovered together last summer. I realized then that she and I were so alike, so eager to explore what has been frightening us since we were children that neither one of us would turn back now.

ॐ

On Monday, the second of our seven days together, we move more deeply into our work. As the professor, I know I have only one week to familiarize the teachers with the theories and practices of teacher inquiry. They will need to understand how to ask questions, how to collect and analyze data, and finally how to write up their results. I set up a tentative schedule: discussion of readings in the morning, a lunch break, conversation about individual work in the afternoon

We begin with Glenda Bissex's book, *Partial Truths*, which describes how Bissex became an advocate of teacher research. The teachers are unanimous in liking her simple style and her reassuring comments and stories. I ask each person to read to us his or her favorite lines.

"I loved what she says about classroom discussions," says Andrea:

> As a teacher I learned what skilled creations discussions were—
> true discussions in which everyone thought aloud together about
> questions that mattered to them.[1]

Ingrid points us to the connection Bissex makes between teaching and living:

> The teacher I wanted to become was also the person I wanted to
> become, which is just as true today as it was forty years ago. I
> didn't envision then that this process would be endless.[2]

"Is it possible," I ask, "that what we set out to learn as teacher-researchers will also affect who we are as people? That the two are not separate?" I notice Margret smiling.

Thomas reads a line that has struck him: " 'An anomaly is the beginning of inquiry.'[3] What she's saying," says Thomas, "is that the things that bother us are the places to start."

"Sometimes the things that are most puzzling offer us the greatest learning," I respond. "Ask yourselves, 'What don't I understand about my classroom? What strikes me as unusual today?' That's where you often find questions worth asking."

Tanja, her thick hair pulled back in a pony tail, likes the way Bissex borrows from the work of scientist Evelyn Fox Keller:

> Keller proposes the concept of "dynamic objectivity" in place of
> an objectivity that is static, detached, and controlling. "Dynamic
> objectivity" . . . relies on our connectivity with the world. [It] is
> not unlike empathy . . .[4]

Margret points out that Bissex also quotes the naturalist Konrad Lorenz who writes, "You must first love your animal before you can study it."[5]

Margret continues, "I agree with Bissex when she says that this sort of love is like empathy, and that it is 'the key to intuition, clarity of vision, and understanding . . . the key to our humanness.'[6] Isn't that what we all want to do—bring empathy and humanity into our classrooms?"

Now it's my turn to smile.

I explain to the class that researchers who design controlled experiments are trained to stand back and to remain as objective as possible. But in the kind of classroom research they will be doing, they will not need to set up an artificial distance between themselves and their subjects. Their caring will draw them closer to their students. "You will begin," I say, "by observing what is in front of you and seeing what calls you."

"But what is the point?" asks Astrid. "In the end don't we have to be objective?"

"I don't think that's the point at all," Tanja responds quickly. "The goal is not to prove anything. The goal is to understand."

"In teacher inquiry," I add, "you study something in order to enrich your understanding of it. What you discover may change with the next class or the next student. Teacher inquiry is a lot like writing, subject to revision. What you discover, as Bissex's title suggests, is only a partial truth."

It is a good place to stop. In an open classroom, as in an open society, there are no final answers, no final solutions.

ÀÂ

At lunch, everyone wants to know about my family. How are my children? Who is taking care of them? How do I like their teachers this year? When I describe my frustration that my daughter's seventh grade teachers assign too much homework and give too many tests, they chuckle. "You mean, even in American schools, tradition dies hard?"

"Yes," I laugh, "the challenges of school reform are not just an Austrian issue."

ÀÂ

In the afternoon, I ask those who did not present their initial thoughts on research to speak. Tanja tells us she is interested in documenting the use of portfolios in her English language classes at a local business school. The group encourages her to explain why. Tanja has to stop and think. "I love what happens when my students keep portfolios of their work, but I am not sure why. I guess I get to know them better . . . I get to see the shape of their learning. But why does this matter to me? I don't really know. I'll have to come back to this."

Martina has come with two different options: evaluating a new curriculum for her school or studying her own work with beginning teachers. "You've worked with student teachers for years," says Christa. "It would be so useful for others to understand what you do." We all murmur in agreement. Martina tells us that our responses make her uneasy. She is feeling coerced as if now she must please us instead of herself. She crosses her arms in front of her chest, saying, "I do not want to be pushed."

"My goal at the university," says Hans, "is to help my students get jobs. I am planning to research the demand for oral English skills in business. Look, I'll be frank. I want my M.A. degree, but I am not in the business of making better human beings. I want my students to succeed, but their values and their humanity are not my concern."

Margret is shocked. "How can you see these as separate?" she retorts, unable to keep the disdain out of her voice. Hans refuses to answer.

The silence becomes uncomfortable. I sense my own uneasiness and the discomfort of the group, but I read these as signs that we are getting beneath the surface. Even if I could resolve this issue, I don't want to. A resolution would be premature. Picking up a point from the morning, I say, "When we think aloud together, we may find ourselves valuing different things. We may discover that we disagree even about what is important. This is what we risk when we teach with such openness. We can make room for differences of opinion here, can't we?"

Everyone nods, except Margret. When we end for the day, she barely looks at me, just picks up her papers and storms out. The next day, at the end of class, she hands me her journal.

> How can I speak my truth if I am not understood? How does anyone dare—in your presence—challenge that the ultimate goal—whether we are teachers or not—is to care for mutual understanding and empathy? The introductory statement of Hans was a slap in my face—to me a slap in your face too—did you feel it? Doesn't he or anyone else here know what this discussion means for us, with our history?

Bissex writes, "Public school teaching stretched and toughened me; it disheartened me and it left me with few treasures."[7]

> I feel the same, but it isn't the kids in school that do that to me. It's the grownups—the speechless men, the assertive women who

always know everything. I do not want to confront any of them anymore. I've done that for so many years now . . .

Later Margret writes:

I'm feeling better now. Hans is my scapegoat for my feelings of inadequacy. My husband can't say to you, Sondra, that he is sorry for what his parents did to your people—not because he wouldn't mean it, but because he can't speak English. I wonder if he can speak his inner voice—in whatever language—when it comes to addressing human beings other than his wife and child. Will these men ever find their voices?

But then aren't we women struggling to find our voices too? Struggling is so painful. Do I abuse you, Sondra, with this journal? With burdening you with all my pain? I beg you to tell me whether this is too much for you. You have to run the course. I have to stop asking my questions in my imperfect way with hidden accusations. I want to concentrate on my research paper. Still will you write back?

Sitting on my bed at Tanja's, wrapped up in a quilt, I write back immediately:

Dear Margret,

It's late at night, I'm tired. I'm having a hard time adjusting to the time change—we've had a long day and I should be preparing for our discussion tomorrow, but none of that matters as much to me right now as what there is between us—what you have written and what there is to say back.

How did we find each other? What forces of life and history have brought us both to this point in our lives? Of course, what you wrote is not "too much." It is the other side of all I think and feel, and to me, it is so brave. I am so glad you decided to write—more than glad—so pleased that you decided to give your journal to me.

You write about our daughters. Yes, I think they will need to understand their inheritance here. But this idea raises other questions: How does one learn to become responsible for others? For the acts of parents and grandparents? When is it too much to bear? And what role will you and I play in showing them what is possible? I hope that our struggles will give us something to pass on to them.

You ask, again, what it means to be Jewish. That is such a good question. I could spend hours and not do justice to its complexity. For many people, being Jewish does mean practicing the religion, but for many others it means something completely different. So, yes, Judaism is a religion, but it is also an identity that is not defined through religious observance—at least as many of my contemporaries see it. And there are many shadings and all sort of nuances in between. I hope we can explore this when we have more time.

You write about Gert. I would like to get to know him—I would like to know who he is, how he lives with his parents' actions, how he understands them. Is it that he has no English—or no German—to express what this means to him?

As for the course, I don't know if anyone understands what you and I seem to be saying over and over again: Who is the person in the research? I don't know what to say about the others. Do people want to stay safe? Don't people have to get their research underway before they are willing to address the personal? To you and me, this is not separate, but if I read the group correctly, they are not so eager, and I must go at their pace.

I know you are upset about Hans and what he has said. Still I must try to reach him, to extend compassion for his struggles too, to offer to have a dialogue. This I must do.

As I close my notebook and turn off the light, I feel lucky to have been given this opportunity to teach and learn in Austria. Luckier still to have met Margret.

ɛ̃ᴥ

On Tuesday, I begin class by placing some questions on the board: Why do we study a student, a class, a teacher? How come we call this work research?

We base our discussion on *Researching Lived Experience* by Max van Manen, particularly chapter one. Van Manen lays out the most thoughtful rationale for classroom research I have ever seen. A philosopher and a methodologist, he often uses difficult words like "hermeneutics" and "phenomenology." Slowly, though, the teachers and I work our way through several important ideas.

The first notion we take from van Manen is that every human being "stands in the world" in a particular way.[8] No one—no doctor, lawyer, parent, teacher—is ever entirely objective or disinterested. Teachers and classroom researchers, van Manen claims, stand in the world in a "pedagogic way," interested in how their students learn, in how they experience the world. This is why we are drawn to classroom inquiry. We are already interested in learning. It is who we are.

The second notion is that human beings know the world through their being in the world, a Heideggerian notion. We are not separate from the world but rather intimately connected to it. "To do research," van Manen writes, "is always to question the way we experience the world, to want to know the world in which we live as human beings . . . In doing research we question the world's very secrets. . . . "[9] Ah, we so easily call ourselves teachers. But, we begin to ask, how is it we know anything?

Van Manen calls the kind of research we will be doing "human science," distinguishing it from research in the natural sciences. In the latter, since Galileo, he tells us, the preferred method of study entails "detached observation, controlled experiments, quantitative measurement in order to explain the laws of nature."[10] In contrast, we will be studying human beings, people who have consciousness and who act purposefully. We will focus on the meaning of events and situations. Our goal is to come to understand the world as our students experience it. "What does it mean?" will likely be the most important question we can ask. This kind of understanding, van Manen claims, is the true basis for a pedagogy of thoughtfulness, based on tact and respect.

Van Manen echoes Bissex. "Lived life is always more complex," he writes, than anything we say about it.[11] Whatever we learn is true for a particular student in a particular situation. In fact, van Manen says, rather than reducing human experience to categories and labels, this work "promotes a theory of the unique."[12]

Little by little, we are chipping away at the standard research paradigm. The teachers will not have to prove anything. They do not have to show that one method of teaching is more effective than another. Instead, they are coming to see that classroom research is essentially an inquiry into meaning—into who they are, who their students are, and the ways they all bring themselves to learning. Anything can be a starting point: how students read and write, the role of journal writing or of poetry or the impact of students' home lives on their development as learners.

Van Manen claims that "description carries a moral force." The research method he advocates asks teachers to address the way they live in classrooms, the way they treat and understand those entrusted to their care: it calls them to examine whether they act "responsibly and responsively."[13]

Unlike last summer, this time around, the group expresses neither surprise nor dismay when the authors they read link teaching to morality. What does come as a surprise is van Manen's discussion of love:

> We can only understand something or someone for whom we care. In this sense of how we come to know a human being, the words of Goethe are especially valid: "One learns to know only what one loves, and the deeper and fuller the knowledge is to be, the more powerful and vivid must be the love, indeed the passion."[14]

It is embarrassing to talk of love. Teaching and research are supposed to be intellectual acts. But it is hard to disagree: love of subjects, love of students, passion for learning, and reverence for life—isn't this what makes a good teacher and, ultimately, a good human being?

ह&

Today we treat ourselves to a leisurely lunch at a Chinese restaurant. It is so warm that we leave our coats inside. As we walk together on a bridge over the Inn River, I notice that the uncomfortable feelings between Hans and Margret seem to have passed. I make it my business to walk alongside the teachers with whom I have not yet spent much time. I talk with Astrid about her summer trip to Spain and with Hilde about her work on the new European Union project for teachers.

ह&

In the afternoon, we address different questions: What do completed projects look like? How does one write up classroom research? To answer these questions, I have assigned *Cityscapes*, a compilation of classroom research projects published by the National Writing Project, the preeminent staff development organization in the United States. Each chapter is authored by a teacher/researcher; everyone in our group has chosen a different chapter to present.

During the presentations, we look at the ways in which each teacher asks his or her research question. We examine how the writers integrate their reading of relevant research into their narratives. We pay attention to the use of the first person pronoun "I." These writers, we conclude, do not distance themselves from their work. They are intimately connected to their students and their classrooms. You can hear their voices. We are particularly struck by Christine Cziko's opening description of a high school in New York:

> I teach in an inner-city, comprehensive high school of over 4,000 students, 99% of whom are African-American, Caribbean or Hispanic. The school is dirty, overcrowded and sometimes dangerous. There are 17 full-time security guards who use metal detectors to search students and scan their book bags for weapons as they enter the building each day. There are 10 deans who use bullhorns in the hallways to order kids to class or race to the scene of fights called in regularly on their walkie-talkies. The attendance is low, the dropout rate is high and the morale is near zero for both students and staff.[15]

And, from a different chapter, Howard Banford's description of a student:

> Every teacher has a student like Maricar. She is the quiet girl, the one I could not remember when I sat down to make out the seating chart three weeks into the semester. She is . . . one of the "phantom students," one of those children whose voices are heard little or not at all . . .[16]

And, from another, Marcie Resnick's framing of a problem:

> For most of the 18 years I have taught at my Philadelphia elementary school, the same sign has been fastened to an easel just inside the school's entrance: PARENTS—REPORT TO THE OFFICE FIRST—IT'S THE LAW. Each morning I have walked heedlessly by this sign. But on one particular morning the sign spoke to me in a new way. On that morning the sign was to become a symbol of the mixed messages schools send to parents about their roles in their children's education. I started to think about how that sign, present in most schools throughout the city, represented all the work that was needed . . . to improve the relationship between families and schools.[17]

Everyone is excited. "They don't sound like researchers," laughs Thomas. "They sound like real people."

"Can we write like this?" asks Hilde.

"I hope you will," I respond, smiling.

I am delighted that the teachers are beginning to see the possibilities of teacher inquiry, pleased when we end on a note of optimism, happy to join Tanja and Andrea for a light meal and a drink after class, and curious to read what Margret has written when she hands me her journal at the end of the day.

ॐ

On Wednesday, when I walk into the classroom, I hand Margret my written response to her journal. As I do, she says, "I've arranged to take you out to dinner tonight. We can sit and have a glass of wine and well—what do you think?" she asks, her eyes twinkling with delight.

I am thrilled. I had been hoping for time alone with Margret, but was not sure I could suggest it without her feeling obligated. "What a great idea," I respond, hugging her in anticipation. "I'd love to."

The work today comes from a group of educators at the London Schools Council who began paying close attention to children's language long before doing so became fashionable in America. To represent this strand of British education, I have chosen *Language, the Learner and the School* by Douglas Barnes, James Britton, and Michael Torbe. The theories of learning presented in their work echo what we have been reading elsewhere:

> Our knowledge of the world is inextricably bound up with the way we feel about the world. . . . It is our values that make us the sort of people we are, and it is on this basis of shared values that we establish our most intimate network of relationships with other people.[18]

They write as well about the importance of the teacher as a learner, as someone for whom learning is a "felt reality."[19]

I have been familiar with this work for years, but sitting in our classroom in Innsbruck, I realize that, without doing so deliberately, I have once again selected work that has an ethical underpinning:

> Teachers must be as "good as their word." Martin Buber goes so far as to suggest that this relationship of mutual trust is the key to all that school education can achieve: trust in the teacher breeds trust in the world—trust on the part of the individual child in his own ability to make sense of the world.[20]

With a slightly different twist, the teachers are hearing a familiar message. Dedicated teachers are learners in their own classrooms. They are aware of their own thoughts and feelings and use these, when appropriate, to guide students. Models of teaching that promote the teacher primarily or exclusively as a transmitter of information do not provide rich, interactive contexts for learning. Such contexts require intimacy, openness, mutual respect, trust, and dialogue.

As I talk with the teachers, I am convinced that each person is deepening his or her understanding of classroom research. It delights me that they are enthusiastic about the theories I have presented to them. But I wonder if they will be willing to put them into practice with me. Can we be who we are in this classroom? Isn't that the real challenge?

ʒ◣

After lunch, we continue our discussion of *Cityscapes*. Once again, the teachers surprise me. They like the carefully crafted openings, they say, but on the whole they are disappointed. Christa, often quiet in class, comments, "These chapters are slim. After all this work, there seems to be so little in the way of findings."

Tanja agrees, "There is something very predictable about the endings of these chapters. No one comes out and says anything very strongly, only that the process of inquiry has been worthwhile."

We have already read in Bissex that teacher research does not necessarily produce "earth-shaking conclusions," that its value often lies in the insights it generates for improving practice.[21] But the Austrian teachers are voicing a criticism that brings us back to van Manen.

Cityscapes has an ambitious agenda. It sets out to describe the ways teachers in urban classrooms deal with wrenchingly difficult problems: poverty, overcrowding, race and class divisions, even violence. While the questions and approaches are fascinating, in the end the conclusions do not directly address the problems that beset urban classrooms. Missing is the "moral force" van Manen claims is the hallmark of thoughtful research.

I respond, "Here's what we can take from this—a lesson in the importance of taking a stand. Like these American teachers, when you do your research, you will have looked closely at your students, your classroom, your school, and the social and political contexts in which you teach. You may discover that you have difficult things to say. I hope that you will think hard about what helps students learn and what gets in the way of learning. And in your writing, I hope you will speak with the full force of your own convictions."

Of course, it hits me: If, as Perrone claims, teaching is at best a moral act, and if the teachers are studying the act of teaching, then in the end, shouldn't their theses address moral issues?

⧉

At Restaurant Kapeller, with its wood-paneled walls, small rooms, fine linens, and candlelight, Margret and I are shown to a table in a corner. The staff seems to know her well. I smile to myself. This is a side of Innsbruck, and of Margret, I have not seen before—an elegant side. Margret orders champagne. Smiling, we clink glasses and tell each other how happy we are to be here, away from family, friends, the class. We have the whole night just to talk.

"Sometimes," Margret muses, "I wonder if I should just be quiet in class. I make people too unhappy."

"No. You say what you think no matter what," I respond, leaning back against the wall, sipping champagne.

"But I'm always like that—too critical, too provocative," she objects.

"I don't think so. You stand up for what you think is right. Most of my life I did not do that. I was too scared to confront authority. I stayed quiet; I was a good girl, the dutiful first-born daughter, always polite. That too is a kind of oppression, don't you think?"

"You're not like that now," she says, her eyes crinkling.

"I'm not a kid any more, either," I say, smiling back. But I know what she means. Certainly in my classroom, I am no longer so afraid to speak.

The waiter comes by, refills our champagne glasses, and carefully places truffles on toasted rounds of bread in front of us. We sit back and allow the food and conversation to fill us. Slowly we move from the class to ourselves, from our families to our histories. We talk of film and music, husbands and parents, Vietnam and protest marches. Given the six-hour time difference between Austria and the States, we try to figure out who was born first, Cara or Sara. Eventually, we find ourselves circling back to the Holocaust.

Margret's eyes cloud over and fill with tears. "I don't know what I would have done if we were alive sixty years ago."

"I know," I say. "It's too terrible to imagine. There had to have been people, women like us, faced with that question." I try to imagine Innsbruck almost sixty years ago after the *Anschluss*. How many Jews lived here? Were the Tyroleans glad to see them go? Did they, like the Viennese, cheer Hitler in the streets? My eyes, too, fill with tears.

"I ask my mum about it," Margret sighs, "but the conversation never seems to go anywhere. I hate that most people won't talk."

I think of my own mother and how she bristled when references to Germany entered even the simplest of conversations. Yet here I am in Innsbruck, with Margret, and there is no way I can continue to hold on to that all-encompassing hatred.

The waiter brings us shrimp scampi and fish terrine. We switch from champagne to wine. I feel as if we are in a movie, as if the setting, the food, the soft lights, the intimate conversation cannot be real.

I look around the room and notice a teenage girl watching us. She looks to be about sixteen, having dinner with her parents. I am reminded of my first trip to Europe with my parents, when, as a teenager, I yearned to be worldly and wise. Now, here I am, contemplating the world's horrors with an Austrian woman whose friendship is becoming increasingly important to me. I feel so lucky to be here, in this place, at this time.

Margret tells me about Gert. She met him at a protest rally against nuclear power in the early 1970s. At that time, he and his younger brother were active members of a radical left-wing Maoist group, something his parents abhorred. But before the political period of Gert's life, there was a time, Margret explains, when he drove a sports car and dressed like a dandy. I laugh at this description. Thin and muscular, with a shock of white hair that reminds me of Andy Warhol, what I see in Gert is a soft-spoken gentleness. "His eyes are kind," I tell her.

She asks me about Arthur. He, too, I tell her, was at one time rather flamboyant. After graduating from Harvard, he lived in Paris, learned to play Beethoven piano sonatas, and became fluent in French. But like Gert, he too was radicalized. For him it happened after he was sent to Vietnam. He worked in Army Intelligence and lived undercover in Saigon. After that, he was never the same. He came back and dedicated himself to understanding the roots of alienation. He initiated a national study on the impact of the war on the men of his generation and in 1986 published a book called *Healing from the War: Trauma and Transformation after Vietnam*. Now he is a clinical psychologist, practicing therapy with individual clients.

We fantasize about our families meeting one another. The prospect makes us smile. Soon dessert appears: tiny chocolates, filigree cookies, marzipan.

"I think you are letting them off too easily, you know," Margret comments, suddenly serious.

"I realize this question of history is important to you and me," I respond, "but I don't think there is room for our agenda here. Half the group doesn't even have a research question yet."

"And if you let it go? How will you feel then?" she prods.

"Well, as if this was a missed opportunity, I guess. It does feel as if there are two agendas. What is happening with all of us in the course and what is happening privately between you and me."

"I know. It's the same for me. But what is happening between us is so valuable. Can you really leave in a few days without saying a word?" she asks, eyeing me closely.

"I don't know," I say shrugging. "Maybe there is some way to open up the discussion." I sip from my wine glass, then approach Margret about another topic. "I had to prepare a talk on teaching for the Carnegie Award. I decided to tell the story of what happened in our course last summer. Naturally, you are a major part of the story. I want to give you a copy and ask you if it is all right for me to write about our relationship—to include your words in my paper."

"I'd be glad to read whatever you write," Margret says easily.

Margret seems not to realize how momentous this is for me. In the paper, I reveal more about myself than I have until now. I fear that she will misunderstand or that my words may offend her. But she has a right to see what I have written. Despite my misgivings, as we leave the restaurant, I hand her the manuscript of "Facing the Other."

ès

The next morning, before class begins, Margret arrives early and finds me in the office next to our classroom. Her eyes are red. "I stayed up all night reading and thinking. This is so incredible. I could not stop crying," she says in a hushed voice, looking to see if anyone else is around. We are alone.

I am relieved and let out a sigh. She doesn't hate it.

"I've thought about this paper all night. You must make copies and give them to the group. They must see this. It is so important," she implores.

"Show it to the group? You're crazy. I can't do that," I protest.

"Of course you can. There is so much in there for them to learn. You don't need to make it part of the course. Just hand out copies for them to read at home," she suggests. "And then, well, why not ask them to write responses? That way you do not have to devote class time to it."

"It's just that it is so personal. I don't know," I say. But even in my hesitation, I realize Margret is right. Not only should the other teachers see it; as students in the course I am writing about, they have a right to see it. We are about to discuss the issue of permissions to publish student work. What could make the issue more real?

Then Margret suggests something even more startling. "I have a friend," she explains. "A historian, an Austrian. He's been documenting what happened in Innsbruck during the Holocaust. If I asked him, I think he would be willing to take us on a walking tour and tell us what he has discovered."

"A field trip?" I say, incredulous. I am immediately drawn to the idea. All along I have wanted to know what occurred in Innsbruck. If I don't take advantage of this opportunity, I may never have another. I am flying home as soon as the course ends. But I am also worried since we have only three days left to complete our work. No one has shown any interest in discussing the past. Won't a field trip be pushing the limit?

I tell Margret that I think she is right about my paper. I will give everyone a copy. But if we do it at all, the walking tour must be optional.

ò•

In terms of course work, we have another full day planned. A few of the teachers have brought samples of student work. We agree that it would be useful to examine some together, to practice how to analyze the writing one collects in a classroom project. Doing so will allow me to introduce the teachers to a documentary process pioneered by Patricia Carini at the Prospect School in Vermont, to show them how they can pool their powers of observation and description so that they can sustain each other in this work after I return to New York.

Hilde has brought poems written by students in her lowest ability group, the "third stream" students in her *Hauptschule*, a typical Austrian vocational school. I ask each person to read the student writing, to offer first a brief comment, then a more detailed observation.

The poems, Hilde explains, were written in response to an ecology project. She was not convinced that low-level students could write poetically. But our observations reassure her. Tanja notices a rhyme scheme in several of the poems. Martina comments on the different tones, one angry, another hopeful. Ingrid points out how some students' drawings seem to overshadow their words. We notice that Hilde's students have articulated deep concerns about the environment, about acid rain, about pollution, about a world that blithely takes from the earth without replenishing her resources.

Once we have immersed ourselves in the details of these drafts, we are able to draw inferences about individual writers, make suggestions to Hilde about what she might do to develop this project through additional readings and music, and suggest ways she can write about it in her thesis.

After an hour and a half of talk focused on close observation and description, we all emerge with a clear picture of Hilde's classroom. Others seem eager to present the writing they have brought with them. We plan to spend the afternoon looking at work from Andrea's class.

Before we break for lunch, I take some time to tell the group about my paper. I mention that as a recipient of the Carnegie Award, I have been invited to give a talk on teaching. I explain that I want to tell the story of what happened in our course last summer, and I would like their permission to quote them. I tell them that I will give each of them a copy of the draft at the end of the day, that I would like them to read it on their own time and to write me a response when they can.

This, I think, is the easy part. They don't know what's in the paper so my request seems reasonable. But now I need to introduce the possibility of the walking tour with Margret's historian friend. This idea, I worry, may not seem reasonable at all.

"Last night, I gave Margret a copy of my paper," I tell them. "I wanted her to read it first because she figures in it so prominently. It is really at her encouragement that I am sharing it with you. As you will see, it has a lot to do with the questions I raised last summer.

"Some of you may be aware that Margret and I have had a dialogue going on outside the classroom. It's been extremely valuable to us and last night we realized that, while these questions move us deeply, they do not belong only to us. So what I am about to suggest I say in the spirit of shared inquiry that Margret and I are finding so powerful."

I notice Andrea nodding eagerly. I think she wants to be included. Tanja, too, and Christa.

I take a deep breath and continue: "The texts we have been studying are more than abstractions to me. They raise questions of what it means to bring the teacher as a whole human being into the classroom. They also talk about the classroom as a place for building trust and practicing dialogue. I am hoping we can do some of these things together. I am hoping we can engage in a conversation that will help us understand our different histories and points of view.

"When you read my paper, you will see that I raise questions about the Holocaust. After Margret read it, she proposed that we go on a walking tour with one of her friends who has been conducting research on events in Innsbruck before and during the war. I would very much like to do this. If any of you is interested in coming along, it will likely occur some time tomorrow, probably late in the afternoon. If you prefer not to go, then you can stay here or go to the library and work on your research proposals. Either way, I want you to know that the choice is yours."

As we break for lunch, Ingrid stops me. She has tears in her eyes and is unable to get up. I sit down next to her as the others leave. "I am beginning to see," she says, her voice trembling, "that my research project is a response to fascism."

"Tell me more," I say, somewhat puzzled.

"I am always concerned about the same thing: structure and freedom. I am always asking, how much structure is too much? My whole life has been one of following the rules, doing what I am told. But I want my students to risk breaking out, to find out what they think for themselves. It all goes back to fascism and learning to think for oneself. Do you see?"

"Are you saying, Ingrid, that fascism doesn't leave room for an individual to think or express her own thoughts? So if you get your students to express themselves, you are making your fight against an old enemy?"

"Yes," she says, nodding, "and the worst part is the silence that fascism breeds."

Ingrid pauses, looks at me, and goes on. "My father, after he came back from the war, was a broken man. He was a child when he went, only seventeen years old, with a machine gun in his arms. And we never talked. We have had no real talk of this ever." She starts to cry.

We sit in silence for a few minutes. Ingrid strikes me as remarkably honest. I want to reach out, to comfort her. And yet, that seems odd. Other than Margret, she is the first to tell me her father was a soldier. Does that also mean he was a Nazi? I would like to ask her. But I sense this issue is far too delicate for such a direct question.

As she wipes her eyes, we realize how late we are. The others have already left for Gasthof Gruber, a restaurant on the outskirts of the Old Town. She tells me to go on without her, but I tell her I'll wait. I don't want to leave her alone. After she has gathered her things, we throw on our coats and rush outside. The sky is gray, and a noticeable chill is in the air. We walk together at a fast clip.

ε∙

We find our group seated in a small private room, gathered around a wooden table. After we order, Astrid calls our attention to a wall hanging. A young woman, apron-clad and smiling, is standing at her kitchen sink. Embroidered in German on the bottom is: "A woman's kitchen should be as clean and pure as her heart." Astrid comments, "This saying comes from that time you people do not like."

I glance quickly at Margret, seated at the other end of the table. Is Astrid saying it comes from the days of the Nazis? And who exactly are "you people"? Me? Margret? The rest of the class? The Jews?

No one responds to her remark.

ε∙

In the afternoon, we examine two drafts by a fourteen-year-old girl in Andrea's class. What can we tell from her writing?

We begin building our understanding from close observations of what we see in the texts, moving line by line, paraphrasing what we have read. As each of us comments, we create a nuanced picture of this girl. Summarizing our comments, I steer the discussion to what can be seen as patterns or themes arising from our observations, modeling for the teachers what they will need to do themselves as they become classroom researchers.

It is a long afternoon, dealing with the nuts and bolts of research. I am trying, in part, to prepare everyone to work without me. They form partnerships, set up study groups, plan future meetings. I spend a lot of time allaying fears. I assure them that their final products do not have to be perfect. They can risk making mistakes. Like teaching, engaging in this sort of research requires a great deal of trust. Given time, they will see the outlines of the stories they want to tell.

"I have no doubt," I tell them, "that you will be able to do this work." But as the day comes to a close, my own doubts emerge. It is time to give them my paper. Who I am—as a teacher, a woman, and a Jew—will now be in their hands.

⁊₰

That night, Margret writes in her journal:

> We went to dinner last night, and I so much enjoyed our dia-
> logue full of mutual understanding. The sorrow, the pain, the joy,
> and the humor we shared. I came home and read your piece, and
> as I sat there crying I knew right away that there was no way to
> keep all these thoughts of yours from the group. Just no way. I
> woke Gert up and told him what I felt, and he said he had
> already started to write a letter to you. It was the first time in his
> life he set out to write a letter. *I* haven't got one from him. And
> when he told me that he tried to do it as an inner monologue,
> I was so grateful to have him.
>   I also spent an hour tonight talking to my mum about her
> arrival in Innsbruck in 1939. She told me a story about her mum.
> My granny, she said, once threw a crust of bread out the window
> to an inmate [from the local labor camp, Reichenau] in the street.
> She was summoned to Gestapo headquarters for this act of dis-
> obedience. A friend got her out. My mum said, "Granny did all
> she dared to. It was not much." My mum sat there crying. It was
> the first time, Sondra, the first time she was willing to talk . . .
>   Martin Luther King, Jr. says in a speech against the Viet-
> nam War: "I agree with Dante that the hottest place in hell is
> reserved for those who, in times of moral crisis, maintain their
> neutrality." I see a moral crisis when standing in the classroom
> and witnessing what is done to our kids. Their will is broken,
> their fantasies cut off, their creativity buried under tons of stone
> having been hurled at them. And still, this is nothing compared
> to the Holocaust.

While Margret is writing this entry, I am in my room at Tanja's, overcome by emotion. Tears stream down my cheeks. As soon as I wipe them away, new ones form. I try to sleep but cannot. I throw off the covers, stand up, look out the window, climb back into bed, turn off the light, turn it back on. I am restless, unsettled, unable to calm down.

Lying in bed, I am surprised at the depth of my feelings. I feel exposed. Vulnerable. I am aware that none of this would have occurred had I not come to Austria. It is a response to being in this land and experiencing my own connection to its history—all unplanned, unforeseen, all shocking to me. I know my tears cannot change the past or alleviate the sorrow. I find them pointless really and, yet, I can't stop crying. I open my journal to write to Margret:

> It is so strange to find myself crying. I rarely cry. And yet I am sitting here at Tanja's and tears come—tears for all of it—you, me, our parents, our daughters, our husbands, my sons, the six million, the children, the ovens, the gas, the sorrow, the pain, the history—I cry for all of it and for none of it—tears of grief and tears of release—for all that we have said and all that we can never say—for all the years that I turned away, turned my back on so much sadness, so much sorrow. And now I am flooded with images and with what it means to me to be here, to take this on and to do so with you. . . .
>
> Tomorrow we will walk and bear witness to what? I don't even know—to what was once there? To the absence? I know we will be there together—I want us to be there together—but suddenly I also feel self-conscious. Not with you but with the others. I have lost touch with why we are doing this—why we thought it would be a good idea. I experience my own defensiveness right now. I don't want their pity or knowing looks or to be examined for how I take this in. I don't want to be on display—the token Jew.
>
> And yet, I know what is speaking here is my fear of being vulnerable. I know that to keep this just between us as our private communication is to engage in a kind of selfishness—it is so obvious that this does not belong only to us. So we are inviting them to join us in confronting what is before us—we are making it possible for them to experience this for themselves in their own ways. Well, that brings me back a bit—to us, this quest.

ॐ

On Friday, February 14, the sky is dark and threatening. As a treat from the States, I have brought Valentine candies to place at everyone's seat. But when I walk into the classroom, I gasp. Christa and Hilde have come early and placed tiny vases of flowers and little bits of chocolate at each person's place. In contrast to the bleakness outside, our room is bursting with color. After five days of focused work, it is lovely to find a lighthearted surprise. My gift, old-fashioned, pastel-colored candy hearts with messages such as "Be Mine" or "Write Soon" or "Hug Me," brings smiles of delight. I am tickled by the modern flourish on one: "Send E-mail."

We have another busy day. I plan to meet with small groups of teachers still unsure about their research topics. Margret will present her project. We will discuss additional articles on case-study research, share a working lunch of pizza and salad in the classroom, and then, after lunch, those who choose to will join Margret and me as we walk with her friend, the historian, Horst Schreiber.

Margret and I exchange journals early in the day, but I have no time to read hers until later on. I am meeting with Martina, Ingrid, Christa, Thomas, and Astrid, none of whom has entirely settled on a project. As I begin, Martina interrupts me. "I cannot go ahead with our work without first saying something about your paper. I am so sorry," she says, her voice catching. "I just didn't realize last summer how much this meant to you."

The others nod. "We didn't know, we weren't aware," Thomas says. "I remember Margret's questions from last summer, but that's all. I never even knew you were Jewish."

"But didn't my group say anything to you?" I ask, incredulous.

Now they look surprised. "You told us that our group discussions were confidential," says Christa gently. "We wouldn't have mentioned what happened in our group to the others."

"You wrote about a grapevine," says Astrid, a defensive edge in her voice. "But there wasn't one."

I am truly surprised. I do instruct participants of writing groups not to talk about the content of people's writing and to honor the agreement of confidentiality. But my being Jewish was not disclosed as a secret. It struck me as a particularly relevant piece of information in this setting. I never imagined the teachers would see it any other way.

"Mainly," Martina continues, "I see now how silent we all were. It's as if we heard you but we didn't. It's really as if we ignored you," she says slowly, looking away from me.

Christa nods in agreement. "Your writing . . . there is so much to think about," she says softly. "I will need more time to understand what happened. But then I will write to you. Right now, all I can do is think."

Ingrid looks away. She will not meet my eyes.

I take a minute to compose myself and say, "I am really interested in your responses. But this is too difficult to discuss in a group. I thank you for not letting it pass by unnoticed today, but why don't we get back to the research? As you find yourself thinking about my paper, would you jot down your thoughts and send them to me? I'd welcome that."

We return to the task at hand: formulating clear projects. Most need just a bit more discussion before settling on a focus. Only Thomas is still unsure. But Ingrid's silence worries me. As we leave the room, I ask her to wait. "Is something wrong?" I inquire.

"Yes," she says emphatically. "I did not close my eyes last night. I just don't understand. How could you come to Innsbruck feeling the way you do about us? I cannot believe you would come here thinking we are all alike—that we are all Nazis. How can you?" she asks, her eyes flashing angrily.

Ingrid is furious with me. I want to explain, to show her that there is more here than she sees. But when? I must return to the group. All I can say is, "Ingrid, I know I say some hard things. You certainly have a right to your response. But I would hate to leave it like this. Can we find some time to talk later?"

She nods, not very convincingly.

❧

We gather together once again as a whole group. It is time for Margret to present her research project. She wants to describe her work and asks us to respond by pointing to what we see as most promising.

The title for her thesis is "Classroomscapes," in honor of the American teachers in *Cityscapes*. "I feel thankful to those teachers in American urban classrooms," she says. "The environment in which they teach is so different from mine and so scary to me, and yet they do not complain or lament, at least not in this book. They try to do their best in a modest and caring way. Their work is full of wisdom and love. I am glad that they did not present lots of findings. I can see them as human beings very clearly. For me they are beacons of hope—as are my students.

"But," she continues, "my thesis would never be complete without an afterward called 'Homescapes.' I want to interview my mum and also my mother-in-law about what they experienced during the war, maybe write about a day in each of their lives. My home life and my family life are not separate from my life in school. And all of these must come together in my thesis. For me, none of the issues I am talking about can be separated."

I am, once again, amazed at how Margret has integrated her personal and her professional lives. But I do not want to speak first. I wait for others to respond.

"I enjoy listening to you talk about your project. You are so sure of where you are going. How many students will you include?" asks Christa.

"I've got two here for you to look at," answers Margret, "but I have not really decided which ones to focus on."

Others are impressed too. "It sounds as if you've already collected so much data," comments Andrea.

"I knew last summer that I would do a writing project in my classroom, so I have been saving everything my students write," Margret answers.

We spend some time looking at the samples Margret has brought with her, and we can see just how much writing and thinking occur in her classroom. We hear student voices that strike us as open and honest. We read a handful of Margret's written comments to them and recognize her voice. It is hard not be struck by the force of her convictions.

Thomas comments that "Classroomscapes" and "Homescapes" remind him of landscapes. "You will be showing us the land, the territory of your classroom and your home. I really like that."

Then Tanja reminds us of another related word, "scapegoat." "Is there a connection? Will your homescapes have anything to do with scapegoats?" she asks. We all sit for a moment with the resonance.

At one o'clock, the pizza arrives. As we gather to eat, we also talk informally about research projects. Thomas asks if he should tape his adult students as they talk in class. Should he examine their textbooks for underlying assumptions? What about videotape? The group has learned how to answer him. "What interests you the most, Thomas? Where is your heart? What do you want most to learn about?"

I smile. They would not have asked such questions six days ago.

I go off by myself and take a moment to read Margret's latest journal entry:

Just read your note and again I feel ashamed and protective at the same time. I do fear that others may not understand. What if they do not see what I see? What if they do not ask the only question possible: how come I do not see?

I want to take this walk with you in silence — walking on the same ground people walked 60 years ago—knowing how different walking would have been for us then. I so hope that the groups' stares and speechlessness don't hurt you too much. No one feels pity for you. We feel humiliated by our own history. You'll see, there will be some in our group who do not put you on display but who see our walk as a dialogue, a sharing of something that cannot ultimately be shared.

When lunch ends, it is time to meet Margret's friend. This whole undertaking scares me. I know I am taking a risk with the group, that I am inviting them to address their own relationship to their history. Her note confirms for me that I should say something before we leave.

I stand up and ask for everyone's attention. I take a deep breath to calm myself. "I want to frame what we are about to do by returning to van Manen. He tells us that as teachers we stand in the world in a pedagogic way. On this walk, we will be standing not only as teachers but also as Austrian or American citizens. I think it might be helpful for each of us to ask, 'Who am I here? What am I bringing? What history? What memories? What silences?' This is, I think, the place where we will each come up against the question of what this history means in our own lives.

"As you know, this inquiry has become particularly compelling for Margret and for me. I am inviting you to join us. But please know that if you prefer not to come, you can stay here and work on your proposals. Whatever you choose to do is fine with me."

As we put on coats, scarves, hats, and gloves, I look around the room. Everyone is getting ready. I cannot tell if this is a good sign or a bad one.

5

Whipped by the Wind

s we leave the university, snow begins to fall. I look up. Although it's only 2:00 P.M., the sky is dark. Margret and I lead the way to the Old Town.

I cannot take a step without thinking about the past. All the questions I had as a child come rushing back. Especially the big one. The God question. Where was He? How could an all-powerful God let this happen? Doesn't the Holocaust prove God does not exist? Since I was thirteen, I have been unable to resolve this question. In fact, I have not wanted to, preferring to use the Holocaust as justification for turning away from Judaism.

Raising my voice above the wind, I ask Margret, "Do you have faith or a belief in God?"

She does not seem surprised by my question. "I don't know," she answers slowly, drawing closer as we walk. "Certainly not the God one finds in church. I was raised a Catholic, but I can't stand their hypocrisy."

"What about Cara?" I continue. "Are you bringing her up without belief?"

"Gert would," she says brushing her hair out of her eyes. "He is opposed to all organized religion. When she was a baby, I wanted her to be baptized, so we had to search for a long time to find a priest who would be willing to baptize her without a fancy ceremony. Finally, we succeeded, but it was a real battle. Now, she goes to church occasionally, sometimes with my in-laws. We rarely go. What about you? Do your kids go to religious school?"

"They do. Arthur and I wanted to provide our children with knowledge of their heritage beyond the few holidays we celebrate. But we didn't want to do this in a perfunctory way. So we helped organize a Jewish study group with a few other couples in our neighborhood. We've been studying with a rabbi, reading Jewish texts and commentaries for several years now. Our inquiry is helping me grasp what Judaism is. It's helping me to get beneath the surface, to understand what makes Jewish life and observance meaningful."

We pause at a stop light and draw our coats tighter around us. The wind is blowing hard. I continue, "I didn't want to give the kids the message that religious training was something only they had to do—a message I got when I was growing up. So now, mainly because of the kids, I find myself studying and trying to understand Judaism, trying to figure out what it means to me."

"What about God?" Margret asks as we continue walking.

"Oh," I sigh. "It's so hard to say. I can be touched by so many things: people, nature, music, painting, my children. The rabbi we study with claims being touched in that way is an experience of God— of awe. I know I've experienced that."

"I have too," Margret responds, nodding.

"But to call that God?" I shake my head. "I keep searching. I'm not closed to the idea any more. But once I learned about the gas chambers, I honestly stopped believing in God."

We have met up with Horst Schreiber whose light eyes meet mine as Margret introduces us. A slight, trim man in his mid-thirties, Horst is a high school teacher of history and French. His long-standing interest in the events of the Holocaust has led him to conduct several documentary projects, uncovering what happened to Jewish Austrians living in the Tyrol at the time of the Third Reich.

As the group gathers round him, Horst suggests speaking in German. Margret and Tanja agree to take turns translating for me. He tells us he has six places to show us but much of what we will hear is the untold history—what Innsbruck officialdom wants suppressed.

We are standing on Franz Mair Gasse, a nondescript, quiet street that borders the Landesmuseum. "We begin here," says Horst, "because Franz Mair was the only teacher in Innsbruck to resist openly National Socialism. He was a brave man who refused to go along with the prevailing view. He was also an unusual teacher."

"In what way unusual?" asks Thomas.

"I've interviewed people who were his pupils in the 1930s and '40s. They still mention how important he was to them. He lived near the school and spent private time with students. He took them hiking in the mountains. He was enthusiastic about culture, literature, and music. He was what we would call *Schoengeist,* a man of letters, exceptional for that time and place."

We are standing in a semi-circle around Horst, listening quietly as the snow starts to fall faster.

Horst continues, "Franz Mair found a way to get inside his students' hearts and to show them a world beyond Nazism and Catholicism. He encouraged their spirit of resistance. Later on, many of his students joined the Tyrolean resistance groups."

"What happened to him?" Christa asks.

"He was shot by the SS at the very end of the war, but I'll tell you that story as we finish our walk."

"You say that Franz Mair was different. So are you saying that all the other teachers went along?" I ask.

Horst smiles wanly. "It's always complicated to explain. Approximately seventy to eighty percent of the teachers in the Tyrol and Vorarlberg—we think of these areas together—were members of the NSDAP [the National Socialist Democratic Workers Party] or waiting to be accepted. It was not so much that they wanted to be Nazis. They were too Catholic for that. But everyone wanted jobs. People who could not get work saw the benefits of aligning themselves with the Nazis."

"And so, after they got the teaching jobs, they just looked away when times got bad?" Margret queries.

Horst continues, calmly, not patronizingly, "You also must realize that the Tyrol was an anti-Semitic place long before the Nazis arrived."

Horst's calm tone contrasts sharply with what I am feeling. I hate listening to this. Centuries of anti-Semitism right here where we are standing. Hundreds of teachers who couldn't care less, who, in all likelihood, felt justified hating the Jews. I want to rage against the injustice of it all, against the blindness and hatred.

Tanja's question brings me back to the group. "Were there teachers here who were Jewish?" she asks.

"Only a few," Horst responds, shaking his head. "And they left for Vienna. It was clear early on that they could not continue to work in the Tyrol. But to my thinking what is more disgraceful was the treatment of Jewish students, students who were born and raised here and considered themselves Tyroleans."

Similar to the Jews of Germany, I think, who believed they had become a part of the social fabric. "What happened to them?" Martina asks. I notice everyone leaning closer to catch Horst's words.

"They were told flatly to leave the schools and to secure private tutoring."

"Well, that's not so terrible, is it?" asks Thomas.

I understand his question. Compared to being murdered, being asked to leave school doesn't seem so bad.

"What is terrible," replies Horst, "is that there was no protest. The students left, and everyone was happy to go along. It was a quiet kind of oppression. Very Austrian."

I think of how much silence still exists in this land and in this group as Horst continues, "We are standing here so we can see just what this street names: a great man who was murdered, but what exactly is on this street?"

I look around. We are standing in front of a small fountain in the middle of a tiny plaza. To my left is the Kleider Bauer department store, next to it what appear to be warehouses or offices with graffiti scrawled on the walls. To my right is the side wall of the museum.

I am surprised when Andrea says, pointing down the street, "My school is right over there." She is directing us to the *Academisches Gymnasium*, the most prestigious secondary school in Innsbruck, a school, Horst later explains, with an impressive history, the most important school during the monarchy, one that was always conservative and always aligned ideologically with the ruling authoritarian position, during the Third Reich and now.

"Yes, there it is," Horst nods, "but is this the street address you use?"

"No," Andrea responds, shaking her head.

"This is a typical Austrian compromise," says Horst. "In the late 1970s, a man on the Innsbruck Community Council argued it was time to recognize the victims of the Nazis as well as those who resisted them. In all this time, except for one small plaque, which we will see later, there had been virtually no public acknowledgment of Innsbruck's past."

We listen quietly, waiting for Horst to continue. In an attempt to stay warm, a few of us stamp our feet.

"Naturally, there was a lot of talk of commemorating Franz Mair. Since he taught at Andrea's school, some people lobbied to change the school's name. Most teachers and politicians were opposed. A questionnaire went out to parents. They, too, opposed the idea. So eventually this street was given the name Franz Mair. But if you notice, it is a back street. There are no buildings that open onto it.

And her school still refuses to use this address. It uses the name of the street on its other side. So we have a nice compromise. We name a street to honor the man, but it is a street no one uses."

We have been standing the entire time Horst has been talking. My legs are beginning to ache. I'm relieved when he says it's time to move on to our next site, two blocks away. The snow is falling harder now, and I know walking will feel good.

But as we begin to make our way along Museumstrasse, a large thoroughfare, an ambulance siren pierces the air. It has the two-toned wailing sound I associate with the Gestapo, the sound I'm accustomed to hearing in World War II movies. For an instant, past and present merge. I am filled with a sense of dread and instinctively grab Margret's arm. She looks at me puzzled.

"Don't you hear it?" I ask, my eyes imploring.

"Hear what?" she asks, surprised.

"That sound," I respond. "That siren."

"Yes, I hear it, but so what? Is there a problem?"

As we walk I explain my associations: Anne Frank, the Gestapo's arrival, the roundups. There is not a movie or play I have seen in which this sound does not signal foreboding and fear. Margret claims never to have heard about such sirens. We decide to ask Horst and wait for him to catch up to us on the street.

"When the Gestapo came," he tells us, "they didn't need a siren to announce their arrival. In fact, they usually arrived at night," he pauses, "in silence."

I am surprised, but I think to myself that it does make sense. Much easier to enjoy public support if your worst acts are unseen and unheard. More frightening, too—the isolated knock on the door, the abrupt awakening, the immediate disappearance, the fabric of one's life suddenly ripped apart.

Then, as we turn the corner, I gasp. In front of us is a synagogue. It is set back from the street, recessed underneath a four-story apartment building. The larger building is nondescript, no window boxes or wooden shutters. Just a plain facade of gray stucco. But behind its supporting columns are a pair of steel-gray metal doors; above the doors, Hebrew letters in gold; surrounding the letters, white marble and beige cut stone. It is small, elegant, and easy to miss.

I am stunned. I had no idea there was a synagogue in Innsbruck. Last summer when I read through tourist information, I could find nothing that spoke of Jewish life now or in the past.

We stand across the street as Horst describes its history. "This synagogue stands exactly where the old one once stood. The building was defaced on *Kristallnacht*, destroyed during Allied bombing raids in 1943, and it remained closed until just a few years ago. Rebuilding it was the inspiration of a woman who works at the university."

"Do people come to worship here?" Margret asks.

"There are not enough people to hold a service every week," Horst explains, "but on the large holidays services are held." Later on, he tells us that after the Holocaust very few Jews returned to Innsbruck.

For me, standing in front of the synagogue, my eyes riveted to the familiar Hebrew letters, it's a wrenching moment. Knowing that Jews once worshipped here and are beginning to do so again makes my heart ache with sadness.

Horst then leads us behind the synagogue to a small open area. It is here he recounts what happened on *Kristallnacht*, the night of violence against Jews in all parts of Germany and Austria. "According to the best available records," he says, "from the early 1900s, about 400 Jews lived in Innsbruck. In 1938, on the night of November 9 and in the early hours of November 10, the synagogue that stood here was damaged, many stores were destroyed, and the Jews of Innsbruck were taken from their homes and beaten."

We are standing closer now, trying to keep warm. I feel dizzy and lean up against Margret. Horst continues, "People like to say that *Kristallnacht* was a spontaneous event. But that is not true. It was planned very carefully. We now have documentation, written orders from Munich to the SS in Innsbruck. They were instructed to kill Jews and to destroy property. Names and addresses were distributed. If someone was missed, it was an oversight."

"Was it only the SS?" Hans asks.

"It is hard to supply numbers," answers Horst. "The SS led the pogrom. But the locals had to have helped. Certainly they did not protest. They knew where everyone lived. These were their neighbors. Four men were murdered, one was thrown into the Inn River. In terms of percentages, more Jews were killed in Innsbruck on *Kristallnacht* than in any other city in Germany or Austria. It was a cruel situation."

"Did all Innsbruckers feel as if they had to go along?" asks Tanja, her face white.

"It is hard to say. You have to realize the role the church played. When the Nazis came, 800 years of religious anti-Semitism met up with modern political anti-Semitism. The ground had already been prepared."

"What do you mean?" Andrea gasps, her mouth dropping open.

"For centuries, Tyrolean peasants were taught to believe in the blood libel," Horst answers. "Even today, there are villages like Erl where the passion of Christ is staged, where Jews are portrayed as the killers of Christ."

I see nods among various group members. Clearly, some of them are informed about these events.

Horst continues: "The Tyrol, as you know, has always been a stronghold for Austrian Catholicism. We came to industrialization very late. The influence of the priests on the peasants has always been profound. They preached anti-Judaism for centuries. It was not racial, it was religious. And in many parts of the Tyrol, it still exists."

"No," says Andrea, shaking her head defiantly back and forth. "I cannot accept that. It cannot be true. Not the leaders of the church."

"It's true," says Horst, quietly. "The Tyrolean bishop in 1938 never protested the November pogrom. He and the Catholic priests had their differences with National Socialism, they disliked the *Gauleiter*, but what they had in common was their hatred of the Jews. The church fathers have been demonizing the synagogue for 1,500 years."

Andrea, visibly shaken, turns away from Horst. She is a devout Catholic, and it appears this is the first time she is being confronted with the church's complicity. I notice that she glances at Christa. Their eyes meet, but both women remain quiet.

The snow is coming down heavily now. My hair, despite a hat, is wet; my toes, numb. "We'll move on," says Horst, "but before we do, there is one last story about this site. In the 1970s, there was a plaque erected where we are standing, commemorating the Jewish neighborhood that once existed here." He reaches into his briefcase and pulls out a picture in a plastic covering. We huddle together to get a close look.

"What happened to it?" Martina asks.

"Well, people need housing, don't they? The apartment building you see in front of you is what happened. No one was asked, and no one knows where the plaque went. It just disappeared."

"What do you make of that?" I ask.

"Innsbruckers, in general, do not want to be reminded of their past. It is best to put it behind us. Not to talk. To bury it or dispose of it, just like the plaque."

With this, Horst turns and we follow him to the next site. By now we are buffeted by the storm. The snow is coming down in clumps, sticking to the ground, our shoes, our coats, our faces. We walk briskly, heads down, shoulders hunched against the wind, to a large open plaza. We stand, shaking, in front of an imposing monument. With tall columns rising to over forty feet and an eagle on top, it stands opposite a building that served, Horst tells us, "as Nazi headquarters."

"Both, you will notice, are huge. They were designed to inspire awe. The monument was given to us by the French who occupied Austria for ten years after 1945. It was designed to commemorate the liberation of Austria from Nazi oppression, but if you examine it architecturally, you will notice something very odd."

We look back and forth from the French monument to the imposing five-story government building with its rows of white casement windows.

"What message do you get from these structures?" Horst asks. "What do these columns suggest to you? Can you see how the aesthetic is typically imperialistic? There is a symmetry here. The French monument does not oppose the German architecture. It mirrors it."

I notice that human beings are dwarfed by each of these towering structures. The scale is neither human nor comforting. And each glorifies power.

We nod, shivering, stamping our feet. "What you see here is a cross between French imperialism and German nationalism. I don't see them as terribly different," Horst says.

Hilde, wearing only a cloth coat and loafers, is soaking wet. She tells us she is feeling ill and has only recently recovered from a kidney infection. She must return to the university. Horst asks if the rest of us are able to continue.

Cold or not, I have no doubt as to my answer. But I look at the group to check. Everyone seems to be waiting for me to decide. I nod yes.

We walk to Maria Theresienstrasse, Innsbruck's main boulevard. We huddle together in an archway, momentarily protected from the wind and snow. Horst removes two photographs from his briefcase— views of the same street in 1938. Bright red Nazi banners, the swastika boldly outlined in black, hang from the upper floors of the buildings. In one photo, smiling soldiers in small jeeps wave at the crowds of onlookers. Horst explains that this picture was taken on March 12, 1938, the day of the *Anschluss*.

He shows us the second photo in which Innsbruckers, some with umbrellas, stand in the rain with their right arms raised in the *Sieg Heil*. "This photograph," Horst comments, "was taken on April 10. Notice that only one shop is without a Nazi banner. The Bauer Schwarz department store was owned by Jews. It would be Aryanized in the coming days; the owners had already been removed from the management. But on April 10 the store was still their property."

We lean against each other, peering closely, examining the details. The photographs have no plastic coverings, and Horst is understandably anxious. He doesn't want them to get wet.

"Do you notice the trolley lines in the picture?" Horst asks. "They are the same lines that existed here until the 1960s and 1970s, when they were removed. They were installed by inmates from the camp at Reichenau on the outskirts of Innsbruck. Today people claim they didn't know, they didn't see anything. But inmates were here, daily, in their prison uniforms, installing those lines. They were visible to anyone with eyes."

I compare what I am seeing to the street today. Things look remarkably similar. I ask about the camp. "It was a labor camp, not a death camp," Horst explains. "But that doesn't mean people didn't die there. Life was brutal. The guards were brutal."

"Who was in the camp?" Tanja asks.

"Political dissidents, rebellious Tyrolean workers, and foreigners—those put into forced labor, most likely some Italian and North African Jews. For them, it was likely a stop on the way to Poland," Horst adds gently.

By now, the cold has penetrated my clothes and lodged in my body. No amount of shaking or stomping will rid me of it. My toes ache. My cheeks are raw. Horst tells us he has planned two more stops. As we gather ourselves, Astrid asks if we might shorten the tour. "My feet hurt," she says. "Couldn't we walk quickly past the other sites, but not stop to talk? Maybe Mr. Schreiber could continue later once we get warm again?"

Horst looks at Margret; she looks at me. I have an immediate, visceral response. There is no way I want to cut Horst short, no way I want to make it easier for us when, half a century ago, people's suffering was far greater. Astrid's concern for her own comfort annoys me. But I have to admit she has a point. We are shivering; our bodies are numb. And it is likely that she may be speaking for others as well.

To me, experiencing a few hours of physical discomfort while listening to such painful stories is uncannily appropriate. Yet, as much as I might wish others shared my sense of poetic justice, I cannot assume they do. I turn to Astrid and tell her that she and the others are free to leave. I will complete the tour as Horst has planned it. Margret nods, indicating she will do the same. But when given the choice to leave, neither Astrid nor any of the others does.

Horst now takes us to the corner of Meranerstrasse and Maria Theresienstrasse where the current government building or Landhaus sits. Here he points out a plaque commemorating the Austrian resistance movement and tells us the end of the Franz Mair story.

Horst calls Mair a "rhetorical star," his greatest skill, his ability to undermine Nazi ideology by turning Nazi language inside out. Only those subtle enough to hear the nuances understood his subversive intent. Students loved it. But it was his impact on students that ultimately got him reported to the Gestapo. In 1944, he was arrested and lost his job. When he was released, he devoted all of his time to the resistance movement. He was shot on May 2, 1945, just days before the end of the war. The Americans, Horst explains, were not far from Innsbruck; the SS had already withdrawn. Mair lost his life when a few remaining German soldiers fired into the street at random.

But Horst's stories, I have come to expect, always have a twist. This one has to do with the plaque itself. Austria, Horst explains, enjoyed presenting herself to the world as Hitler's first victim, a title conferred on her by the Allies in the Moscow Accords in 1943, when, in an attempt to spark resistance against the Nazis, the Allies recognized Austria as an occupied country. As a result, right after the war, it was in Austria's interest to portray herself not only as a victim but also as a country that resisted Hitler's onslaught. Suddenly, Franz Mair and his actions became useful to Austrian politicians. The plaque, describing the Nazi years as "Seven years of oppression . . ." was hung on the Landhaus in the early 1950s, while Austria was still under the supervision of the occupying armies.

"But as soon as the occupying forces left in 1955 and German tourists began visiting Innsbruck, complaints were lodged. The Germans," Horst explains, "knew that the resistance movement was small and had arrived relatively late on the scene. They knew that the majority of Tyroleans welcomed National Socialism. They objected strenuously to language that described them as oppressors in a town that viewed them as brothers.

"How did the local government respond?" Horst asks us as we stand shivering in front of the bronze plaque. "First," he explains, "they removed the offending sign without any plans to replace it. Then after protest from resistance groups, they replaced it," he pauses, "but with the offending words gone. Now, as you can see, it says, 'After seven years of being unfree . . .' "

"Another Austrian compromise?" Thomas asks sardonically.

Horst nods as he directs us to our last site. It is close by, in a small open area behind a federal high school. We are standing in front of a small, partially broken stone monument that resembles a coffin.

"This was originally erected to honor the memory of soldiers who fought in World War I," Horst explains. "If you look at the inscription on the left side, you can see that it says, 'The Teachers of Tyrol for their Heroic Brothers' with the dates 1914–1918 carved underneath."

We nod, chilled to the bone, huddling even closer.

"But," he points out, "look on the right side. They have added the dates for World War II over here. Now it honors the soldiers of both wars."

"Is there something wrong with that?" asks Christa. Even through the wind, I can hear her shock.

"For me there is," responds Horst. "You cannot compare them. It defames the memory of those who fought in World War I to add the soldiers of World War II."

"How can you say such a thing?" Christa asks, her voice rising sharply now. "My grandfather fought in the First War and my father and uncles in the Second. They all suffered. How can you not want to honor their memory? That is the least we can do."

"For me there is a big difference. It is bad enough to glorify any war. But World War II was a race war. It was a war of extermination. It had nothing to do with national defenses. You cannot compare it to World War I." This is the first time I have seen Horst become passionate, his eyes flashing. "As for the soldiers," he continues, "they are also victims. They gave their lives for nothing. Even worse, for a crime."

I watch Christa's face. Such strong words cause her pain. She turns away, horrified, shaking her head, pulling her coat tight around her body, her scarf even tighter over her mouth. It is completely dark out. The wind cuts like a knife. Everyone is shivering terribly. But Horst claims our attention for one more minute. "National Socialism and all those who contributed to it," he concludes, "are a disgrace to us. For me, the Nazis represent the absolute failure of German humanism.

All educated people revered Goethe, but no one knew how to live his ideas. For a long time, German universities lectured about humanism, but it was pure theory. It led directly to the cult of superiority. This is a huge failure, one that should not be masked by monuments."

Horst's final words ring in my ears. I don't know anything about him or how he came to make this work his own, but I feel grateful to have met him, to have walked with him, and to know that people like him exist in Austria. He gives me hope.

We have reached the end of our tour. Drenched and shaking with cold, we decide to look for the closest coffee shop, to warm ourselves before returning to the university. Hans knows of a nearby cafe. Horst agrees to come along.

As we walk, heads bent against the wind and snow, I ask Horst a question that has nagged at me since childhood. "With all your study," I ask, "have you come across anything that makes you think the Holocaust is a particularly German phenomenon, that there is something unique in the German character that allowed it to happen?"

"No," he responds calmly, "I think that committing atrocity is not the province of any one group of people. We are all capable of such things. What's sad is how easy it was. And how devastatingly ironic. The same German culture which produced Goethe, Heine, Schiller, and Rilke gave birth to horror and bestiality. That's what I find so hard to reconcile."

"As you were saying," I muse, "people could quote humanist ideas, but did not know how to live them."

"Right," Horst nods. "And it was so easy for the Nazis to bend them to serve their own purposes. Very few spoke up against that. That is another part of the failure."

Yes, I think, another huge silence. As we all walk quickly now, wrapped in our own silences, I realize I am one step closer to knowing what happened here. Shaken and grateful at the same time, I also wonder how the group will come to grips with this experience. In my own desire to face the evil that happened here, I have asked a great deal of my students. I have asked them to face the horror that touched the lives of their parents and grandparents. By listening to Horst, each of us has, in our own ways, opened ourselves to questions regarding hatred and complicity. Will we now stand in a new relation to this frightening and frightful legacy?

❧

We have reached the cafe. In another moment, we are out of the blizzard, hanging up our coats and hats, rubbing our hands together to bring back the circulation. Over hot chocolate *mit Schlag,* conversations begin slowly. Many of us express our thanks to Horst for his thoughtful presentation. He tells Margret and me that he has had a hard time finding an audience who wants to listen to him. He has tried to interest the Ministry of Culture in his research, but so far the ministers have not shown any enthusiasm.

"I have no doubt," I say, "that many Americans visiting Innsbruck would want to walk with you. Last summer I looked in all the guidebooks for some mention of the Holocaust or of Jewish life in Innsbruck but found nothing. I had no idea there was a synagogue here—I'm still stunned. I think this is important work. I hope you can make it more public."

Horst nods, grateful, I suspect, to have someone outside of his culture validate what he is doing.

Astrid is saying across the table: "What right do we have to question our parents? They have their own crosses to bear, don't they?" When she sees me looking at her, she directs her question to me. "Would you as a daughter, Sondra, confront your own father, the father who loves you?"

The anger I felt towards Astrid during the walk flares up again. At this moment, I have no desire to listen to her. I do not want to be her teacher, modeling a dialogic response. At this moment, I want to be a Jewish woman in Austria. "I suppose that it would depend upon what I thought he did." There is an edge to my voice.

Christa, who is sitting next to me, says she has a question too. I turn to face her. "Is it really possible," she asks hesitantly, "to change who we are?"

"What do you mean?" I respond.

"In your paper, you say you came here assuming that in our hearts all Austrians are Nazis. Can you really change that belief? Can your experience here really make a difference in the way you see us?" I detect no accusation in her voice, only a desire to understand.

I am glad that Ingrid is sitting next to her. I have not had a chance to respond to the anger she expressed in the morning. Maybe my answer to Christa will also speak to her.

"In some ways, I don't yet know the answer. I will only be able to answer you seriously as time goes by," I reply. "But even at the end of last summer, I saw things differently. All we are saying to one another and all we are doing are opening me up in ways I could not have imagined before I came here."

I look closely at her and Ingrid. They are pensive, waiting patiently as I attempt to articulate what I am coming to understand. "You are no longer just Austrians to me," I continue. "You are friends, women I have come to care about. Don't you think that makes a difference?"

"Perhaps I am not so optimistic," Christa answers softly. "Your prejudice took hold so many years ago. Can you just give it up so easily?"

I take a sip of my hot chocolate, letting the cup rest between my palms, letting its warmth penetrate my hands. I continue, "Before my trips here I never wanted to let go of my prejudice. I wanted to believe that all Germans were evil. Now, I feel differently. It is not possible for me to think like that any more. For me, this has to do with the issue of responsibility, of what it means for each of us to be responsible." My eyes search hers and Ingrid's.

"Are you saying we are responsible for our parents' actions, that we have some responsibility for what happened?" Christa asks, a hurt look on her face.

"No, of course not," I say hastily. "You are not responsible for the past. But I think you do have, that we all have, a responsibility to the future. That our responsibility has to do with what the Russian philosopher Bakhtin would call response-ability. The ability to respond. The ability and the willingness to take another person's words and questions seriously. Not to turn our backs. Not to be silent."

Ingrid smiles. "I like that idea," she says. "Responsibility with an 'a' instead of an 'i.' To me it makes the idea of responsibility less filled with guilt."

"I agree. We cannot change the past. We cannot condone it. But we can attempt to take one another's questions seriously and to enter into what Bakhtin would call a true dialogue. And we can begin to think about how we carry this history forward. That, to me, is our responsibility."

"That's obviously what Margret did last summer, isn't it?" Christa remarks.

"Yes," I say, putting my empty cup down. "Margret took my question seriously and responded fully, out of her own sense of the issue. My questions gave her an opening to speak. And her responses gave me room to keep questioning. And as Bakhtin would also say, there is never a final answer here. This is why dialogue as a model for teaching matters so much to me. Because it makes room for an unending conversation in which all speakers and all points of view are valued."

Christa and Ingrid both nod. "It's what fascism does not allow," Ingrid adds quietly.

Sitting in the cafe, warmer now and more comfortable, I don't want this moment to end. But I know it is time to return to the campus, to collect our books and make plans for our last class. Slowly we gather ourselves, pay the bill, and say goodbye to Horst. Putting on our wet coats and limp scarves, we brace ourselves for the blizzard. But as we enter the street, we are astonished to find that the wind is gone, the snow has stopped. All is peaceful and quiet.

èā·

Back in the classroom, I expect everyone to pack up and hurry out. We are all spent. We need time to clear our minds and hearts. But no one leaves. People take their seats around our familiar table. It is as if no one is ready to part. In the cafe, conversations were subdued and occurred in groups of two or three. I sense that the group wants some closure.

"Would you like to write reflections?" I ask.

No one has the energy to write. "How about a go-around, then?" I suggest.

Hilde begins. "I waited for you to return because I have something to say to the group. First, I want to apologize for leaving. With such thin shoes, I could not take the cold any longer."

"Hilde," I say, "please, no apologies. I'm glad you took care of yourself. I'm just surprised you waited here. Why didn't you go home?"

"I waited because there is something I must say to everyone." She looks around the room. "Last summer, you all remember that Professor Soloway stayed with me?"

Nods all around.

"She felt comfortable with me, I think. More comfortable than she felt in the group. We used to go out to dinner, relax, and have a drink. One night she told me she was Jewish. But she asked me not to say anything."

I glance at Margret.

Martina interjects, "When Hans and I drove her to the airport, she told us, too. It was so strange. We didn't know what to say to her."

"And what are we supposed to do with this information now?" asks Margret, always sensitive to the slightest hint of judgment or pity.

"Nothing really," says Hilde. "I just thought the group would want to know."

"I am really surprised," Andrea comments. "Now that Sondra has talked to us, I feel as if I have a much better understanding of what it means when someone says he or she is a Jew. Before I never even thought about it. About what it would be like to be Jewish and come here . . ."

"I am not sure you can know what it means for a Jewish person to be here," I say, "unless you ask. Maybe it was hard for Beth Soloway to be in Austria. Maybe talking to Hilde was her way to begin exploring this question. City College invites us to teach, but these issues are not discussed in the States. As I've said, it was a shock for me to see how deeply I was affected just being here. I wasn't prepared."

"I keep asking myself what would have happened if Margret had not been in this course," says Thomas.

Martina responds. "Me too. If Margret had not responded to you as she did last summer, what would have happened?"

"It's hard to say," I answer. "Perhaps someone else would have taken on her role. When a question is asked, usually someone emerges to answer it. But the point is, she was here and she did respond. And all else has followed from that." I smile at Margret, sitting across the table from me.

"I want to comment on Horst. I think he was wonderful," says Tanja. "He is so gentle, and except for the very end he presented his research calmly. There was very little blaming in his tone even when he expressed his own opinion. He did not want anyone to feel guilty."

"Yes, I thought so, too," Hans responds. "He was very professional. What he said is not new to me, but this walking with him, I think, was a very good idea."

"I think he is a fine person," reflects Christa. "But I find it hard to listen when someone criticizes the church. The church holds an important place in my life."

"For me as well," says Andrea. "I found him too harsh on the church. I am upset about it all and very tired."

Ingrid adds, "I am tired too and still cold. I need a long, hot bath. But I have also learned a lot. I am wondering more about the Jews. I wonder if you, Sondra, could suggest some books for me to read."

I nod, pleased.

As the conversation winds down, I say, "As we've been sitting here talking, I have had Thomas's comment in the back of my mind. After I asked my questions last summer, had no one responded to me at all, I suppose I would have returned to the States with my prejudices confirmed and not wanted to come back to Austria."

"And then can you imagine what would have happened to our research projects?" asks Tanja lightly. "They would not be turning out the way they are now."

I smile, continuing with my thought: "I want you to know that I did not think I could take on the task of mentoring you once this course ends," I say. "But as a result of this week together, I cannot imagine trying to find someone else to do the job. I don't see how anyone else could pick up where we are leaving off. And to be honest, I don't want to stop now. I want to see you through your research projects, if you still want me."

"Of course we do," exclaims Martina.

"Well, Martina," I respond. "I hope you are speaking for everyone. I'd like all of you to think about it tonight. We can find additional mentors. But you should know that if you want to continue working with me, I am more than willing."

"We're so glad you came back," seconds Thomas.

"I am too," I say.

❧

Martina and Hans have invited Tanja and me to eat dinner with them. Soon we find ourselves in their flat, having walked up a few flights in a modern apartment complex located on a hill overlooking the city. We immediately sink into an overstuffed couch, glasses of red wine in our hands. It feels good to relax, to let the day's images recede, to enjoy the warmth of the room and the friendship.

Hans, who has been noticeably quiet in the course, especially after his confrontation with Margret, explains his point of view over salad and a spicy dish of beef wrapped in a flaky crust: "I am not an English teacher as the others all are. I already have a master's degree and a secure job at the university. I enrolled in this program because I was interested in what was going on in the States, and I value the way in which I learned English. At this point, I would like to finish and move on.

"I think my English skills are what enabled me to get where I am now. I still want to conduct my survey on the need for oral English in business. For me, it's a good question and one that can be useful to me in my work at the university," he explains between bites.

I nod. "I think that your thesis should serve whatever your purposes are, Hans. You need to do whatever fits for you."

"I knew you'd say that," Hans says gratefully. "You know," he continues, "I don't disagree about values. Of course, they are important in teaching and in everything. But the world is becoming increasingly capitalistic. That is the system we are in. I find it hypocritical when people spout left-wing politics and criticize the system while all the time they are benefiting from it."

"You said in class tonight that you had already heard a lot of what Horst told us. Was any of it new to you?" I ask.

"Not really. I have been making many studies about the Holocaust. I don't like to talk about it because everyone here says, 'I had nothing to do with it.' They are all liars. It makes me angry that the Germans are willing to admit their guilt and say they are sorry, but the Austrians still want to claim that they were victims.

"Everyone here was affected by it, of course. My father lost both his legs in the war. I can remember when I was a little boy he would say to me, 'Bring me my feet.' He meant the attachments we used to strap on to him so he could walk. Looking at him and my mother, we can never forget."

Hans and Martina keep our wine glasses filled as we reflect on what happened among us this day. We all recognize that we bring different perspectives to what I have come to call "our historical inquiry." Each person, it seems, has had to face his or her demons. From Christa and Andrea's Catholicism to Astrid's resistance, from Ingrid's anger to the group's curiosity about Jews—no one is leaving the course untouched.

ε✿

In my room at Tanja's, I cannot fall asleep. My thoughts are scattered, but I write to Margret nevertheless:

This is the last time I will write to you during this trip. Today was so immense, what words are there to describe it? The weather, the sky, the snow falling, the bitter wind . . . Each person in the group moves me in a different way, but what I feel for you is so strong, I wonder how obvious it is. This is a tricky dynamic, and I worry that my bond with you leaves you alone and isolated once I am no longer here. Can the group make room for what you and I have together? Does it matter if they can't?

I also wonder what other reactions will surface about today. We would not have done otherwise, but confronting all of this must leave at least some of the group reeling—upset, shaken. I am not suggesting that you or I need to protect them, but I do believe that as the teacher I am responsible for each person, accountable in a different way to each one. I think I am trying to sort this out in preparation for tomorrow.

But this isn't really why I began writing. I want to say thank you for all of this. For dinner—I have the same picture of it that you do, I think—the two of us smiling, laughing, crying, drawing strength from our connection. And thank you for Horst, for the walking tour, for all that will grow from this. How will we ever say goodbye?

I wake up on Saturday morning at 5 A.M., just as the sun is rising. I spend an hour writing out what I want to say in my final remarks. Then, not wanting to disturb Tanja, I tiptoe outside. More snow has fallen during the night, and as the sun appears over the mountains, ice crystals twinkle on the trees. Everything is white and tranquil. It is so beautiful. It must have looked the same sixty years ago. The same startling peaks, the same open fields and rolling hills. And yet, so different.

Margret wakes early, too, and writes to me:

It's morning and I have one hour left before I have to rush to the bus. I wish we had more time—more time to take walks together, to sit in cafes, to meet leisurely and to talk seriously. Also to walk to town and get some presents for you, for your kids, and for Arthur. I have got it all in my mind. I wanted Sara to have a book, just to show her what this place you have now come to for a second time looks like, and maybe for your boys . . . ? And here I am thinking that all I can give you are my words, with which I try so hard to express what is on my mind and in my heart.

Of course it would be great to have you come back as our mentor . . . What a great time this would be. And then—do I dare suggest that you come and stay in our place, maybe meet my in-laws, see their outstanding friendliness and hospitality, yet knowing. . . .

How far you will go, Sondra, to confront this world of ours. What we have encountered so far is only just the beginning. Understanding and learning with one's heart take a long time, and yet the group now thinks they have understood, that now they know.

I am not pessimistic at the moment. I know that people have started to ask themselves, "Who am I?" but have they realized that the answers are not easily gained in one day? I am saddened when thinking of all the backlashes ahead, of never being sure how thick the common ground has become. Can I walk on it safely? Do I have to be cautious for the rest of my life? It's sometimes so tiresome and life is so short.

How will you go back—lightheartedly? I doubt that. Maybe you will go home with the feeling that you took one more glimpse into the abyss—from a slightly different angle.

ะ๑

People arrive slowly on the last day of class. I put a schedule on the board. Hans and Martina bring the leftovers from last night's dinner. Christa places a homemade quiche on the table. Hilde lays out some pastries. Silverware, plates, and napkins appear along with wine, juice, club soda, chocolates, and fruit. Our plans are to work through our agenda, to eat lunch in the classroom, and in the evening to have a celebratory goodbye meal at a restaurant overlooking the city.

I begin with individual conferences, the first one with Ingrid. I want to make sure she has settled on a research question, but she refuses to talk about her research just now. "There are other things I want to say to you," she begins, "things I must say. I have had another sleepless night, but now I realize why I have been so angry at you."

We are sitting alone in the office adjacent to our classroom.

"All along I have wanted to believe that the Holocaust has nothing to do with me. But your questions forced me to ask about my own responsibility. This is something I have never done and never wanted to do." She looks at me, then looks away.

"I wasn't prepared to read your paper. I could not hear your message. I saw only one line. And I could not accept that you, the perfect teacher, could come here and be prejudiced. It hurt too much."

I nod. I can see her struggling.

"And I kept thinking that what you wrote has got nothing to do with me. I was angry at you because I have never wanted to face this question. But last night I finally asked myself, 'What is my responsibility in all of this?' And I found the answer."

With tears in her eyes, Ingrid continues: "I would not have seen the truth," she says. "I am one of them—the people who are too stupid to see through the lies, the ones who would go along. I would have believed everything they told me. I am not brave. I would not have had the courage to stand up. I am so ashamed." She is calm, but her voice breaks at this last admission.

I know Ingrid does not lack courage. I look at her pale face, her earnest expression, and can see the toll her soul-searching has exacted. She has examined herself with remarkable rigor. "There's more," she says. "Yesterday when Mr. Schreiber spoke about the war memorial for the soldiers, he was angry. He said we should not memorialize the soldiers from the Second World War along with those from the First. I did not understand his anger. But after last night, I do. We should not call it the 'Monument to our Heroic Brothers.' We should call it the 'Monument to the Followers of the Crowd.'"

I am stunned. Ingrid has opened herself fully to this encounter and has already moved through so many different responses and reactions. I want to go on talking, but I know others are waiting to see me. All I can do is thank her for her honesty and her friendship. We embrace, briefly, knowing we have only touched the surface, knowing we will keep talking.

Next I meet with Christa. She, too, wants to talk about the walk and what she has been thinking since yesterday. The research project is clear in her mind but these other issues are not. "When I think of my life," she begins, "I see now that it has always had to do with the Holocaust in some ways. My father was the mayor of our town. Both he and my grandfather," she pauses and gathers herself together, "they were both members of the Nazi party. They were . . . " she hesitates, looking away, "jailed after the war. But," she continues, "we never talked about it. We never talked about those times. I never asked my father why or what it meant to him. It never even occurred to me to do so. No one talked.

"I devoted myself to the church. I thought it was true that if you speak no evil, there is no evil. I have tried to live my life like that. Doing good, being good within my own little world. I thought that was enough."

I look at Christa's face. She is so pretty, I think, so earnest, so much the Aryan beauty. "Yes, Christa," I say, "your goodness is apparent. I remember feeling it as you read last summer about your mom and the way you cared for her as she was dying, the way you obviously care for everyone in your family."

"I do care," she says, "but I have put a boundary around my caring. I think it is too limited now—that one must do more than care about one's own children and family."

I am deeply moved that our work has brought Christa to this point. "These issues raise questions for all of us," I say. "When I first leaned about Auschwitz, I was about thirteen. I was shocked that people would willingly and happily destroy a whole race just for who they were, for what they believed in, for what they looked like. I was also deeply hurt. I experienced it as a huge betrayal, Christa, not only by people but also by God."

She nods, listening intently.

"From that point on, I could not believe there was a God. For if he exists, how could he allow Auschwitz to exist? I have carried this sense of betrayal with me for my entire life. And it is only now, as we have all begun to talk about this together, that I sense I can begin to let go of this feeling of betrayal. You asked me yesterday whether one can really change. This is the beginning of my answer."

Christa looks at me with tears in her eyes. "I am not very good at writing," she says, "but I will try to stay in touch and I promise to write to you about your paper."

"Good," I say. We hug.

Margret and I have exchanged journals at the beginning of the day. It feels strange, sitting down together. So much of our communication has occurred through writing, through notes and journals passed back and forth, through looks across the room. But here we are, face-to-face, with only a few minutes before us. Already she has written back a note to me:

> Here it is again—reading your lines and thinking: How could this happen? You are saying exactly what's on my mind as well. I sense that the others are stunned or even taken aback—is this the right word?—by what is going on here between the two of us. When we were talking, standing in the corridor, I was struck by the impression that the group "handles me with care" because they esteem you so highly. When you are gone it doesn't really matter to me how my relationship with the group will develop. I am not their teacher, and isolation is part of my life anyway— with great moments of symbiotic experiences in between.

I know in my heart what our talks and shared feelings mean to both of us and the wish to be close is interrupted by sudden feelings of panic—wanting to run, to flee, not wanting to cry any more, not being able to bear a glimpse at harmony, knowing that it will be gone the moment I look into—let's say—Astrid's eyes.

I feel as if I am going along a path, being constantly interrupted by people who ask for the way. This disturbs me and I do not want to be stopped too often.

I look up from her words. "It's uncanny, isn't it," I ask, "how often our thoughts run along similar lines?"

She nods. Smiles. "Our questions are so much the same. I saw it again when I read your paper. You knew just what I was thinking without my having to tell you."

My turn to smile. "You know," I say, "these private conversations I am having with people? They are struggling, too. Each person is coming to me and talking to me very honestly. They are not where you are, but most of them are also on this path now."

"That's good," Margret responds, "I'm just more suspicious than you are. I'm so used to people starting to open and then closing up again. I fear the backlash that will come. It scares me. People may retreat."

"This has been hard for everyone, but you are not alone on this path, Margret," I say.

"But," she says, "I am always the one in the group to speak out, always the one to challenge. It gets so tiring," she sighs.

"It's true," I respond, "if it weren't for you, or I guess for both of us, we wouldn't be at this point now. But sometimes you seem so angry at the group, so vehement, you don't give them much room to struggle."

"I think it's that I care so much—and that they seem so unwilling to look," she explains, not defensively.

I am coming to see how painful it is for Margret to live in this culture of silence and denial.

"I know that. I can see that," I say. "But all they see, I think, is your anger. You have such a huge heart, Margret, and you care so deeply that I think it is hard for others to deal with that. To deal with your bigness. It's scary for them." I pause, looking at her. "Can I say something else?"

She nods, looking back.

"I think your vehemence gets in the way. Can't you see that you are already the one who stands up and speaks for justice?"

Tears begin to form in her eyes. "You can see that about me?" she asks softly.

"Of course, that's what I see. Your beauty and your heart. How loving you are. I think people could hear what you are saying much better if you were able to say it in a softer voice."

"I think my voice is so loud," she muses, "because I feel always as if I am speaking for more than one person, as if," she falters, "I am also speaking for Gert. It means so much to me that he is writing to you."

"Yes, me too," I respond smiling, then add hesitantly, "you know, it's a bit unsettling to me that I might become the occasion for bringing him to words."

Her eyes light up. "It has just occurred to me," she says excitedly, "perhaps when Gert finds his voice, I can soften mine."

For years, I realize, Margret has felt alone, carrying the burden of who her in-laws are by herself, as if she were the only one in the family able to give voice to the pain their actions inflicted. Gert clearly shares her anger, but until now he has remained silent or expressed himself only through actions.

"I would be so happy to see that," I say, my own eyes teary.

We know it's time to return to the group. We cannot say goodbye. Instead Margret comments, "I am so glad you will be our mentor, that you will be coming back."

"If it works out, if I can come in the fall, if I can convince Arthur to come with me . . ." I say. "But in the meantime you must get e-mail. That way we won't have a week's delay between letters."

She wrinkles her nose. "I like writing longhand."

"I know. But trust me, e-mail is great. You'll really like that too."

"How can I not trust you?"

۶♣

The afternoon is busy, filled with work and a wonderful sense of accomplishment. We talk about the hard steps that lie ahead. Once one has collected data, it takes enormous courage to begin going through it. It takes time and patience and even faith to sustain this sort of work.

We return to Bissex to remind ourselves of the overall purpose of classroom inquiry: "We show proofs to other people," Bissex writes, "so that they may be convinced. We share meanings with each other in the hope that the meaning of one person's story will help others seek and find the meaning of their own."[1]

We return to van Manen to remind ourselves of why teaching is an enactment of human values. Christa reads to us her favorite line from *The Tone of Teaching*, another of his books we have been using: "True pedagogy requires an attentive attunement of one's whole being to the child's experience of the world."[2]

Margret reads hers:

> There are educators who believe that their own education is complete. They will probably try to impose a taken-for-granted set of beliefs and values. Inevitably such 'education' turns into a pedagogy of oppression—an authoritarian form of domination of adults over children.[3]

I read mine:

> . . . [I]f a teacher discusses poetry but is unable to poeticize life, if a teacher talks about responsibility but does not live a responsible life, . . . if a teacher knows many jokes but lacks a true sense of the joy of being, . . . if a teacher asks students many questions but does not know how to be addressed by a question, . . . then . . . what the teacher is doing overtly is a profound contradiction. . . . When a teacher fails to be what . . . he or she does, then that teacher is really an absence, is not at all genuinely present.[4]

I remind the teachers that they can return to these passages when I am not here. In these books, I tell them, they will find another kind of comfort and companionship.

Then I realize that in the press of all I want to cover, I have forgotten that Tanja has yet to present her students' portfolios. How thoughtless of me: Tanja, who has housed me, taken care of innumerable details for me, handled hundreds of course arrangements from duplicating articles to ordering books, Tanja, who has served valiantly as the course coordinator, dealing frequently with everyone's needs and everyone's complaints. I apologize and ask her to describe her work.

With skill and ease, Tanja takes us inside her course for business students; she shows us their written work and has us grapple with the question of the level of English language proficiency necessary for Austrian adults to succeed in the business world. Her presentation is just what we need to tie the research work together: a serious question, lots of data, practical applications.

Even Hans's interest is piqued. Tanja's portfolios show the written work of students who are in the business world. "These are fascinating," he comments. "Perhaps my students could bring portfolios as part of their interviewing packages. These portfolios are so much more interesting than tests. You can see what the students can do."

Now even Margret is smiling at Hans.

Partners and small research groups have been formed. Promises to meet have been made. The teachers will keep journals, save student work, tape small groups of students as they talk about books or read their writing to one another, try their hands at field notes, collect interviews and learn to proceed with patience. When Margret says that her first step is to get e-mail, I can't smile broadly enough.

We are coming to the end of the day. I have one last opportunity to speak to the group. I know I have spoken a lot in this course but I want to try, one last time, to reach them, to leave them with some words that might help them make sense of all we have encountered together.

Everyone is sitting calmly around our table. I feel the swirl of emotions rising inside me. I take out the notes I made early that morning and take a deep breath to steady myself.

"As this course ends," I begin, "I want to emphasize that a lot of what happened in the last two days was unplanned. It is what emerged from our asking questions and responding as human beings. Clearly, there were risks involved. This has been hard for each of us. So hard it can bring us to tears."

I inhale deeply, blink back my own tears, and continue. "This is historic ground." I say this slowly, deliberately, giving them time to let my words sink in. "When I came here last summer, I sensed that. Ever since, I have hoped that my questions would lead us to engage in a dialogue.

"Yesterday, Andrea began to consider what it must be like for a Jewish person to come to Austria. I hope you have glimpsed what it means to me, but I am only one person. Van Manen writes about a 'theory of the unique.'[5] This is, I think, what he is referring to. You can't know what coming here means unless you ask, and for every Jewish person, that answer will vary.

"But," I say, looking at Hilde, at Astrid, at Ingrid, "I want to stress that I did not come here last summer to challenge you. I did not say to you, 'I am Jewish. How are you going to handle that?' I said, 'I have questions about what happened here. If you would like to tell me, I would like to listen.'

"This, to me, is the ground of dialogue. One does not accuse. Instead, one invites others to engage in a discussion of meaning. It begins with the kinds of questions that lead to openness, to uncertainty, and when it works, to a real exchange.

"Our course last summer was unique. It was what we created together, and it led me to question prejudices I carried from the time I was a child. I am not the same person you met last year. If you reread what I wrote at the end of my paper, you will see that even then I was beginning to realize this. And in this, I see the possibilities inherent in teaching. It lets me grasp more fully what it means to embody a pedagogy based on hope."

I pause, take a breath, look again at each person sitting quietly. Some, I notice, are taking notes. Most are just watching me.

"I say all this but this is only my part of the story. The other part belongs to each of you. I have asked you for responses to my paper. Whatever you say, I will treat seriously. If there is something you do not understand or if something I have written upsets you, please write to me and tell me.

"Yesterday, as we stood in the snow and listened to Horst, we stood as witnesses to history. Having done this calls on us to face enormous questions. I don't think we quite understand yet what it will come to mean or how it will live on in us.

"But," I say, looking this time at Thomas, at Christa, at Hans and Martina, "here is what I do know: whatever happens, we have had a confrontation with history. Some of us have been moving toward facing this history for a long time. We embrace it although that doesn't make it less painful.

"For others, what we did may raise difficult issues. So I want to warn you that the tendency will be to push it all away, to consider it a mistake, to withdraw. I hope you won't do that, and I want to suggest an alternative.

"If you notice yourself getting upset, see if you can find a way to express it. Write, talk, take a walk, get angry, but try not to suppress what you feel. Let it touch you.

"From what some of you have told me, your parents could not do this, but perhaps you can. You can at least ask yourself: What is this for me? What does it say to me? And, even more important, what do I have to say in response? I am inviting you to take your rightful place in this inquiry as a person who inherits these questions in dialogue."

I look around again. The room is so quiet. I take another breath and push on.

"Last summer we asked, what does it mean to be a full human being in the classroom? To this question I would now add, what does it mean to bring the world into our classroom and us into the world, to encounter the other in some sort of full recognition? I think there are implications here for what might happen when you return to school.

"I am not suggesting that you go back to your students and do what we did here. But someday a student might ask you a question about the Holocaust, or you might decide to teach about the Holocaust, and you will have your own story to tell. It might include what happened here among us or what you will come to learn through this inquiry. And in this way, you will be bringing a trace of me back to your classroom—just as I will be bringing parts of you and our conversations back with me to my work. I feel this is what it means to learn from and with one another."

My voice nearly breaks at this last admission. I look down at my notes and steady myself.

"In the last few days, differences have surfaced among us, differences about politics, about religion, about research. I think it would dishonor the work that we have accomplished together if people retreat now into judgments. So I want to end by asking you to proceed with empathy for one another and for our struggles, to treat what we did, what we have begun here, with respect. And for all that you have given to me, I want to conclude by saying thank you."

The course is over. I feel a profound connection to each teacher in the room, one that will extend beyond the ocean soon to separate us. I realize I have expressed what I don't normally express so openly in a classroom: gratitude and love.

As we pack up and prepare to leave, I experience a sense of relief. I feel as if I have been able to speak for who and what I am in a way that might encourage them to speak too. I have attempted to ask, in the tradition of van Manen, the questions life has called me to ask.

❧

At Chalet Buzzihutte, high up in the mountains, we are gathered in a small, wood-paneled room, illuminated only by candles, around a large oak table. The lights of Innsbruck twinkle down below. Everyone is here except Christa and Thomas who had prior commitments. Margret has invited Gert to join our final goodbye party. I am glad he has come and eagerly shake his hand in greeting.

Everyone orders large mugs of beer. I realize that I am so exhausted that even deciphering the German menu would be too taxing. Ingrid, noticing my fatigue, offers to order for me. We agree to share an Austrian specialty, *Kaiserschmarren*, a pancake made with eggs and flour and liberally sprinkled with sugar.

After we order, I overhear Martina, Astrid, and Tanja joking about the name of a new lipstick. "Oh," I say, "finally we're having a really important conversation." They grin.

Sitting there, I realize how strange it is that with all the serious talk, we have had so little conversation on women's issues. Feminism is a topic I take seriously. And yet, these women and I have hardly talked about how we live our lives.

Who cooks dinner? Who cleans? Is there equal pay for equal work? Who gets promoted? Who is responsible for child care? Once we start, it's clear we can go on for hours. Hilde tells us how as a single mother she raised her son and worked full time; how her son needed to learn to cook so he could have dinner ready when she came home; how hard it was to leave him when he was little. "To this day," she says, "I regret not being able to stay at home with him when he was young."

Ingrid explains that she chose to stay home to raise her children. Now that the younger is of school age, she will be returning to full-time teaching. Andrea, with three children, the youngest a toddler, is already back at work. Martina and Margret each have one child. Both have husbands who help. Astrid's daughter is grown, so she and her husband travel when they are not working.

I recount stories of raising twins: the sleepless nights, the constant earaches, the airplane rides with two howling babies. We laugh at what I describe as the early years of strain, now thankfully over. It is good to be able to be women together, sharing family stories.

When Tanja regales us with funny episodes of her romantic interludes with Austrian men, everyone starts to laugh. Then Martina tells a joke in German that I don't understand, but it leaves everyone else in stitches. I sense that their laughter is a necessary release from the hard work of asking hard questions. This laughter is well earned. It comes from struggling together and growing in mutual respect and love.

During the meal, I turn to Gert. He is quiet, sitting between Margret and me, patiently watching us as we talk and laugh. I have the urge to engage him in conversation, but it is hard to know what to say. I realize that what we have in common is our love for Margret.

"It's been wonderful having Margret in this course," I tell him.

"Yes. And for her too, it is good," he says slowly, working for each word, his head tilted toward me, his blue eyes bright in the dark room.

"I hope that I can come back in the fall and that my husband can come with me."

"Margret has told me this. Your husband . . . he is a doctor?" Gert asks.

"He is a clinical psychologist. That means he has a degree in psychology, not medicine. He works with people." I try to speak slowly too.

Margret looks on, smiling. I can tell she's working hard not to translate.

"Your husband, he was a soldier too, in Vietnam?" His words are halting.

"It's a long story. I hope he can tell it to you. He can speak some German. He was not really a soldier. He lived in Saigon and worked undercover. Do you understand?"

"I think so," says Gert, leaning towards me, tucking strands of long, white hair behind his ears.

"When he returned," I add, "he joined a group called Vietnam Veterans Against the War. Like you, he found himself protesting the actions of his government."

"There are many things I did not, I do not, like about Austrian government," he says with a great deal of effort. "But now I do not protest. I am more private. I prefer that."

"We are all different now, I guess." I would like to ask about his parents, but instead, I say, "I hope we can stay in touch."

Gert responds, "I am writing you a letter."

I smile, saying, "I will look forward to receiving it. In fact, I will walk to the mailbox every day to check."

"Where is your mailbox? Do you have the kind on a post?" Gert asks.

"Yes, it is at the top of our driveway, so you have to walk up a short distance to collect the mail."

Now he smiles.

Margret turns to me and says quietly, "I think Gert's English is so much better when I am not around. When he has to, he can do quite well for himself."

"So he and I just need some time alone," I joke.

As we place orders for coffee and dessert, Tanja starts to hum. Many Austrians, it turns out, especially those who are teachers of English, are familiar with all sorts of American songs. I am delighted to hear this, and soon we are all singing. We begin with classic Simon and Garfunkel—"Bridge over Troubled Water" and "Hit the Road, Jack"—switch to folk songs from Peter, Paul and Mary, and then move on to American spirituals. Their favorite is "Let My People Go." I can't tell if they are aware of the irony here, but their enjoyment is palpable, singing and harmonizing in English. From Broadway show tunes to standard Christmas carols, we are unstoppable.

Sitting in this dark, wood-paneled room, relaxed and relieved, I know we could continue drinking, laughing, and singing for hours. But it has been a long and exhausting week. When I mention the hour, everyone seems as reluctant to leave as I am.

Slowly we put on coats and walk outside. The air is crisp and cold. A few snow flurries fall gently on our coats, our faces. The lights of Innsbruck sparkle down below. I spend a minute or so with each person, exchanging hugs, promises to write, making plans for next time.

"It's been wonderful," says Martina.

"Thank you," says Hilde.

"I'll write to you," promises Ingrid.

"I will too," says Astrid.

"We all hope you can return in the fall," says Hans with a hug that is warm and full.

My flight is scheduled for 8:30 in the morning. Margret tells me she will be at the airport.

"You have your family," I protest. "You don't need to come. Give yourself a rest." She looks at me as if I am crazy.

"O.K., come," I say, shaking my head at her stubbornness, knowing, of course, there is no way she won't.

❧

Back at Tanja's, I finish packing, then join her in the kitchen for a last cup of tea.

"I'm sorry," I say, "that I overlooked your presentation today. I feel terrible that I could have been so thoughtless."

"It's fine," she says. "I had already told you that I didn't need to do it."

"Even so, I should not have forgotten."

"Well, in the end I'm glad I did present, but there is one good thing about your forgetting," she says smiling. "It reminds us that you are not perfect, that even the Carnegie professor can make a mistake."

We both laugh. It's been a long day.

"What worries me," I say, turning serious, "are the mistakes I am not aware of. What I may inadvertently have said or done that has left someone feeling hurt. This wasn't just an ordinary course."

"No," she comments. "It was a remarkable course. You have raised questions that many of them have avoided asking for years. I have written to you about your paper so you can take my response home with you. But what has been most powerful for me has been watching everyone open up. I think you have really started them thinking. I think this course will really make a difference to everyone.

"You should also know, Sondra, that it has been a wonderful experience for me. I have learned so much. As an American, I heard your questions differently from the others, but you have made me think about what it means for me to be living here."

"I'm glad," I say, "but mostly, I am the one who is still learning."

Tanja's students' portfolios are piled on shelves in the kitchen. "Look at all that work," she remarks. "I'll be writing my thesis forever."

❧

On Sunday morning, Tanja and I arrive at the airport and just like last summer find Margret, Hans, and Martina waiting for us. We order coffee and croissants. Martina asks me about home. "Have you heard from Arthur? Is everyone O.K.?"

"You don't want to know," I respond, laughing. "His last e-mail said that he and the boys have the flu. Sara's still fine. But I think I'll be walking into chaos."

When it is time to go through passport control, I say my goodbyes. Margret and I take a moment to embrace. She hands me one last note. Somehow she found the time to write between last night's late dinner and our early morning arrival at the airport.

"We'll keep writing," I whisper.

"A friendship journal," she whispers back.

"A dialogue journal," I add, looking at her, blinking back tears.

"How can we say goodbye?" she asks me, her eyes mirroring mine.

"We don't have to," I respond. "It's not over."

❧

From my seat on the airplane, I look out the window and see my friends, my Austrian friends, waving to me, watching until the plane disappears. Once we are above the clouds, I sink back in my seat and open Margret's letter:

> We have just come home. I would so much have loved to be together for a little while longer—you and Gert and me. I love his way of trying to communicate with you. I can see his attempts and read his thoughts. He would have liked to embrace you when saying goodbye, but he surely thought he had no right to. Spontaneity isn't his thing, but yet there is so much caring in him.
>
> Anyway, what can I say now? I loved what you said in class and how you said it. Now I hear you saying, "They can't carry your bigness." How do you, within such a short time, see all the love I have for other human beings, all my caring and empathy, when others that are so close to me can't see any of it? I am used to working so hard to make people take a second look and stay with me. But I sense things are changing and that feels good.
>
> You are sitting on the plane right now and although at the moment I have no words left to say, I want to go on talking with you, staying with you on the plane. I will be thinking of you all the time, and your kindness, your caring, and your courage will help me to go back to the place I am in, knowing that I am doing the right thing with my students and my family...Here's another big hug from me.

Reading Margret's letters again, wiping away tears as I give in to all the emotions of the week, I recall a line from Zora Neale Hurston's *Their Eyes Were Watching God:* "Mah tongue is in mah friend's mouf."[6] It is said by Janie, the protagonist, about Phoeby, the woman to whom she entrusts her story. For me, it has always been a startling and unsettling line, and yet I have never understood it so well.

ଛ

Eight hours later, on the map at the front of the cabin, I notice that we are approaching my favorite landmarks: the Labrador Sea and the Goose Bay of Canada, evidence that we have nearly finished crossing the Atlantic. Soon New York will appear.

My mind returns once more to the course, the readings, the teachers. Suddenly I am visited by Hannah Arendt's insight that the banality of evil can be understood as the absence of thought.[7] Struck anew by the power of this idea, I open my journal to jot down one more note:

> Now I know why Margret and I must teach our children how to make this history their own. It is not to carry the burden of guilt nor to atone for the sins of forebears, but to enable them to walk in the world with their eyes open—full of thought.

Synagogue on Sillegasse in Innsbruck

Close-up of synagogue on Sillegasse

Monument commemorating the end of World War II
built by the Tyroleans under the supervision
of the French Allied forces

Government building that served as Nazi headquarters

Maria Theresienstrasse, March 12, 1938:
Arrival of first motorized German troops

Maria Theresienstrasse in 2002; same view

Maria Theresienstrasse, April 10, 1938: Innsbruckers with right arms raised

Maria Theresienstrasse in 2002; same view

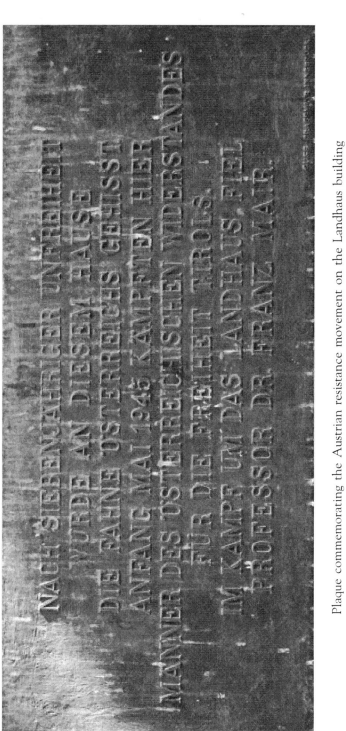

Plaque commemorating the Austrian resistance movement on the Landhaus building

Stone monument with inscription:
"The Teachers of Tyrol for their Heroic Brothers"

Anna and Luis Fessler during the war

Anna and Luis Fessler after the war

Monument commemorating *Pogromnacht*

6

Interlude: Winter-Spring 1997

ebruary is mild in New York City. There is no snow on the ground and almost no wind. As I walk to the mailbox, I wonder who will write. When will I hear from Margret, from Gert, from the teachers? Two weeks after the course ends, I notice an airmail envelope in the box from Ingrid. Quickly, I tear open the back flap. As I begin to read, my heart sinks.

"How dare you?" Ingrid writes to me. "What right do you have to come here and ask us questions about our past? You came here with the desire to gain answers to your personal problems. I am sorry to say, but to my mind this is unprofessional."

I am mortified. I should have expected this. Actually, I realize, *I have been expecting this.* I knew I had gone too far. I never should have given them my paper, never should have suggested we take the walking tour with Horst.

I walk back to house in a daze, sit down at the dining room table, and begin again:

Dear Sondra,

After a week of very little sleep, I am so relieved to be back home with my family. For me, group dynamics in our course took over: I was confused, sad, felt guilty. On the way home, I was falling to pieces . . .

My goal was to gain more focus, to work out a clear structure for my research project [but] 80% of my energy went into building up a feeling of guilt: "We live on historical ground." "We must be beaten for what our parents did or did not do." . . . I spent all those nights wracking my brains: "What is my responsibility for the Holocaust?" And sure, I found something: I probably would not be courageous enough to resist openly, to risk the lives of my children. I would not even have brains to see through that intricate web of dictatorship, steady propaganda, and the pressures of the economic situation.

If not being a hero means to be a Nazi, I wonder how many there are in this world.

Sondra, it is wonderful that you came to Austria in spite of the terrible fate of your people here. It is admirable that you searched for dialogue in spite of the deep resentment you felt towards everything German/Austrian. For the second time, though, you should have come on a private basis.

I think you know far too little about me to write about me. Therefore I ask you to delete my story from your paper and not to use any of my data in the future.

Yours,

Ingrid

I sit still, unable to move. My face feels hot. I read Ingrid's words over again. I try to imagine what has happened. She left the course having glimpsed the larger questions. Of this, I am sure. But now, she's angry; she thinks I have called her a Nazi.

It stings to be called "unprofessional." I know I took risks in the course, allowed my own questions to take us where we would not have otherwise gone. And now I realize I must be willing to face the consequences. This pains me. But I also know I have only one real option—to write back:

Dear Ingrid,

I received your letter on Monday and have been thinking all week about what you wrote. First, I want to say I appreciate your honesty and your willingness to let me know just how strongly you are experiencing what went on, how upset you are, and how difficult the course and the conversations were for you. I am truly sorry for whatever pain my actions have caused you. I hope in time that you will be able to accept my apology and come to some peace about all that happened both in the course and between you and me.

One thing that seems crucial to say is that I never had any intention to make you feel responsible for the Holocaust. None of us was alive then. None of us needs to bear this burden. For me, the questions always were: "What is relevant to raise here, in this course, as we talk about what it means to be a human being in our classrooms? Can we make any sense today of what happened here so long ago? Can we engage in a dialogue about this?"

I have never said much to my children about the Holocaust because, like you, my desire is to protect my children from horror and pain—certainly, I did not want to instill in them the same hatred my mother instilled in me. But now I see that perhaps there is another way. Perhaps I can teach them about this history without also teaching them to hate. Perhaps being responsible does not mean carrying guilt but rather being open to think and ask and talk and respond—as we said to each other in the cafe, to hold oneself accountable through one's commitment to respond. But once again, I hope you can hear from me, I do not consider *you* blameworthy. What always mattered most to me was your willingness to ask the question: What is important to say now, in dialogue, to one another?

You spoke to me of your father and of what happened to him as a soldier. I know that soldiers are often forced to do things they would never do if given a choice. Hearing your story allowed me to see the issue I raised in a different way. I came home feeling gratitude for this tiny glimpse into life as you knew and experienced it.

Now, should I have allowed the course to take such a turn? All I can say is that I did not come to Innsbruck with this issue as an agenda. From Rosenblatt's words to those of van Manen, I was looking to be "a human being" in the classroom. Obviously this became tricky and more emerged than I had planned. Given your critique, I will continue to think seriously about this whole aspect of teaching and what I can learn from this . . .

But one part that stays with me from February is the way we laughed on our last night together at the restaurant where you and I shared a meal—it struck me as the kind of deep, heartfelt laughter that only comes when people have truly worked well together, have learned in each other's presence, and in so doing, have honored one another's humanity. Doesn't any of that stay with you too?

I also want to add that I don't think we can ever fully judge how we would respond under terrible circumstances. But in my mind the only alternative to "not-being-a-hero" is *not*, as you suggest, being a *Nazi*. And I certainly did not mean to leave you with such an impression. I also want to say that no matter how much you wonder about what you would or wouldn't have done, what I saw in you was someone willing to look deeply into profoundly troubling questions and to speak her heart and mind. That, to me, already shows tremendous courage.

Finally, I will do as you ask and remove your name and any reference to you from my paper. It saddens me to do so since you were so much a part of that course, and it saddens me that you feel the need to take yourself away now, even if only on paper. I regret not being able to tell the story of the "paradigm shift" since it does reflect real learning that took place in the course last summer. . . .

When it comes to teaching, I think I am always, as Bissex says, in the "process of becoming." Your letter has given me much to think about in terms of my own flaws, the mistakes I made, and who I might become out of this experience.

My best,

Sondra

A few weeks later, Ingrid writes back:

Dear Sondra,

Thank you for your considerate response! I knew that my picture of the course would become more differentiated, and it has. I felt I had to give feedback of the turmoil the issue of the Holocaust had left in me, wishing and knowing that this could not be the endpoint of this learning sequence but rather the middle of the crisis. I had to separate what, for me, had gone too far on a course level and why this had hit me so much on a personal level.

On the classroom level you raise the question of how much the teacher should reveal of herself. I think we all experienced you as a wonderful and thoughtful teacher because in class you are present as the human being, Sondra. I was and I am impressed by this. In the last course it became difficult for me when our roles, teacher—researcher—student—human beings struggling for response—were not clear any more. Don't worry, some distance and your response [to my letter] have helped to sort this out. Therefore I find no need to take myself away from the group, neither in reality nor on paper.

On the personal level, I, too, ask how much to reveal of myself. I would like to imagine this is a talk we could have under my apple tree, human being to human being. I had to probe further, ask more what is important here in order to be response-able to myself and to you with regard to this choking and silencing issue, the Holocaust. As a result, I would like to say that from the February course I take away your notion of "response-ability." It is a great concept, and you live it. I begin to see that we can be response-able to others only when the different aspects of our personalities can respond to each other. Now . . . I can see the aspects within me that were contradicting each other, unable to respond when faced with the Holocaust. A way of healing, I think, is looking closely at those [aspects], getting to know their nature and potential. Then they will also show a way to coexist with each other . . . We must find a way to integrate whatever is within us. This work is painful but also exciting and fascinating.

I do not know whether I can make myself understood. I try to explain with the most horrible example I know: Never could I understand [how] the most bestial torturers in the concentration camps could be caring fathers and lovers of literature. Now I do. They cut off some aspects of their personalities completely from others, with hardly any relation or connection, no RE-SPONSE among each other. Their personalities were terribly split, and they failed to become whole.

This becoming responsible and whole is a lifelong task. Being asked what I make of the Holocaust raised very troubling questions in me, but it has also given me some glimpse of an insight and has opened doors. On a group-dynamic basis, I had to learn that there is no one answer, neither for all the Austrians, nor for our Innsbruck group. Each of us has to find his or her individual response, due to personal history and personality. I respect the responses of the others, but they are not necessarily true for me.

All this sounds a bit heavy, but I do remember the laughter we had, the warmth, the exciting journeys to our research questions, Bissex, van Manen. I also feel good that I could write to you about what was troubling me. In the meantime the whole course has fallen into place (within me), and I am ready for new adventures.

Thank you again for your letter. I would have found my own way, but reading your letter shows what the ability to respond can be.

Love to you and your family,

Ingrid

Reading Ingrid's words, I let out a sigh of relief. The worry that I had hurt her and the charge that I had been unprofessional never left me. It was as if I had been holding my breath, hoping the promise of what we engaged in together would speak to her again.

And it does. We pursue this inquiry, writing back and forth, every few weeks. But eventually Ingrid's attention is taken up with writing her thesis, and her questions focus increasingly on her classroom research. We are not finished with this topic, but during the time of her thesis writing we put it on hold.

Few of the teachers in our group respond with Ingrid's outrage. Nor do they continue to keep the dialogue alive in the ways she does. Most write once about the past and then limit their letters to research-related issues. Hans and Hilde do not write about the past at all, but everyone else astounds me with his or her first attempt at dialogue. Martina writes with uncharacteristic openness:

Dear Sondra,

Our February week has left me shaken, with the feeling that makes it hard to breathe. The paper you gave us left me sleepless. How could I have been so thoughtless, blind and tactless, not seeing, feeling, hearing your questions? That first sleepless night my mind wandered back to my childhood, when I didn't learn anything about [the past]. Was this innocence or did it arise out of active silence?

I grew up in a mountain village (born 1951) where everybody was poor. We went to school in hand-knitted cardigans and stockings half an hour up the mountain. The winters were cold, so cold my feet and legs were frozen sometimes, and I knew that I couldn't hold my white, frozen hands under warm water at home because that would hurt terribly. I had to hold them under cold water to warm them up slowly. None of us knew that boots with fur linings and quilted anoraks even existed. I got my first winter coat when I was twelve.

On our birthdays we were allowed half a cup of sugar and to mix in a teaspoonful of cocoa powder. It came nearest to the taste of chocolate, which was not in the house. But the other children in the village didn't have it either, so we were very happy with this dry mixture.

There was a strange man in the village where the elementary school was. He was the owner of the old inn between the church and this huge tree where notices were hung. As children we laughed at this man's odd nervous behavior. Somehow I learned that he had been a Nazi. The question if he was the only one never crossed my mind. I did not see, I never looked, never researched.

When I was ten, I learned about the Holocaust. It was terrible, but hadn't we heard hundreds of terrible stories in our history lessons? This one didn't seem more connected to my life than the others.

When we learned about the Holocaust again three years later, it was with more depth, and we learned what happened where we were living. But I understood that the war happened here, the Holocaust happened in Vienna, in Germany, in Dachau and Buchenwald, wherever that was.

Then another question. Were my parents innocent or guilty? War criminals? My father was in the war in France. He had to reconstruct bridges. He brought home a piece of fabric [big] enough to sew two children's dresses. It was green with white butterflies. The dress was handed down to me. I wore it on Sundays and was so proud of it. Remembering this, I now ask, "Was the cloth stolen? Did it come from a Jewish store? Could it have belonged to a Jewish family?"

Those were all my questions. I didn't ask, "What did you see?"

When I first met Hans, he had a very different agenda about this issue. I had always assumed that everyone was innocent if there had been no rumors about someone being an old Nazi. Of all the people I knew, I had heard of only three: the odd innkeeper back home, the boss of a friend (whose daughter is married to a Jew, and I think he loves his grandchildren), and an architect who built the Landhaus you saw. All the other Nazis were people in books. This is clearly not true, but I did not see it.

Hans assumed that everybody above a certain age was guilty (an old Nazi) if not proved otherwise. After many discussions with him, I began to see it his way. By the time you came here, I had been ready "to take the beatings of the world." But your questions still left me helpless and speechless. The biggest question

I have now is this: can you heal from the past? Can you bury a corpse through writing? . . .

Thank you for coming here again. Thank you for giving me a voice finally. Thank you for seeing, feeling, listening.

Love,

Martina

Reading Martina's letter, I am immediately reminded of her reticence to write in the first course. What a difference there is now. I write back to her, thanking her for her honesty, pointing out the detail and the depth in her writing, and remarking on the power of the voice I see emerging in her letter.

Christa, whose insights in the February course came slowly and painfully, also moves slowly with writing. It takes her several months before she can put her thoughts on paper. But when she does, she speaks from the strength of her convictions, with her characteristic searching honesty and her deep compassion:

Dear Sondra,

I have thought about you often while jogging in the woodlands above St. Kathrein. Despite the enjoyable experience of your writing course, I sometimes ask myself if I truly am a writer. Somehow I seem to do literally everything else before I start writing—from school preparation and responding to my students' texts and logs, to household chores, not to speak of working in the garden or reading. Yes, I really have become a reader again . . . Now I read into the small hours of the night, I read while I dry my hair, I read when I roast onions for the goulash . . . I certainly read more than ever before since we parted in February.

But I don't think I am a writer. It takes me such an effort to start. But not writing does not mean not thinking. Those large questions we were living through in February are instantly recalled when I listen to the reports or interviews on the radio, when I read your words or talk to Margret, when we watch *Schindler's List* together in our family and speak about that deplorable past of ours. I see it that we had this individual "exchange of burdens" on our shoulders—not just you and me but all of us who engaged in the process of opening ourselves up to a hidden, covered, wanted-to-be-forgotten guilt. And it's not an exchange . . . it's more. *If it hadn't been for you, I never would have started changing . . .*

One thing that is important to me is to be considerate and put myself in other people's shoes. And last July I thought I did see through your eyes. How totally I misjudged your feelings I only found out seven months later. I did not hear you; I did not.

I did not sense the deep-rootedness of your distress, of your pain, of your hate. You were the first Jewish person I ever met in my life (I should add, knowingly, after hearing about Professor Soloway). I heard you read your piece, but your words didn't "stay" with me. They didn't ring into my heart as they did into Margret's.

All my life I have been covering my people's and my family's political history with a fire blanket. Nobody (with the exception of our youngest son) has ever truly tried to lift that cover. I haven't either. No teacher. Neither of my parents. Not the rest of the family . . . In a way I showed the same attitude as those thousands who didn't want to know what was happening around them. I didn't want to.

Now I can honestly say that I listen with a different memory and react with different emotions and feelings when the Holocaust is addressed. I no longer feel silenced in my thinking, and at least I started talking about it after [seeing] the Spielberg film. Still I haven't done enough reading and informing myself about the Holocaust. Still there is not much exchange of thoughts with others. Still there is not enough true caring for those who were killed or damaged for life . . . In a way the shift and change of attitude leave me recognizing that I must work toward greater wholeness in that part of my life. . . .

You, Sondra, . . . have made me set out for new shores . . . Before I met you, there was never any need, nor even a chance, for a dialogic encounter with a Jew. I have only been able to give up the safety game of the postwar generation because it was you, the stranger, who opened up a dialogue with us.

I'll end now by wishing you pleasure in your work, but above all with your kids, and in the many strolls along the river with your dogs (I assume that there is a river in Riverdale!) and sending you my love,

Yours sincerely,

Christa

I have always been touched by Christa, seeing beneath her physical beauty a caring and sensitive soul. I respect her struggles and her strength. It is easy to respond to her comments and to return the compliment she has given me, to tell her that she and the group occasioned in me as much learning as I may have occasioned in them.

Astrid waits until the end of the school year to write to me. I am taken by surprise, having been convinced that Astrid did not welcome this inquiry. But time to reflect has given Astrid room to respond:

Dear Sondra,

I have read your paper once more and thought I could now try to answer the questions you raised in our class last July. You asked how I cope with the knowledge of what happened here during the Third Reich. I did not feel comfortable with these issues in February. I did not want to be confronted with them. But now, I will try.

At first, I accepted the stories we were told . . . At grammar school we heard a lot about World War II, facts about battles, which cities were bombed, but my teachers were relieved not to have to explain in more detail . . . We were told that "poor Austria" was taken over by Hitler. Only in the 80s was the film sequence of Hitler's speech in the Heldenplatz in Vienna in 1938 with the ovations of the masses shown on TV. This was the same time that everybody was talking about Waldheim's quote of the 'Pflichterfullung' [the obligation to do one's job].

What had I learned at home about this time?

My parents were born into anti-National Socialist backgrounds. My mother's mother was a believing Catholic; my father's family lived on a big ranch, producing everything themselves, even electricity. But they told me how careful they had to be when talking about the government. One could not trust anybody.

My father seldom talks about his four years as a soldier in Russia (age 17 to 21). He still feels those were lost years. When two of his brothers deserted the army in Russia and walked home all the way to the Tyrol, the Nazis gave his family a terribly hard time. As it was common practice to punish the whole family if someone deserted, my father and his six brothers, who still served in the army, had to do the most dangerous jobs on the front. My father was wounded several times.

What astonished me was he did not seem angry with his two brothers. Those two were hiding in the mountains in summer and in stables in winter for two years until the end of the war. To protect the members of the family in case they were arrested or tortured, nobody knew the places they were hiding except one brother who provided them with food. So when my grandmother was put into the labor camp in Innsbruck, Reichenau, she could not tell the officials anything. She was released after two months because of heart problems, after having signed a document that she would be shot if she talked about anything that had happened to her in camp or about what she had seen there. She never talked.

SS officers came to look for my two uncles nearly every night. They used hayforks and dogs for the search. Because of the guard dogs on the farm, they were not successful. It is astonishing that nobody in this family was driven crazy. Maybe they are very good at "pushing away" the past? . . .

It has been much harder for my husband to understand his father's role. He was one of the 80% of teachers who were party members. He even got promoted to inspector of schools. He never told his sons which role he played, but he seemed to be a lecturer in one of the colleges for SS officers. He was in an American camp in Salzburg for three years after the war. After some years as a salesman in books, he was allowed to enter the teaching profession again. Since 1955, every teacher has [had] to sign a document saying that he will be neutral in what he says in the class. This means that one should not express any political opinion in order to avoid influencing the students.

I am sure that my father-in-law was very careful about what he said in school because he never talked to his family about this time. He destroyed all letters and documents. He spent lots of time in his garden, which was immaculate, and he would read stories to my daughter for hours every day. Before I got married, my parents inquired about my fiancé's family. They were told that my father-in-law had been a "good Nazi"—such a statement was often heard. It is still hard for us to understand why he was fascinated by Hitler and his ideology. My husband, his brother, and I have not joined any political party because we find there are parts in the ideology of each party we cannot accept. A reaction? I agree that nothing should be forgotten.

Here is a poem that I have written about my father-in-law:

Eye Contact (Silence)

A humble old father
cannot look into other people's eyes.
He talks about his garden only.

Nobody, especially not his son,
asks any questions about the past.
Years later his granddaughter
wants to know
but he cannot talk.

Astrid's candor reminds me of a comment Tanja made to me on my last night in Innsbruck: Austrians may take their time, but when they are ready, they will speak.

Andrea also takes her time in writing to me. When she does, she explains the reason behind her silence. She has been hurt by what I wrote about her in my paper. In describing the lightheartedness a group of us felt one night at a local bar when Andrea asked me about visiting "New York's Jewish quarter," I originally wrote that it might have been "Andrea's naiveté" that led us all to laugh so wholeheartedly. She has been upset ever since.

Dear Sondra,

It has taken me a while to sort things out after the February course. I found myself physically and emotionally worn out . . . I set all that had happened aside for a while, which proved a wise thing to do. Slowly I moved toward collecting data, toward reading about poetry, toward cautiously trying things out. But I do not yet know what to focus on for my thesis. There's been a big shift in my research question, which has got a lot to do with what I experienced in the February course. Well, here's my story.

The questions of responsibility—of my "ability to respond"—has haunted me for a long time but now it is center stage. The more I encourage my students to write about their own topics, the more I invite them to inquire into themselves, the more I want them to be full human beings, the more I am confronted with texts that openly show deep personal agonies. There's Esther, who was in tears while writing about something personal, though later she wrote in her reflections that it had been " . . . good for cleaning her soul." There's Michael, who wrote about how he watched a 12-year-old boy commit suicide because of a bad mark. There's Hanna, who wrote a text about a grandfather attacking a character in her story with a knife.

What right do I have as a teacher to teach with an approach that releases my students' most personal, inner agonies? To collect their texts and turn these revelations into a research paper? Where am I when those agonies are released? Who is there to deal with them? I cannot and do not want to take on the role of therapist or friend. I've got my own troubles, I've got a husband, a 10-, an 8- and a 3-year-old, who need my support, help, and strength. I've got a job and a master's thesis to write. I've thoroughly questioned myself whether these are just cheap excuses, but I've become clearly aware of my own personal boundaries and the limits of my energy.

I wonder if the traditional approach to teaching isn't more honest in this respect. All a traditional teacher can do is ruin students' concepts of school or their love of a subject. But isn't what I am doing here more dangerous? They open up to me in ways they haven't before, and then they are left alone or written about in a research paper, and still I am the one who decides about [their] passing or failing. Am I not pretending a trusting relationship with my new approach? Isn't this fake? Betrayal?

How can I ever believe in being able to listen closely enough to how each student feels in a class of thirty (and I do have more than one such class) if—and this is definitely the hard part—when you, the best and most experienced teacher I know, who has opened this new approach to teaching for me—failed in doing this with a group of ten?

I know this is hard talk but I hope I can enter into a dialogue with you about how I feel about the February course. I feel I have not been seen as a full human being. When you label me "naive" [in your paper], I feel you saw only one facet of me. I have never been to the United States, I didn't know anything about Jews in New York. Moreover, knowing that nothing but this minor, negative facet of myself is being publicized in your paper hurts.

I understand that coming to Austria released your own personal agony, and I was deeply moved by your text. It has started a new and important awareness about my own share of responsibility for the history of my people. I know that pigeonholing me was the last thing you intended to do and I also know you tried and still do care about everything that was and is going on in the group. I am writing this not to make you feel guilty, but to help you understand why the above concerns have become so predominant and have influenced my research question.

The point I am trying to make here is that it is probably impossible to listen to everything, to see everything, to care about everything, to respond to everything that is going on in a group of ten, twenty-seven, or thirty learners. How could you possibly know I felt like this? How could you possibly see, care, respond to everything?

So I question myself whether taking on the responsibility of being a full human being in the classroom and responding fully to other human beings is not expecting and demanding too much of everyone concerned. This has blocked me and it still does. I do not know how I'm ever going to find an answer to this. I guess I'll need a lifetime.

I welcome your response.

Yours,

Andrea

Andrea's questions allow me to write about teaching, about why I teach the way I do, and what is at stake in such a model. She also allows me to make an important distinction between therapy and teaching. Writing teachers are not therapists and need to know when to send students who reveal troubling issues for help. But most of all Andrea's questions allow me to engage in the dialogue I have been claiming is so important.

I begin with an apology, telling her I am sorry to have caused her pain and explaining that to me the word *naïve* is not negative, but rather conveys a kind of openness and even innocence. I explain that I never meant to prescribe how anyone else should or might teach, and that she, rightly, needs to be guided by her own values and the very real limits on her time and energy. I comment on the issue of authority, writing that teachers do have power, and to pretend otherwise is dishonest. And I tell her that most teachers I know struggle with what it means to be present in the classroom—that we see this as a worthy goal but frequently feel as if we are falling short.

Six of the eight Austrian teachers who attended the course in February write to me about my paper. Tanja and Thomas, the two Americans in the group, had responded during the course, writing into the wee hours of the morning and handing me letters on the last day of class.

Tanja uses my questions to analyze her reactions to life in Austria and to the racist undercurrents she has begun to notice in her community and in her classroom. When she hands me her letter, she tells me I do not need to write back. The value for her has been in having this opportunity to sort out her thoughts:

Dear Sondra,

I just finished reading your paper and looking over the reflections I wrote last summer in the course. I was surprised to find several of the themes you mentioned recurring in my notes: the shift that occurred in the room when you named "the paralysis," the openness and safety we all felt, the beauty of the pieces we each wrote, and the topic of moral neutrality.

I remember reacting strongly to this, too, because I had had to sign a form at that time that said I agreed to remain apolitical in order to renew my contract at the university. I remember being disturbed by the document even after colleagues told me not to take it seriously. Only now do I realize how profoundly immoral that policy is. It applies to all teachers—ironically, a preventative measure to protect against National Socialism. Essentially, the state denies teachers the right to be human in their classrooms. I heave a sigh here; there is so much to be changed.

Looking back on our course, I realize I had little faith in my Austrian colleagues; I hadn't known any who truly dealt with the issue except on an intellectual level, and those people were at the university studying contemporary history in the safety of university walls. I remember talking with Andrea in 1993, when our friendship was still in the early, tentative stages (as friendship often develops here), and asking her about the concentration camp that existed near her home. She was stunned; I can still see the expression on her face. She denied the possibility. I remember feeling disappointed and confused, and I dropped the subject because I had quickly realized neither of us was equipped to discuss it.

Margret is certainly an exception to the rule, and I admire her strength and humanity. Last July, after our brief talks on what you were experiencing (just how deeply I only now realize!), I wondered how far the Austrians in the group would/could go with the issue and how much time they would take to reflect on it. I am curious to see what happens in the months ahead.

The horror of what happened here is something every human being has to confront if they are to live healthy lives. A few years ago, I became aware of the fact that some of my neighbors had been collaborators. I began to ask myself if I could really live here and how much tolerance I would have for the right-wing party as it carefully positioned itself solidly in the government. I went to see Haider speak and was terrified by how similar his rhetoric was to Hitler's. I participated in a peace demonstration for the first time in my life. Little did I know that Lee Anne, my American friend, would be attacked by skinheads on her way home. Two years later, Ozcam, a Turkish boy who came to visit me, was harassed by the same group on the train.

In my second year of teaching here, I had a Haider fan in class who brought in a rune and told a story that was clearly linked to the Aryan folklore of the Nazis. When he finished, the silence spoke for itself—the atmosphere was thick with dis-ease. I made a carefully worded, ironic comment and the group eventually recovered, but I only knew intuitively what had happened. Later that evening, I checked with a friend and found out that indeed his entire presentation had been loaded with Nazi overtones. I later confronted him and told him to keep his politics at home. Another student, who was a member of a dueling fraternity here (illegal but with a long Nazi tradition), was more difficult to cope with. I had to throw him out of class because of his hostility—something I realize now was illegal—which makes me angry. I just saw him a few weeks ago at the university ball, and he greeted me with his usual threatening nature. He truly hates.

I have heard more stories from people I know here: one is of a woman who, like Margret, married into a prominent Innsbruck family. She only discovered that her grandmother was Jewish while sifting through papers after her mother died. Her family denied her this knowledge in an effort to protect her. She is confused and lost. There is no one to tell her the stories, and she can only piece them together with the little bit of evidence she has found in attic boxes.

The subject has manifested itself in my teaching in many small ways. I often point out how enriched American English is by Yiddish and list many words my students understand as a result of their German. Each time we discuss this, there is a palpable shift in the group triggered by the word Yiddish. And we have worked the issue into our business curriculum in other small ways. One of our scenarios for discussion when working on effective ways to agree and disagree is: "You are having a discussion with your 80-year-old grandfather who was a Nazi in World War II." Students' reactions vary from "I wouldn't bother arguing" to "Of course, I'd tell him what I think." The discussions occur in small groups, and I mainly listen in, not wanting to interfere because I am an outsider. I realize now that I should seize the opportunity when it arises, be open about my views, and invite them to do the same.

In thinking about my experiences here, I realize how troubled Austria is by her past, how much damage has been done by sweeping it all under the carpet, and how difficult it will be in the future to confront it. There is a profound sense of self-hatred here, and it seems to eat away at people in different ways. Whether this self-hatred is a cause or an effect of genocide, I don't know. It is a question I now have. Suffice it to say that reflecting once again on all this has helped me to learn even more about this culture I am living in, and the review has been good for me . . .

These are some of my stories. I am sure there are many more trapped in attic boxes, most of which will never be revealed. Others are lost because they won't escape the boundaries of the limited circles in which they are confided. So few are written down. Thanks for writing yours.

Love,

Tanja

Unlike Tanja, who has often analyzed her encounters with Austrians and reflected on Austria's history, Thomas is facing these events and his German family's role in them for the first time. He is in turmoil, weeping at his computer. Writing a letter to me is cathartic for him:

Dear Sondra,

I've just finished reading your paper. It's 1:30 in the morning, and my head is reeling. I have so much to say to you.

There are so many things I cannot grasp. I mean I'm aware of things; I go through moods and feel my emotions tiding and ebbing. But yet I feel they elude me. It is perhaps the feeling that there is something more behind all this, something beyond comprehension. Take the fact that you are here with us. You literally dropped out of the sky, and you taught us to open our hearts. I don't know why as I sit here and think of you, think of us, tears well up in my eyes. On one side, happy tears for the person you are, your soul reaching out and yearning for understanding; on the other side, deeply saddened tears, for there are not many like you.

Now the choking up has passed, but I think I've captured the moment! You are here, as the result of many efforts: Tanja's to get the M.A. program started, our wishes to have you return. Then there are the doubts you had to overcome the first time you were here. So many things had to work to bring us together.

Maybe the thing that eludes me can be called "destiny." I am not satisfied with that word. It sounds so hollow and doesn't really capture the magic. So I'll write for a while and see if things get clearer.

Thank you for sharing your most honest writing with us. You chose, with Margret's support (and prodding?), to expose the dilemmas inside you, the struggles with your beliefs, the tearing feeling as you try to define yourself. I'm glad we got to hear your thoughts. Don't you feel now as though some great burden has been lifted from your shoulders? Don't you feel now all those wonderful things like trust, faith, friendship, and love converging at some point in your heart?

I'm glad, too, that you recorded the happenings of last summer's course. I hardly remember any of the things people said except for Margret's statements about National Socialism. She was so outspoken about her concerns and fears that it's no wonder I remember. I cannot recollect, however, how you tiptoed your way through revealing a little of your life to us. When I reread my daily reflections, I realize I made no mention of the discussions regarding you and how Nazism affected our lives. Did those things just pass over my head? Was I just suppressing some uncomfortable feelings inside me and passing off the discussions as interesting but irrelevant to my learning? How do I, as a born German, stand up to what happened fifty years ago and what's still going on today?

I grew up in America. As a child entering school, I realized my family was different: we were first generation immigrants. I was embarrassed at my parents' accents and did everything possible to hide my heritage. It had less to do with jokingly being called a "Nazi" by my classmates than just plain trying to be like everyone else. "Nazi" didn't mean anything to me. How could it when nobody ever explained to me what had happened? My father told me stories of running from Allied bombs, the nights hiding in shelters, or the weeks spent in the country away from the target centers. From my readings, I understood that the good guys were the Americans, and the bad guys were the Germans. School didn't help either. How could it when World War II was a chapter in the textbook we had to get through by the end of the year! Nazi Germany was so distant, temporally and spatially.

When I was a teenager I went to Germany a few times to visit my relatives. To me they were distant people who played virtually no role in my life. My father's mother was full of stories about the war. By that time, I knew of the horrors and was relieved to hear that my grandfather had a job in a cemetery burying German soldiers. My grandmother said she helped the Jews when she could. She once showed me antiques, porcelain figures, in her living room, gifts for potatoes or shelter she had once given. Chills are running through my body right now. Now they turn to flooding tears. They are subsiding . . . I can continue. A deep breath . . . The stories are so vague. I regret not talking more with her. My grandmother died last year. Now, more than ever, I want to hear her stories, to know about her and my grandfather. For what they were is some part of what I am today.

My eyes fill with tears again. This writing is tearing me apart. All horrors past, present, and future are becoming real to me now. Is writing that powerful? Yes—the more I write, the more I want to say to you.

Past, present, and future. What I can't believe is that over all the millennia of human existence we have not advanced. What happened fifty years ago is just inconceivable, but similar things are happening all over the world today. Will they continue to happen as long as humans exist? How can I remain silent when an old man in a supermarket blabbers to himself what a wonderful man Hitler was? How can a young man remain quiet as a bunch of skinheads make racial remarks at his Bosnian girlfriend? How can politicians remain quiet as human rights are violated everywhere? Where is all this silence coming from?

There are only a few who dare to speak up, a few who have managed to overcome their fears, a few like you, Sondra. But you can only reach a few at a time, and the population is exploding. I'm beginning to sound very pessimistic, and the more I think about it the more furious I get. We can be angry at Hitler and the Germans for what they did. We can be angry at Stalin, too, or at the Europeans for what they did to the Native Americans. The Chinese Communists. The Serbians. What's going on in the Near East, Africa, South America? What about America and Europe? Hasn't anybody learned anything?

I don't want to apologize for my race and what they did because my apology is meaningless, symbolizing nothing except my recognition of what happened. I recognize what is going on, and I can cry for all the people who have suffered, who are suffering, and who will suffer. My tears are the only thing I can offer the victims. And I can only be angry at myself for being so helpless, for taking no action. I constantly think about my next vacation, what I will eat for dinner, the shoes I want to buy, but I suppress the images of pain and suffering around me. I am too comfortable with my life, too worried about my own exaggerated problems to worry about what's going on with my neighbor, let alone a neighboring country, let alone a country on the other side of the world.

I have grown up in a world of silence, and I live in a world of silence. You are right, Sondra. Something momentous has happened during our time together. Again, it is rather indescribable. But I can say this: I have never written a letter like this before, not to anyone; and I have never done any writing like we did in our course. Without realizing it, I have been paralyzed, but now I can wriggle my big toe. Thanks, Sondra, for cracking that world of silence. The rest is up to me.

Love,

Thomas

Sensing the urgency in his letter, I write back to Thomas a few days after I return to New York, thanking him for his honesty and for allowing the work we did together to have such a huge impact on him. I also remind him that it is what we choose to do today that matters most—whether we speak up or remain silent.

I expected that most of the teachers would write to me. But I was never sure if Gert would follow through on his promise. Toward the end of February, though, I discover another airmail envelope in the mailbox. Inside I find a letter from Gert written in German, accompanied by an English translation written by Margret. I walk back to the house, make a cup of tea, and sit down to read:

Dear Sondra,

Last summer, Margret told me you were Jewish and that you had great difficulty coming to a former National Socialist country where the most appalling atrocities against Jews were committed. I remember my surprise and inner defense. My surprise came from my attitude: I had not harmed anybody, and my defensiveness came from knowing that my parents had been Nazis.

Then in your February course Margret said that again you were talking a lot about the Holocaust and that she wanted to keep a journal for you. I sensed that she wanted me to take part in this dialogue. This meant for me that I would have to get away from being passive and try to interact with you personally.

Once again my inner voice told me, "I don't have a close enough relationship with her for such an intimate topic." This was one of my arguments. The other one was "My bad English doesn't allow me to have such a deep and complicated talk."

Right away I knew that these were excuses and that as a citizen of this country I had to speak out; and I am of the opinion that it has to be me who takes a step towards you and asks you whether you would like to talk to me about this issue. Besides I do not want to ignore a wish that is important to Margret.

I would like to start with my parents and say right away that I am always inclined to protect them. I hope that the picture I draw of them is not too optimistic but rather is as objective as possible.

Both were very young: my mum was sixteen when the war broke out, and my dad was twenty-one. I think they had little chance to encounter different opinions, and they could not help being influenced by the Nazi propaganda. I kept asking myself how I would have reacted, and I think there probably wouldn't have been a lot of difference.

Both of them were very active Nazis, my mother as the leader of the girls' movement of Tyrol, and my father in war for six years—not enthusiastically but certainly with the strong wish to give his best for the aims of the Nazis in this war.

Both have constantly stressed that they did not know or witness anything about the Holocaust or hardly anything. In this respect, I have to ask myself just how much they didn't want to see, just how much they looked away or repressed reality. I deeply hope they never agreed with the appalling goals of the Nazis or that they never themselves took an active part in the atrocities.

Even many years after the war they had little doubt about the righteousness of their doings. When I was a child, whenever the grown-ups came together, they talked about the lost war. When they were confronted with the atrocities, they tried to fend everything off, never once looking critically at their own deeds. They could not admit that their whole commitment, yes, their whole life, had served one big crime. They were forced to take part in the war, they believed the Holocaust was a lie, and, if they had to admit anything, then they pointed at others who had been worse.

I was taught that our enemies were the Americans, because without them stepping in, we would never have lost the war; the Jews because they owned all the money; the Catholic Church, because of their hypocrisy and the traitors among us.

In those days I believed my parents, but those ongoing talks, which were the same all the time, got on my nerves, and I didn't want to hear any of it anymore.

But there was one basic attitude that influenced me a lot. Part of it is: "Do everything alone, do not trust anybody, be wary of everybody." Another part is: "Weaknesses are not allowed; an alcoholic is weak and has only himself to blame, and we do not want to associate with such a person. Also, fat or unsporty people, for example, are to be despised."

When I was thirty—fairly late in life—I decided to become a member of a Communist group and I was an active member. Since I was also a shop owner, I walked a difficult tightrope. At that time we had a lot of discussions about the time of the Nazis and neofascism and everything that seemed part of this ideology we fought against. At one of those rallies against fascists I met Margret.

Today I know that my discussions about National Socialism did not go deeply, and we never questioned our own actions or thoroughly investigated our personal attitudes toward fascism. Today I somehow have the feeling that my parents (especially my mother) have realized that much had been wrong and downright criminal. I think I constantly have to be aware . . .

For many years I had been proud and self-satisfied that I could say, "I hold nothing against Jews." But because of my discussions with Margret I have come to realize that this is a rather arrogant point of view, especially if I do not add anything to it. It is natural and obvious that I hold nothing against Jews as they have never ever done me any harm. I feel it would be right to ask you, "How do you feel when standing in front of me, and what can I do so that you do not mistrust me?"

This letter is my first try in this direction. For me this topic had always been closed. It was your talks that made me realize this was a lie, and I thank you and Margret for helping me express myself.

Gert

It is more difficult to respond to Gert than to the teachers. With them I have many reference points. With him, there are only the words of his letter and my questions. What is it like to be the son of ardent Nazis? What is it like for him to write to a Jewish woman? Is there any chance of our understanding one another? And if so, to what end? As I sit in front of my computer, I picture him on the few occasions I have seen him: striding easily up the Austrian Alps on a day-long hike, sitting quietly at dinner in a restaurant, smiling kindly at Margret and even at me.

As I begin to write, I realize that each step of this journey has come as a surprise. I cannot know where this next step will lead until I take it. So with nothing more than trust in the future, I write to Gert, telling him I welcome our conversation.

I tell him that reading what he writes about his parents is a bit like taking a bandage off a wound. It hurts, and I am not sure if I can look at what lies beneath the covering. I tell him that I am trying to see both sides: the fact that these two people are his parents and the fact that they were active Nazis.

And finally I explain that, like him, I once believed that the Holocaust had nothing to do with me. It happened in Europe before I was born. It was not my issue to address. As horrified as I might have been by the events and the stories, I did not imagine that I had any reason to address it or speak about it.

But in Innsbruck, standing on Austrian soil, I tell him, I began to recognize that the Holocaust is as much mine as anyone's, that those of us born in its aftermath can choose to look away or choose to turn toward it. I now see, I tell Gert, that there is both power and freedom in embracing this history—in claiming it and addressing it in whatever ways we can.

7

A Dialogue in Letters

Unlike the other teachers, who write to me only once or a few times over the spring and summer, Margret writes often and at great length. Our correspondence becomes a bridge connecting our lives, our teaching, and the larger questions that haunt us. The trust we build through writing strengthens our resolve to pursue together what is too painful to pursue alone.

February 22, 1997

Dear Sondra,

It is one week now since you left, and I have been thinking of you daily. How did you find everything when you arrived? How is your family? How do you live your daily life? What are the moments when you think of us here in Austria, of me? I just unpacked all your letters from the course, and I do not dare to look at them. I am already sitting here crying as I miss you and the certainty to see you again the next morning. . . .

I am thrilled at the prospect of writing my research paper, as I know you will read it and return in October as our mentor. My mum has also written her piece and to me it is really touching—to see her handwriting, her spelling mistakes, and her simplicity. Now I have got her words on a sheet of paper, and we both have the feeling that her writing has woven some kind of thread between us. I send you all my love and a big, big hug.

Margret

March 1, 1997

Dear Margret,

I woke up this morning with two contradictory thoughts in my mind. The first is that we are just two women searching our hearts for truth. Our efforts cannot stop war or abolish racism—we are just two little specks on the face of the Earth who will all too soon be gone. The second is that what we are doing is so profound there is nothing more important. The connection we are creating is not only nourishing for us and those we love, but it is also the most meaningful way I know to live—it is a gift that we will bequeath to our children . . .

Today we attended a Bat Mitzvah service, a coming-of-age religious ceremony, for the 13-year-old daughter of a neighbor. It was surprisingly touching to me. We do not go to synagogue often. I rarely find myself sitting among friends listening to prayers or Hebrew music, but here I was, two weeks after walking through the streets of Innsbruck, sitting in this exquisite synagogue on West 83rd Street in Manhattan with tears in my eyes.

I heard things I had never heard before or never in the same way. As the rabbi spoke of this tradition that is thousands of years old and how no amount of suffering or atrocity has managed to extinguish the urge of this people to pray and to live a life commanded by the Torah, I was deeply moved. I sat there in the pew, picturing the walk we took in Innsbruck, and I felt much less of a burden—much less distaste or need to distance myself from what is good and true in this tradition. I came home feeling touched, wishing I would finally have some word from you, and there in the mailbox, I found your letters waiting.

I also love hearing about your mom and her writing and your research and all that we have to look forward to. I sent my mother a copy of the paper about the summer and she is also touched not only by what I wrote but also by you. I know she has been thinking about where her own hatred comes from and the whole issue of responsibility—so this is now moving into my relationship with my mother too—so much we all share.

Love for now and always,

Sondra

Dearest Sondra,

"I must find room for us—I need it." These are the last lines I posted yesterday in my short note to you. Today I came home from work and stopped to have a look into my post box. And just like two weeks ago, I found your yellow envelope. And I knew right away that tonight I will sit down with a glass of wine and write and write for as long as I want.

So your letter arrived just when mine left—like last time. That is really funny and at first I worried whether we would get mixed up completely . . . would I answer all the questions you asked me, and would I not miss anything? But then I realized it doesn't matter. Isn't it like a piece of art? Sometimes you look at the whole of it and sometimes you look at a detail and study it, but at the very next moment you are intrigued by another aspect, a different perspective, and when you get confused you just step back and just look at the whole and there it is: our dialogue, our mutual understanding, our sharing, and our feelings.

I am sitting here reading the letter you wrote to Gert, helping him to understand what you are saying by just translating it—I want him to have the full impact of your words without my interference, and I see how he realizes that never in his life has any human being (except for his wife) talked to him like that, really being interested in him.

You know, Sondra, what really scared me in Gert's letter? When he said that he thought he would have been like his parents had he been in their shoes then. This is exactly what haunts me. Do you remember when I wrote to you about preparing myself for a time I would really have to be courageous in order not to become one of them too? I am too scared to even imagine that I would not have been different because this means hopelessness. Do you understand? I am always afraid of my own fear. Will it numb me one day? If not, who will I make suffer—my child, my husband, my family? Would I set the fate of other human beings above the fate of those closest to me? Would I sacrifice them on what may seem like the altar of humanity?

One needs always to question oneself. This is why I hesitate to lecture students. I truly believe in learning in dialogue. Sometimes students welcome this, but at other times, they do not. But I dare say that the question of being welcome is of no real importance when it comes to teaching. Once in a while, don't you find yourself in a situation in which you just have to go ahead even if your students don't really understand at that moment? What keeps you going is the belief that you cannot do it any differently and the ray of hope that one day they might understand . . .

I was really impressed that you talked to your mum about your experiences here in Austria. I had wondered whether you would do that. If I meet her one day, will she take my hand? I just imagine what it could be like not to be seen as an individual but as a member of a group. This is exactly what happened to your people. What would I feel if she ignored me? If she didn't even want to hear me speaking—hearing the German accent through my words—being reminded of I don't know what. Would I hate her? Would I really be so understanding when it comes to being confronted with reality instead of discussing theory? . . .

I envy you your experience in the synagogue. It's so touching and it makes me realize that all I can do is have faith without a church. Have you ever seen our churches? One never knows whether they were erected to glorify God or those who built them. There is hardly anybody left in the Roman Catholic Church who can evoke feelings of belonging for me. I feel as if the church has robbed me of a home for my beliefs. Does that make sense to you? I am not an atheist, but I would not know whom to pray to as when I try to do so, all I see is Jesus being tormented, and God punishing me for petty sins.

One day soon I will call you—just to hear your voice. . . .

Goodbye then,

Margret

March 29, 1997

Dear Margret,

Hi—how are you? Not a day goes by when I don't wonder how you are or what you are doing. Like you, my time is full with all the day-to-day demands of teaching and caring for my family. I am so happy whenever I receive a letter from you and can then make the time to write back.

Your last letter is dated the 11th of March, and I will try to pick up from there ... Yes, I did have a start—a sort of scary jump of my heart—when Gert wrote that he suspects he would have been like his parents—but I also respect his honesty ... it takes courage not to pretend. It is so much easier to say, "Oh, I would have been different." But is that any truer? I am coming to believe that nobody is exempt from the possibility of doing evil—different times try us in different ways ...

I agree with you that sometimes one needs to raise hard issues in class and not worry so much whether everyone likes what is going on. But at what point does this turn into coercion? At what point should a teacher back off if students can't or won't follow along in the inquiry? In our M.A. course, I still wonder if I went too far. I wanted to give people room to say no to me, but I'm not sure they felt they could. I, too, believe in dialogue, but what do you do when someone doesn't want to respond? I am also thinking about this in terms of what we might do when we are together next time in October ...

I want you to know that whenever my mother meets you, she would like you immediately. She already knows how important you are to me—and you would respond to her warmth and generous spirit. I will write more about her some other time ... but right now, everyone is out, and I can look forward to some quiet time in the house: home alone with the dogs, cat, snake, birds, and mice! Arthur said yesterday that our having so many animals must reflect his childhood yearning for pets, something his mother wouldn't allow. Other than the dogs, I am not in charge of pet care.

With love and a great deal of missing you,

Sondra

It normally takes one week for our letters travel back and forth across the Atlantic. Then one morning in May, I discover an e-mail message from Margret. The subject line, "It works!" is a heading we use for months. Now our correspondence takes new turns. We find ourselves describing more of our lives at home, going into greater detail about husbands and children, reactions to movies and books. Back and forth, day by day, week by week, we recount events, ask questions, clarify meaning, retrace steps, rephrase an idea, rethink a position, apologize for misconstruing a comment, and ultimately, write our way into even greater intimacy.

Subject: It works!

Dear Sondra,

Finally! It seems to work! It is Sunday morning, and I'm trying to find a few minutes to write to you. I try to picture you at home, what you are doing, and where your computer is. Gert has just entered my study and is pacing like a lion in a cage. He gets really tense when we do not get out into nature. I'd better run. More later.

Love,

M.

Subject: RE: It works!

Dear Margret,

Yes, at last, it works! In answer to your question, my computer is upstairs in my office, which is overflowing with books, files, and, of course, kid things—discarded homework papers, stuffed animals, doodles, even dog bones strewn here and there. One dog lies on my couch as I work. The other crawls under my desk. I sit facing the wall as I work at the computer, but the room has large windows that face the Hudson River, so even in the reflection on my screen I can faintly see water, trees, and mountains. It's quiet and comforting to be here . . . I have "a room of my own"—but without a lock on the door.

When I take my morning walk in the woods with the dogs, I picture your being here and seeing how we live. Today I went to "the ledge"— a landing that juts out near the water. To the south you can see the George Washington Bridge; to the north, the Tappan Zee Bridge. Across the Hudson are the Palisades, rock cliffs that line the shore for miles, and on the river occasional barges, tug boats, and sail boats. It's an amazing spot.

The other day I started reading Goldhagen's book, *Hitler's Willing Executioners: Ordinary Germans and the Holocaust.* As I began, I was thinking how interesting it would be if we could read it together. What do you think? . . .

Love,

Sondra

Hi, Sondra,

We have just come back from a two-day trip to a valley nearby— a one-hour trip by car, which for us seems to be far, far away. The weather is gorgeous (is it English?). We were there with friends, and it was a very nice break in all the work.

Still, I always find myself torn between the wishes of all the people around me. There is Cara, who doesn't want to walk too far, and then there is Gert who keeps on walking and walking and doesn't see that people are tired. All I try to do is satisfy both of them, which is quite complicated. Besides, there is the dog who keeps pulling me in yet another direction.

I haven't read Goldhagen's book but I assume I know what he is writing about. I have read so much about the Holocaust and been to Mauthausen and Dachau. I do not share your feelings—I do not want to know more—to read and see more. Sorry to be so short . . . I've got to run.

Love,

M

May 20

Dear Margret,

I can just picture you on this outing needing to care for everyone's needs. I, too, always feel as if I am responding to the kids, the dogs, and Arthur. There is always this sense of having to juggle what everyone else needs and wants, isn't there?

I read Goldhagen at night. It makes me tired. Like Horst, Goldhagen traces the roots of anti-Semitism back 2,000 years to the church. It's a straightforward presentation but so draining to read about centuries of hatred and persecution.

. . . Yes, we say the weather is "gorgeous"—or we might say, "It's an incredible day."

Love,

S

May 22

Dearest Sondra,

About Goldhagen: I wanted to tell you that on the one hand I have the feeling I know it all, and I can hardly stand any more recollections of the appalling atrocities committed during the Holocaust. On the other hand, I am, like you, somehow trying to grasp how this could ever happen. I have lots of theories about what could have turned human beings into monsters, and I still do not understand. This is exactly what scares me so much: if you do not know what to be aware of, could it not befall you one day? Could I have been one of them? You know all my questions. You are not the reason for me to read . . . You are like a key that helps me open the doors to questions and maybe answers that have been hidden.

The other thing I wanted to say is that there are times when I can hardly breathe because of all the daily fascism around me. Maybe this seems so drastic to me because of our history. I remember how shocked I was when you told us that you had sent Sara to a summer camp where she was not allowed to phone home whenever she wanted. This reminded me so much of the belief so common among people here in Austria that the true things in life are the ones that hurt. . . .

So, I'll go to bed now—and you will just be sitting down in the afternoon and doing what?

Love,

Margret

May 22

Dearest,

I am rushing now because I have to catch the 2:12 train to Manhattan. I have my last class at the Graduate Center today, but before I go there I have to stop at the jeweler's where I had a pair of earrings made for my birthday—a gift from Arthur. They are beautiful, but the spring is too tight. Sometimes it amazes me that I have this life as an academic, and yet I also think about earrings!

I love you,

S

May 23

Dear Sondra,

I loved your comment about the earrings. It could have been my thought, too. Whenever I succeed in getting my fingernails growing really long, I am very proud of myself. Then I paint them red and smile (inwardly) at all the people who—at best—think I am an elementary school teacher or kindergarten nurse . . .

Over the weekend I'll have to prepare 34 oral exams. There has to be a text (from newspapers or literature) and questions of different kinds. The supervisor of this form is an English teacher himself, and sometimes I find myself worrying about my English. I have the experience that when I am stressed and my students do not communicate well with me or cannot express themselves properly, I start stammering and forgetting my vocabulary. So I'll be extremely nervous in these exams, but whenever I start worrying and doubting my abilities I turn my mind to you and my M.A. courses. No one ever had difficulties in understanding me (although I sometimes had difficulties in expressing what I wanted to say). I can vividly imagine what your face looks like at the moment of reading about my language inferiority complex—right?

That's all so far. I love you, too.

Margret

May 26

Hi—

I loved your nail polish story. I also do shake my head in what? exasperation? sigh of understanding and yet wanting to say how silly? that you have any sense of inferiority when it comes to English. You are so clear—your vocabulary and sentence structure are so sophisticated. Silly, silly, silly, how school makes us doubt who and what we are—probably worse than silly—so I am glad you think of me and our courses and can use that as a way to remind yourself how strong you are and how profound your understanding is. A world that makes us doubt what is so good and true in us is really crazy.

Time to go now. I picture you with your students and final exam questions and send you love,

S

July 5

Dear Sondra,

Our final M.A. course with Cynthia Mitchell is going well. She is a delight. She has asked us to do some writing about a time when we "caught sense," as she puts it. So I am puzzling over a question: Why do I always remember the awful moments in my life—never anything positive? I seem always to be drawn to the difficult, the heavy, the negative. I can't remember a moment in which I learned something, a moment of importance, that did not hurt. Why am I always so harsh with myself?

Love,

M

July 13

Dear Margret,

Did you ever consider that being drawn to the difficult is not bad—so much of life is superficial, and so much of who we are comes from the hard times, the pain, being willing to look at it, and if we are fortunate—to move through it and beyond it. I see you as brave enough to go to the hard places, as someone who does not flinch, who is willing to look and see what is there.

Love,

S

July 15

Dear Sondra,

The course ended well. Last night, we had a little farewell party for Cynthia and her friend, Roberta. Gert's parents came. Cynthia and Roberta were the first black people they had ever seen, and his mum kept asking such naïve questions ("Does you hair ever grow?" "Where in Africa do you come from?"). Gert got very angry, and then there was silence. Roberta later said that she was impressed by her soft voice because she always thought former Nazis were brutal people. This is the thing we have not grasped—how schizophrenic everyday human beings can be.

Love, M

July 16

Dear M,

It's hard to make sense of Gert's mother. Or maybe it isn't so hard. The more I am reading, the more I understand how easy it was to get caught up in the whirlwind of hatred. A week ago, I finished Ursula Hegi's novel, *Stones from the River*. It takes place in a German town before and during the war. The narrator is a *Zwerg*, a female dwarf, which provides Hegi with an unusual angle for exploring the issue of difference—of being ostracized and excluded. She makes no excuses, just shows how ordinary people were led—and misled. One of her main points: the devastation silence brings. But recently, I've noticed that I am feeling overwhelmed by the reading I am doing. I have some sense of what you mean about not wanting to read anymore. I often feel sick at heart. We leave for California in a few days. When are you leaving for Greece?

Dear Sondra,

We leave for Greece tomorrow on the ferry from Ancona—return August 17. I have finished packing, taken a long shower, rolled up my hair, eaten too much spaghetti, and opened a bottle of wine.

I just packed my books for Greece. I had Goldhagen first, but then I put it back on the shelf. You wrote that you sensed what I meant when I said that I could hardly read more—still I am interested in his findings. My reluctance to take him along to Greece is mainly due to my conviction that even if I know more facts about the Holocaust, they will not help me teach people humanity. But this does not mean that I do not want to know what you are thinking. Even though I won't be able to write back until we return home, please send your writing about the books you are reading. It means so much to me to continue our inquiry.

Love,

M

Dearest Margret,

Right now I am imagining you in Greece, eating olives and feta cheese and swimming in wonderfully soft, warm water. I hope you are picturing us in California, eating tacos, getting tan, and relaxing under the southern California sun.

You asked to hear about my reactions to what I'm reading. . . . O.K.— As I complete each book, I'll send you my responses on e-mail, but I won't expect to hear from you until you return home from Greece.

As you know, I've been using this summer to immerse myself in Holocaust literature: history, testimony, and theology. I read all day long and even at night. Yesterday, I finished Martin Gilbert's 900 page account of what occurred month by month, year by year, within each European Jewish community. I'm sure you know the stories: thousands taken into the woods, forced to dig their own graves, shot, murdered, piled in huge pits, bodies writhing, later on those same bodies uncovered and burned to destroy the evidence. Millions of innocent men, women, and children locked up in ghettos and then in camps, starved, beaten, brutalized, shaved, gassed, burned. And then in some ways even more shocking and upsetting: After the war ended and the Polish survivors returned to their homes, they were taunted and then massacred by the locals who had taken their homes. Clearly anti-Semitism did not end just because Hitler was dead. What was unleashed—the hatred and the desire to kill—was too strong to dissolve when the Nazis were defeated. I read, and such deep sadness overcomes me.

I keep asking myself why I persist. I realize that I want to look clear-eyed, without flinching, at what happened, facing the knowledge that millions were tortured and murdered. But often I wonder, has coming to love you made it too easy?

The survivors quoted at the end of Gilbert say they will never speak—will never let anyone know the depth of their terror and horror, especially not the Germans. I can understand that, and yet it comes so strongly to me that new generations must find a way to speak.

As this inquiry lodges deeper within me, I feel the need to be informed, to know the details. I no longer want to speak only from within ingrained prejudices. I also find myself reading with an interest in the resisters, those who helped hide the Jews, who risked their lives and often were killed for doing so—those who, I suspect, actually remind me of you. I find myself reading now with a desire to make distinctions.

Love,

S

August 1, 1997

Dear Margret,

I have been continuing to read histories: Dawidowicz, Friedlander, Hilberg. The material is so hateful, the history at once easier and harder to comprehend. Easier, because I now understand the ways the laws worked, how Hitler tested the Germans and the world, how incremental each step was, who the major Nazis were and what their roles were, how things got carried out, etc. But it becomes harder to live with this knowledge—in some ways my childhood dismissals were easier, more protective for me.

I see, too, that if I ever teach a course on the Holocaust, I would not be willing to teach this material merely as topics in an historical drama, highlighting facts and information: the growth of anti-Semitism, the rise of Nazi Germany, the development of the camps, the resistance movement, the current revisionism, etc. In any course I teach, I would want to make room for responses to the material, for probing the question of evil—and examining what we must do to answer. The facts tell one sort of story, but I am more interested in the question of response-ability: Where does this lie for each of us?

I also suspect that this reading raises a personal issue for me: how much I did not want to be Jewish, how I did not want to be seen as a member of this backward, weird race—the parasite, the vermin, the bacilli, the poison mushroom—so ugly. The Nazis produced such effective propaganda—one revolts in disgust—of course, I think to myself, one would feel compelled to exterminate such vermin.

Love,

S

August 5

Dear Margret,

I have moved on from histories to survivor testimonies: Primo Levi, Tadeusz Borowski, Jorge Semprun, Wiesel, of course. As I read about the camps, I wonder if I would have given in and died. How much abuse can one person withstand? I don't think I could have held on. Too hard to live like that—easier to die.

When I was younger, I was convinced I would have fought, would have used any means possible to stay alive, would have looked for the ways out, the loopholes, the signals—but maybe such thinking is a function of age—now it seems pointless to fight just for one more day of agony.

Love,

S

August 10

I knew I would like Charlotte Delbo—and I do—her language is so chiseled—so precise and careful. I have read many times now about the stripping, the shaving, and the showers, but I have never before read anyone who conveys the utter humiliation of standing naked and helpless in front of one's children. Or what it must have felt like for children to witness the disgrace of their parents. Delbo gets to it immediately:

> My mother
> she was hands, a face
> They made our mothers strip in front of us
> Here mothers are no longer mothers to their children.[1]

I've never seen this scene conveyed with such immediacy, in so few words, from the daughter's point of view—and yet for me it has always been the act most humiliating—to witness one's mother standing helpless and naked. And again the hate rises within me—that human beings could do this—is it inexplicable or all too easy to explain?

Love,

S

August 20

Dear Margret,

A few days ago, my friend Mark accompanied me to the Simon Wiesenthal Museum of Tolerance in Los Angeles—an incredible place— a place designed to summon responses.

In the first exhibit, you are confronted with your own tendency to judge others. Staring at pictures, words, and videos, you are asked to examine your own reactions to those who are different from yourself; you watch an eight-minute film documenting atrocities that have occurred since the Holocaust—in Cambodia, Bosnia, Rwanda. You come upon pictures of white supremacists in the States, many wearing the robes of the Ku Klux Klan, and then a series of photos and videos of the civil rights movement including some gruesome images of black bodies hanging from trees. The message is clear: we never learn—we only continue to hate. And this is just the beginning.

In the main exhibit, you walk through a series of dioramas that re-create life in Berlin prior to and during the Holocaust. At each scene, a voice describes what is happening: how Hitler came to power, what life was like in the 1930s, how Jews were persecuted and ultimately locked up. Next you see how the camps developed. There are maps, one showing all the train routes. In one area, you come upon a re-creation of the Wannsee Conference: staring at a formal table, with glass goblets and crisp folders neatly displayed, you hear voices imitating Eichmann and Heydrich, discussing "the Final Solution to the Jewish problem." Finally, you stand over a scale model of Auschwitz where clouds of dust obscured the sun, where birds never flew—and then you enter a dark cement room that resembles a gas chamber—solid, solemn, cold.

After this exhibit, Mark and I needed a break, so we stopped for a drink; we then returned to see a video called *The Way We Were,* a documentary on Jewish life in Europe before the war, focusing on *shtetl* life in Poland and Russia. Mark thought it presented too narrow a view; he would have preferred to see more on the lives of assimilated Jews in Berlin. But I found it powerful to see observant Jews wearing black hats and prayer shawls bent over the Torah; poignant to hear the stories of the rabbis, to listen to their parables, to witness life the way it once was for so many Jews. The last part of the film was a listing of the names of all the *shtetls*, so many now recognizable to me from my readings—all the *shtetls* that were destroyed by the *Einsatzgruppen.* So sad. Such a rich inner life of study, of belief in God, of holidays and services, of observance—gone.

I know it is easy to romanticize. Obviously, life was hard, and *shtetl* Jews were not necessarily more decent or better people than their neigh-bors, but to me, there is something so touching about traditional Jewish life—which, while full of its share of hardship, was not without singing, dancing, laughter, and love. The images reminded me of my grandfather, my Poppa, and his family, and my dad's mom, my Grandma Rae, and hers—Jews who came to the States from Poland and Russia. The world they came from is gone forever. Not that customs or styles wouldn't have changed with the advent of modernism, but these lives and this kind of worship ended so abruptly, were wiped out with such fierce determination.

Then we saw one last short film on genocide—on the Turks' murder of the Armenians, with gruesome shots of heads piled on shelves, then hundreds of skulls; on Pol Pot's massacres, and then on the current situation in Central and South America concerning the extinction of indigenous peoples.

It is truly an incredible museum; it was a deeply moving experience. I came home exhausted, spent, and that night I got sick. It is possible that

I caught a twenty-four-hour virus from our neighbors. I cannot be sure. But it honestly felt to me as if I were having a physical reaction to having immersed myself in so much horror.

With chills and shakes and my stomach cramping, I lay awake all night, unable to find a comfortable position. Nauseous, I would run to the toilet, bend over, and retch. Images of the camps assaulted me: the inmates, the men, women, and children, those whose names have become known to us because they survived, and the millions who remain nameless, who filed through the lines, who disappeared, the endless numbers of people disappearing.

Sitting on my own clean toilet, all I could picture were the latrines and the stench, the overflowing buckets of excrement, and wonder how anyone with loose bowels could make it, could stand it, how people with severe illnesses, dysentery, fevers, managed to pull through, to stand for hours without collapsing, and also how many could not do it, did collapse, were gassed.

Names—Himmler, Heydrich, Goblochnik, Wirth, Wagner—kept running through my mind—and the Wannsee Conference, the plans for the Final Solution, the Germans comfortable in their uniforms and their power, planning the destruction of an entire race. My mind would not stop and I felt so sick, so full of hatred and wanting to scream and vomit it all up, get it out of me, push it away from me, and yet I know I have been taking it all in, presumably for some purpose.

In the morning, in Arthur's arms, I was able to cry, to sob for so much loss, so much agony. And I was aware of how much one needs to be humble in the sight of all of this and to find the way to compassion: not for the Nazis—that I cannot find in myself, but as a way to bear witness to what in many ways one wants to turn from. Once again, I realized that if I ever teach a course on the Holocaust, I would need to muster both strength and compassion, and I would want my students to focus on questions for today: How do we live in the aftermath of the Holocaust? What is to be learned here?

August 25

Dearest Sondra,

I was sitting in a small room next to the X-ray apparatus waiting for the doctor to come (a routine mammography). I printed out your texts at home, took them with me, and had already started reading in the waiting room. I just couldn't stop. I get so absorbed when I am reading your words.

You know what I was thinking all the time when reading? Before each new thought of yours, each next line, I knew what it would be, and it felt like a relief.

Why? Well, whenever we talked about the Holocaust I had the fantasy that you must have read all the books and reports, knew all the details and yet somehow overcame it, somehow managed to live with it. When I now read how sick you became, I was immediately reminded of my sickness when standing in Dachau, when looking down the quarry in Mauthausen, realizing that I live in the midst of it. Witnessing the Holocaust in retrospect has robbed me of any lightheartedness I might once have had. I do not know whether my words in English say what I want to say. How can you, Sondra, a Jew, not become sick, not become nauseated at what you read? I couldn't understand why there had never been a word from you about the horror. I thought why is there no outburst of emotion? Do you understand now what I mean by "relief"? You cannot be a supernatural being and just carry no hatred and anger in your heart once you immerse yourself in the reports on the Holocaust. I cannot, and I am not Jewish.

I also had to think of us talking about our children and about talking to them, and I thought you so brave and courageous and wise when you said that we have to talk and that you do. Yes, I also do, but deep down in my heart I want to protect Cara from feeling all the feelings I had when I immersed myself in pictures and stories and places and people. I don't know how to do it. I don't want Cara to feel guilty for the rest of her life. But how can you teach compassion and empathy for the victims without teaching hatred for the murderers? Without teaching them to hate their grandparents, without getting sick?

They, the older generation, themselves cannot stand acknowledging what they took part in. It is so huge, and all I can do is stay in contact with you and thank God for that. I understand every line you write, and I know many people would not. Do you remember when I wrote to you that I cannot read any more about the Holocaust? Do you understand this somehow differently now? I have a book about fascism with lots of photographs, and whenever I look at it, my stomach turns. The images are so real, so personal. Do you know the picture of the small boy when the Warsaw Ghetto was taken? His expression in his face, his arms up, looking and not knowing what is happening? Do you know the picture of the Nazi soldier who is shooting a mother with a child in her arms? How can one ever feel safe in a country like ours?

I was sitting here in this surgery, and the doctor started to tell me about his kids and how they hate school and so on. And I was just thinking that I am living in the midst of people who do not see things the way I do ... I felt so sorry for this father and his sons and so grateful for knowing you and being able to talk to you on a level that I so rarely encounter.

Gert and I talked about your texts at noon. He understands everything we do, everything you write, but he has such a hard time talking about his feelings. Finally, he said that he does not feel comfortable having me learning more, talking more about the Holocaust, because deep down in his heart he feels guilty and he doesn't know what to do. This feeling did not develop through knowing you—it has always been there.

He also talked a bit about his days with the Communists, when he and his brother confronted his parents daily and tried to force them to see things the way they should be seen. Today, he says, he doesn't confront them any more because he knows their answers. So he has become resigned to this and has made peace with them. I understand that.

It is painful and hard to talk about these issues but with the help of you and your questions I am convinced we will proceed. I also understand when you say that even if you can make peace with me, this doesn't necessarily mean you have made peace with all of us Germans and Austrians.

Hope to hear from you soon.

Love,

Margret

September 2

Dearest Margret,

It matters so much to me that you understand and respond so fully. It felt scary to send my reflections to you, but I am glad I did and glad that you can express your relief. Isn't it interesting that even after all our intimacy, we still are finding ourselves being careful about what we can risk saying? It's as if we don't want to say too much, intrude too far, or overwhelm one another with our fears and pains, and yet, now that we write again about our emotions, it is so real and matters so much.

Yes, I understand your not being able to continue to read Holocaust books. It was/is fascinating to watch as I go in and out of this process—wanting to read more, then not being able to. One of the hardest things for me is looking at the propaganda pictures of the Jews that circulated in Germany in the 1930s. Do you know the children's book *The Poison Mushroom*? The drawing on the cover is a picture of a mushroom, and the cap is shaped to suggest the head of a Jew with a big, hooked nose. I cannot tell you how sick it makes me—and yet there is, at the same time, this desire in me to know, to see, to witness this too . . .

I want to say something about Gert. I believe there has to be a middle ground between feeling as if he must confront his parents and silently carrying the burden of guilt. These cannot be the only two options open to him. Being human carries more possibilities than just those two extremes. Don't you think so?

Love,

S

September 3

Dearest,

Viktor Frankl died today. He was 97 (or so). I think it takes a lifetime or longer to make peace. All I can say is that I am thankful that I have been able to start.

Love,

M

September 6

Dearest,

I have saved Victor Frankl's obituary from the *Times* for you. Have you read his work? He writes of the absolute necessity of endowing suffering with meaning. Of course, it's nearly impossible to imagine doing so when walking into a gas chamber.

I spent the morning watching Diana's funeral on TV. Did you see it? I thought her brother spoke beautifully. How did his criticism of the royal family and their suppression of emotion strike you? It's sad to think of how vibrant she was and her two grieving boys. What a sad week.

Love,

S

September 7

Dearest Sondra,

I watched a bit of Diana's funeral. Gert does not share my feeling of how tragic the whole thing is. She was one of the very, very rich and he doesn't think she really gave a damn about the poor. Besides, he thinks it's not the *paparazzi* who are to blame, but the owners of the media. His heart is always on the side of the exploited. But once again I was amazed that you and I remarked on exactly the same things about the funeral. I also loved her brother's speech. He was honest and took a clear stand for his nephews and for Diana. Of course, we noticed the criticism of the throne and the Queen's behavior after the accident. The only thing I like about the Queen is her English!

Love,

M

September 9

Dearest Margret,

I've been meaning to write to you about one of the other books I read this summer: Bjorn Krondorfer's *Remembrance and Reconciliation: Encounters between Young Jews and Germans*. He discusses the third generation—Cara, Sara and many others older than they are—who have inherited what he calls the "conspiracy of silence." He feels that it is up to us, the second generation, and our children to find a way to break the silence. He asserts that we need cross-cultural meetings to begin to build bridges and experiential methods to help us find common ground; that we must share our histories and our (mis)understandings. In so many ways, he is describing what happened in our courses through the writing we did. And he makes Gert's silence even more understandable. It's as if anyone whose parents were involved in the Third Reich in any way at all got a very clear message: don't ask, don't talk.

Love,

Sondra

September 10

Dearest Sondra,

Gert and I have often talked about the conspiracy of silence (a very widespread term when talking about our history here). What is so amazing about it is that Gert and many more, I believe, were never told to be silent when they wanted to talk about the past. On the contrary. The parents started talking immediately, telling stories about the war. What was taboo, however, and still is, is talking about one's disbelief and feelings of horror. I am saying that the older generation, especially those people who still cannot believe they have taken part in committing crimes, talk all the time. But within a family there is this unwritten law that children must not confront their parents. There is no room for the child's worries and feelings. The conspiracy of silence is difficult to grasp as on the surface it does not exist, but it is really there.

Sondra, about this silence and our past, there is a related issue I want to bring up. When you come in October for the mentoring work, do you want to meet my in-laws?

Love,

M

September 11

Dearest Margret,

I don't know. It's a scary proposition. Arthur is coming with me, and he speaks some German. If we told your in-laws (I realize I don't even know their names) that we were interested in history—their history— would they be willing to talk with us? Why don't you think about this and let me know? . . .

Love,

Sondra

September 12

Dearest Sondra,

About my in-laws: if you ask about their past, I think they would be puzzled and find no words, as they have not come to understand their own motives for joining the Nazis in their youth. They will try to explain to you that they didn't know what was going on, but they will not say they are sorry as they always say they didn't mean to be part of such a regime—remember my poem? But never in their lives will they make you feel bad or not welcome. They will marvel at themselves and at you—like kids—just the way they did with Cynthia and Roberta, the first black people they have ever come in contact with.

In less than three weeks we see each other again. Isn't that breathtaking? (Breathtaking reminds me of Gert. In preparation for your visit, he has started to learn English. He is very serious about it. He learns whatever words he reads so he can say the most unusual things already. "Struck dumb" is his favorite at the moment. It is funny and so sweet.)

Love,

M

September 14

Dearest Margret,

How great about Gert. Arthur has been brushing up on his German, working with a tutor. He is thoroughly enjoying it. Last night he said how different I am now when he speaks German in the house. I responded, "How can I not like German when it is Margret's language?" About your in-laws. I keep wondering what it will be like to meet them. Of course, it will be fine on one level, but on another there will be those unspoken questions. Have they ever known any Jews? What do they think about Jews? Scary to ask but am I supposed to pretend that I am not thinking this?

Love,

S

September 15

Dearest Sondra,

Of course, they have not met any Jews, and they would not know any. They will not talk about the war unless we invite them over for dinner. You are staying for such a short time we will not even see much of them. So the question is: would you like to confront them? There is no pretending that you are somebody else than you are. It will not be an issue for them. So what is it you want?

Love,

Margret

September 18

Dearest Margret,

The more I think about the question of meeting your in-laws, the more I think we should. I don't see this as a confrontation with them—I am hoping that there will be the possibility of having a real dialogue. And if not, well, that's O.K. too.

Love,

S

September 21

Dearest,

I agree. I think it would be foolish for you not to meet my in-laws. They live here, and you are very likely to meet them in passing anyway. Of course, I know this will not be a confrontation. On the other hand, it will be just the same. You know what I mean? Gert said that he suddenly has the impulse to protect his parents—then he said maybe he is protecting himself because he has never found out—never asked—how involved they had been. I realize that we are caught in our lifelong way of talking and not talking about the Holocaust. So I'm excited to think how you will experience them and what you'll say about them. If you want to confront them yourselves, it is like a gift I am not entitled to have, but am very grateful about. In ten days, you'll be sitting in my kitchen, and we'll talk and talk for hours.

Love,

M

September 25

Dearest Margret,

O.K. If it really is O.K. with Gert, and you think it's a good idea, let's set it up. Can you also do us a favor? Our trip coincides with the Jewish holidays. It would interest us to see what Jewish life is like now in Innsbruck. Can you check to see if the synagogue has services while we are with you?

Can't wait to hug you—one week from today at the airport, 9:20 A.M.

Love,

S

I had not foreseen that my trips to Innsbruck and my friendship with Margret would lead me to make such a disquieting choice: to look directly into the eyes of people who, since the time I was a child, represented the embodiment of evil. But, in the end, it is the choice I make. It is, to me, hypocritical to advocate dialogue in my classroom and then to refuse to engage in it with those whose views I cannot tolerate.

8

Unexpected Lessons

ednesday, October 1, 1997, the day before Rosh Hashanah, the Jewish New Year, I am off once again to Austria. Only this time, my husband, Arthur, is with me, and this time, I am eager to return.

On Thursday morning, when we arrive at the airport in Innsbruck, there is neither shyness nor hesitation. Margret and I embrace, eagerly throwing our arms around each other; Gert and Arthur shake hands. We are laughing, joking, pleased to be together, the four of us, for the first time. Arthur's recent work to recover his German is paying off. Margret and Gert are immediately impressed with his command of the language and his accent.

At her home over lunch, Margret recounts her conversation with the secretary at the synagogue. There are New Year's services scheduled for this evening, tomorrow morning, and then again next week, on Saturday, for Yom Kippur, the Day of Atonement. My work with the teachers is scheduled to begin the following day, so I cannot attend. But Arthur's time is his own. He says he'd like to go to services in the morning. Today, we both agree, it would be best to unpack and settle in. After the course ends, Arthur and I plan to go hiking in the Dolomites, the mountains of northern Italy, but we decide to return to Innsbruck in time to attend services together on Yom Kippur, the most sacred day in the Jewish calendar.

The afternoon passes leisurely. Cara comes home from school; we distribute gifts—pierced earrings for Cara, a book about astronomy for Gert, a book of poetry for Margret—and show them photographs of our children and our dogs. Relaxing in the living room, we talk about plans for the next two weeks and how best to arrange all we want to do. Arthur, most of the time, tries to speak in German. Gert tries to answer in English. When the conversation gets too complex, each returns to his native tongue and Margret translates.

As the light begins to fade, Margret begins preparations for dinner. Arthur and I set the table. Gert pours the wine. We have been together all day, but no one has yet raised the question of when we will meet Gert's parents. Then, as we are eating a typical meal of *Knoedel mit Salat*, Gert asks, in his halting English, "You would like to meet my parents?"

"Yes, we would," I respond, a bit surprised by his question. I thought it was clear from recent e-mails that we had already decided to arrange a meeting.

"When would be good?" he asks.

Again, I am surprised. We've been writing to each other about this for weeks—whether or not we should meet, our desire to hear a first-person account from the other side, Gert's worry that it might be too upsetting, our reassurances that it will not turn into a confrontation, Margret's insightful response that of course it will be no matter what.

I glance at Arthur. He glances back. "Well," I ask Margret, "do you want to set something up for tomorrow night or next weekend? Outside of the course and our hiking trip, we have no plans except to spend time with you." But inwardly, I feel uneasy. What is going on that Margret, always so organized, has not yet organized this meeting? The three of us look at her as she busies herself with her dumpling.

"We aren't sure what is best to do here," Margret says, hesitation in her voice. "We don't usually invite them over for dinner . . . , but I guess we could . . . or maybe we should just introduce you to them and see what happens."

I'm not accustomed to Margret sounding so tentative. I am also surprised that this meeting has become important to me, surprised that I want to move closer to the horror, to explore the wound.

For months, I have wavered about whether I want to meet them at all. A few weeks ago, I wrote to Margret that I didn't even know their names. For more than a year, she and I have referred to them as "the in-laws," "Gert's parents," "the Nazis." But when I first encounter their names in an e-mail, I blanch. Until that moment, they have been abstractions. With first names—Anna and Luis— they have become people with identities. I am no longer sure if I am up to this challenge.

My stomach tightens, and I feel myself pulling back. Do I really want to pursue this path? What, after all, is the point? But then, I tell myself, they are old. The opportunity to sit down and talk with Nazis, in the home of my friend, will not exist much longer. I do not entirely understand what is driving me, but sitting in Margret's kitchen, I realize that I do want this chance to confront my demons in the guise of Gert's parents. Am I willing to be so bold, I wonder, only because Arthur is here with me?

Margret gets up from the table and returns with apple strudel and freshly brewed coffee. As she serves dessert, I realize that she and Gert might be having second thoughts. Turning toward both of them, I ask, "Do you think this is a bad idea? Should we just drop the whole thing?"

"No," Margret responds slowly, keeping her eyes focused on each cup as she carefully fills it. "I just don't want you to be disappointed . . . to expect too much. Gert's father wears a hearing aid, and frequently he just turns it off. He doesn't listen. And, well, they always say the same things about the war: how hard things were, how much they suffered. We get so tired of hearing it."

"But," Arthur answers, "we want to hear what it was like for them. It is never easy to have lived through war, no matter what side you were on."

"Talking to us," I offer with some optimism, "might be different." Then I raise the question that has been plaguing me. "Have you ever told them we are Jewish?"

This time there is not a drop of hesitation. "Of course not," Margret exclaims, a frown creasing her brow. "We don't talk with them a great deal. And something like that, well, I think it's up to you to decide whether to tell them or not."

"This is the trickiest part," I say, searching her face, trying to discern her feelings. "If we don't tell them, it feels as if we are deliberately hiding something; but if we do mention it, how are they supposed to respond? Will they think we've come to accuse them?"

"That's what my brother and I did in the 1960s," says Gert. "We'd confront them with their past. We'd argue for hours. It led nowhere." He shrugs his shoulders in a gesture of resignation.

"But maybe that is why they were always so defensive. Because no one ever asked them what it was like to live then, to be them. I am not saying they were right . . . ," I add, taking a sip of coffee, my voice drifting off.

"What are you saying, then?" asks Margret, a challenging note in her voice.

I take a long breath, wondering whether I will regret what I am about to say. "I am suggesting," I say calmly, "that if they were always being attacked, their natural response would be to defend themselves. I think we are more interested in hearing them describe what they thought they were doing—how life appeared to them as they were living it. Who knows? Maybe they will be able to say things to us they could never say to you. Or maybe I am just being naïve. Maybe it will just be a social evening that doesn't go anywhere."

Margret and Gert look at one another. Something is still worrying them. What are they not saying? I wonder.

Gert stands up, places his coffee cup in the sink, and says conclusively, "I'll talk to my mum in the morning. I'll find out when they are free and ask if they'd like to come over."

Margret adds, "If we invite them, they'll surely come. We just can't predict what will happen."

"Maybe we shouldn't try," I respond.

෴

The next morning, at 10:00 A.M., Margret and I are sitting in her kitchen. Arthur has already left for synagogue. Over soft-boiled eggs, toast, and coffee, she tells me that Gert has already spoken to his mother. They would be pleased to come to dinner that night, although Gert's father has an appointment in town and will need to leave by 8:30 P.M.

Suddenly, there is a short knock at the front door, and before Margret has time to get up and answer it, a woman comes bursting into the kitchen. I am not prepared for this. But everything about her demeanor tells me it's Anna Fessler, Gert's mom. Her familiarity with the house, her nod to Margret, her age. As she strides over to greet me, I feel panic rising inside.

She is stretching out her hand to shake mine. I suppress the urge to recoil. I do not want to touch her. Yet what excuse can I give for refusing? She has reached the kitchen table and is standing there, waiting for me to greet her.

"*Gruss Gott,*" she says in German.

"*Gruss Gott,*" I respond.

"My English is very little," she says, smiling ruefully.

"My German is even less," I say, looking up into her face and extending my hand after all.

I am caught off guard, but my surprise does not prevent me from noticing Anna's bright eyes and gracious smile. At seventy-five, she is a robust woman, muscular and energetic, her thick white hair cropped close, her blue eyes crinkling at the edges.

I know I have just greeted a woman who fifty-five years ago proudly led the Tyrolean girl's division of the Hitler youth movement, the *Bund Deutscher Mädchen*. And yet, I also know that had I met this woman at a party in New York, I would have been impressed with her warmth, her openness, and her good will. I would have wanted to get to know her.

Margret confirms the arrangements for that night. "Sondra and I will be leaving shortly for the university, but we will all meet back here tonight for dinner at 7:00 P.M."

Anna nods and leaves, smiling. I sink back in my chair, speechless.

❧

On Friday afternoon, the teachers and I find ourselves, once again, gathered around a large table in a classroom at the University of Innsbruck. Since February, they have been attempting to document aspects of their teaching and then to look closely into the meaning of what has occurred. This weekend is planned as a time for people to receive responses to their research, to receive encouragement as well as critique, and to ask whatever questions they need to ask as they begin the final stages of completing their theses. As requested, everyone has brought at least one chapter to share with the group. After warm hugs and heartfelt hellos, we settle down, eager to get to work. I begin by handing out copies of a poem by Thomas Lux and asking everyone to read it.

The Voice You Hear When You Read Silently

is not silent, it is a speaking
out-loud voice in your head: it is spoken,
a voice is saying it
as you read. It's the writer's words,
of course, in a literary sense
his or her "voice" but the sound
of that voice is the sound of your voice.

Not the sound your friends know
or the sound of a tape played back
but your voice
caught in the dark cathedral
of your skull, your voice heard
by an internal ear informed by internal abstracts
and what you know by feeling,
having felt. It is your voice
saying, for example, the word "barn"
that the writer wrote
but the "barn" you say
is a barn you know or knew. The voice
in your head, speaking as you read,
never says anything neutrally—some people
hated the barn they knew,
some people love the barn they know
so you hear the word loaded
and a sensory constellation
is lit: horse-gnawed stalls,
hayloft, black heat tape wrapping
a water pipe, a slippery
spilled chirr of oats from a split sack,
the bony, filthy haunches of cows . . .
And "barn" is only a noun—no verb
or subject has entered into the sentence yet!
The voice you hear when you read to yourself
is the clearest voice: you speak it
speaking to you.[1]

I ask the group to consider how this poem frames the work we are about to do. We will, after all, be listening to one another's words all weekend; we will be hearing each other's words in our heads and transforming them by putting our own voices and meanings to them. The word "student" or "classroom" will be the student or classroom each one of us calls to mind, that we see in our mind's eye, not necessarily the student or classroom the writer wants us to see.

"Our job," I tell everyone, "is to let the writers know what we are seeing and hearing as their words take on private resonances within us—to listen carefully and to convey to each writer the meanings we make as we each repeat their words in our own private voices."

"You mean," adds Thomas, "we have to bring our own barns here." As usual, he gets a laugh.

The teachers and I work together from Friday afternoon through Sunday evening, taking time for a dinner celebration on Saturday night. Most people choose to read their drafts to the entire group. A few, including Margret, prefer to work in smaller groups. By Sunday afternoon, everyone will have had a chance to present his or her work and to hear it reflected back in the comments and suggestions of peers.

What impresses me about the research projects, as soon as we begin hearing them, is the way each teacher has found a style to convey what has become important, and above all, how readable the writing is—all in English, a second language for most. Hilde, for example, grabs me immediately as she reads aloud her description of the first moments of class with her lowest level *Hauptschule* students:

> Rene shoots through the door like a rocket, reaches his seat sliding along the polished floor and simultaneously slams his bag on top of his desk. He tries to hit the seat of his chair, misses, and finds himself sprawled just underneath my feet, looking up and grinning. There are loud comments from the boys on his lack of timing, laughter from the girls, and general excitement. I stretch my neck to get a glimpse across the desk of the outstretched body, inwardly hoping that he did not hurt himself, and tell him to sit on his chair, not the floor. The noise around us increases, the jostling has finally penetrated into the classroom and will not stop until the corridors and classrooms resound with the ringing of our school bell . . .
>
> And here they are now. My fourth-form third-stream students, making up a group of 26, four girls and 22 boys between the ages of 13 and 16, standing to attention facing me, four rows deep. Their faces reflect many questions revolving in their heads: Why do I have to attend these classes when I am stupid anyway? I am not interested in learning English—or anything else, if you want to know—so why must I sit here wasting my life? I'll earn my money snowboarding anyway!! But there are also "I wonder if we'll start something interesting new today?" faces in the crowd . . .

When Hilde looks up, she smiles shyly. Not everyone in the room teaches in a *Hauptschule*, but it is clear from the number of knowing nods that everyone recognizes this scene. "This reads like a short story," Tanja tells Hilde, "and yet it is so real."

"You have really captured the way it feels," Christa says admiringly.

"Your barn," Ingrid jokes, "is just like mine!"

But in her next passage, Hilde moves beyond what is readily recognizable, creating a powerful metaphor for the challenges involved in learning English as a foreign language:

> Time is passing and silence finally embraces the group like a layer of snow. It is time to sit down, collect our senses, and take this stallion called "English" by the tether, twist it and tear it, almost strangle it, and tame it until it acknowledges us as its master and can be trusted to hold us as its rider, at the beginning for short moments only. By stroking and loving it, we can extend the periods to a point where riding the stallion becomes a pleasure, and the feeling of being in command gives each one of us a feeling of contentment.

To Hilde, who for a year and a half has hesitated to share her work, I say, "Please keep on writing like this. You've taken my breath away."

"O.K.," she nods, smiling.

Christa's writing, with its fine observations, makes me want to read on, to discover how she introduced her students to a learner-centered classroom. She begins with a description of her school:

> The iron gate opens to a straight drive, demarcated by one of the school buildings and a sheltered area for bikes. That's all a passerby can see of the three schools for girls, which the Order . . . has been running for decades. High walls prevent sight of the beautiful garden, where benches under old apple trees invite the "inhabitants" to take a rest in peaceful surroundings. The large complex of buildings added to the convent nucleus through time, but now unified through a geometric design of wall painting in ocher, amber, and maroon, exude a pleasant atmosphere of long-lasting seclusion.
>
> For fifteen years I have been teaching English as a foreign language at one of these private schools. Safety and protectiveness have been the slogans in this small school for some one-hundred 10- to 14-year old girls. All the pupils and teachers know one another. Standards in teaching are high . . .

But then she describes how, within these striking buildings and underneath the pretty picture of her success, she began to sense something lacking in her teaching:

For a long time I especially appreciated the willingness of my girls to follow the teachers' ideas and suggestions. I tailored curricula around the skills approach of the Austrian national curriculum. Year after year, my pupils improved their listening skills, they became more or less fluent readers, they enjoyed acting out sketches, and they were able to communicate orally in English. They dutifully completed grammar worksheets, and they wrote texts that were neat, accurate, and uniform . . . My students and I had the feeling of achieving a lot . . . Frequent tests informed me about their language skills. But only rarely could I glimpse the adolescent girl behind the facade of growing language competence.

Christa writes that she began to feel as if she were "working too much on the surface . . . the stress was on what I wanted to do in 'my' classes . . . The neat and clear-cut curricula were a well-loved safety net," but still, she admits, "I was dissatisfied. I wanted to see my pupils as learners who could indeed be trusted." The M.A. program enabled Christa "to look at teaching and learning differently," and at the end of her introduction, she writes, "about this venture, which has become a truly satisfying one, I will tell."

All I can say is, "Christa, please do." The appreciative nods of the teachers around the table show me I am not alone in wanting to hear more about Christa's journey.

Listening to the teachers read their writing, I am impressed by the quality of their work, and at the end of our first day together, I say so. While no one has yet completed the thesis, everyone we have listened to has made significant progress. The end is in sight, and I already sense the end of our working relationship. This, I know, is the inevitable conclusion to all educational programs. But in the back of my mind all day are thoughts about the less predictable lessons awaiting me at home that evening at Margret's.

è&.

At 7:00 P.M. sharp, Gert's parents arrive. The dining table is already set. Margret has planned a simple meal consisting of melon wrapped in prosciutto, a selection of cheeses, roasted chestnuts, artichoke hearts, salad, and sun-dried tomatoes. The wine is already poured.

As we gather in the front hall, Gert introduces us to his parents. This time, I am prepared to shake hands. As I do, I inspect Gert's father for signs of evil. All I see is an old man with bushy white eyebrows, who stands a bit shorter than his wife. His face is an older version of Gert's; at one time, I think to myself, this balding, bespectacled man with a crooked smile must have been handsome.

As soon as Arthur greets Anna and Luis in German, they want to know more about him. "How did an American learn to speak German so competently?" Anna inquires. Margret beckons us to sit down at the dining table as Arthur briefly explains his history. After college, he went to Paris to learn French. After nine months in France, he traveled to Germany to study German, at a Goethe Institute in Braubeuren, but he could only spend two months there.

"You learned so much in two months?" Anna asks admiringly. "Why did you leave?"

"The draft board came after me. America was fighting in Vietnam, and I did not have a deferment. I ended up in Saigon, working undercover for Army Intelligence."

Luis's eyes brighten. He sits up just a bit straighter. I can tell he is intrigued. He asks Arthur about Vietnam, about America's misguided role in the war, about the failure of American foreign policy. His relish in criticizing America is apparent.

Arthur is a clinical psychologist. In the 1970s, he conducted a national study supported by the U.S. Congress on the impact of the Vietnam War on the generation of men who came of age during that era. In 1986, he published *Healing from the War*, a book that received critical acclaim, and he has always devoted a part of his clinical practice to work with individual soldiers. He knows how to talk to veterans. He does not mince words.

Looking directly at Luis, he says frankly, "Like you, Herr Fessler, I am a veteran of a failed war."

I am shocked at Arthur's audacity. I could not have imagined raising the topic of war so early in the evening. But Arthur doesn't stop there. "When I came home from Vietnam," he explains in German, "I needed to understand what had happened, to make sense of my actions, to think about what I did. How was it for you, Herr Fessler?"

Luis shakes his head, refusing to answer. But I notice that he does not turn off his hearing aid. He continues to pay attention to the conversation as we pass the salad and refill our wine glasses.

Cara, who has been sitting quietly, asks, "Did America really lose the war?"

"Yes," Arthur answers. "In 1973, we left Vietnam, and in 1975 the North Vietnamese marched south to declare their final victory.

Nixon called it 'peace with honor' but there really wasn't much that was honorable about it. You don't study this in school, do you?"

"Not really," Cara responds, smiling, reaching for some chestnuts.

I explain that it was unusual for young men of Arthur's background to go to Vietnam. A Harvard graduate, fluent in several languages, he did not imagine that he would be sent to a war zone. Even as an enlisted man, he expected to conduct research in Europe, following the path of his famous professor, Henry Kissinger. He was shocked when he got his orders. But by then it was too late. He could not arrange for some other form of duty, nor did he try.

"Unlike Bill Clinton?" Luis asks, raising his eyebrows ever so slightly. I don't know German but his derisive tone is not lost on me.

"Right," I say, feeling defensive. "Most men of Arthur's background did what Bill Clinton did—found a way out. They joined the reserves, became conscientious objectors, or left the country for Canada. Those who ended up fighting were primarily boys from the working class."

Anna, reaching for some cheese, brings the conversation back to her home ground. "For us, it was different," she comments. "Our parents were thrilled by National Socialism. They wanted Germany to be great again. Hitler promised that. They were convinced that the Third Reich was a wonderful thing for Austria and Germany. We thought so too."

Luis seems pleased to pick up this thread. "Times were hard. There were the reparations from the Great War—the debt, the Depression. There were no jobs, no work." He shakes his head again, as if trying to expel the memory.

As Cara goes to the wood-burning stove to retrieve more chestnuts and Margret pours more wine, Arthur turns again to Luis. "I can understand the appeal of restoring Austria to its former place in the world. Vienna, under the Hapsburgs, had been the seat of power and culture for much of the nineteenth century. And after World War I, it is true that there was much suffering in Europe. It is well known that the Treaty of Versailles was not fair and a great burden was placed on Germany. But my question is a different one: How did it feel to you after the war, Herr Fessler? For me the greatest lessons of the war came after I returned home."

Luis answers: "I put it all behind me. I was treated like a criminal. I had planned to become an architect, but I was forbidden to enter architecture school." Luis's tone is flat, and his lips tighten in anger.

I shoot a look at Margret. Did she expect such a remark? "Right after the war," Margret explains, "Nazi party members were excluded from public life and future schooling by the conservative politicians who were then in power in Innsbruck. Ordinary soldiers could return to school; Nazi leaders were often jailed; party members, like Luis, were ostracized."

Luis continues, "I had two sons. I had to work. You do what you have to do. That is all."

Clearly, Luis sees himself as having suffered. I wonder if he ever imagines what sort of suffering he imposed on others. Is there a shred of remorse in this man or is he still living with lost illusions, justifying his actions without considering their impact?

Anna describes her most vivid memory of the war. "I gave birth to Gert during a bomb attack in December of 1943. I was alone, up in the mountains. No one came to help. I had no choice but to deliver him myself."

There is no self-pity in her voice. "Luis did manage to get a leave for a few days," Anna continues, "but he soon returned to the front. I was hungry and alone with Gert, born two years before his brother, Friedl."

I find myself feeling sympathy for this woman; her life during wartime could not have been easy. But what about those mothers whose children did not survive? What about those who walked with their babies into the gas chamber? I feel anger rising but remind myself that I came to hear Anna's and Luis's stories. I did not come to interrogate them. They are speaking openly to us—and we haven't told them we are Jews.

Gert explains that Luis was in the infantry for six years. "He fought from the beginning of the war in 1939 until the end in 1945—on the eastern front, in the Caucasus mountains, and along the route to Norway."

Arthur comments, "It is hard to imagine the impact of six years' combat on a human being."

Luis regards Arthur carefully, but he has said all he is going to say. It is 8:30 P.M., time for him to leave. He stands up, shakes hands with everyone, and bids us goodbye. I cannot tell whether he is reluctant or relieved. But it is clear that Anna wants to continue talking and so does Cara. Excusing herself from the dining table and settling into a more comfortable chair in the living room, Cara continues to listen.

Anna, voluble now, tells us that what she liked most about the Hitler youth was its emphasis on sports and the outdoors. "We all had to have copies of *Mein Kampf*," she tells us. "But no one ever read it. It was unreadable," she comments, a laugh in her voice.

Margret asks Anna, "You did see Adolf here in Innsbruck, didn't you?"

I can't believe my ears. "Adolf?" I interrupt, my voice rising.

"Oh," Margret responds, taken by surprise. "It's very common around here to refer to him that way."

I am shocked to hear Hitler's first name roll off Margret's tongue. My entire life he has always been Hitler, the embodiment of evil. How can my friend speak about him so casually? Then I remember: Her in-laws not only served him, they loved him and saw themselves as part of his Reich, as members of his Aryan family. To them, he is Adolf.

Anna describes how frightened she was when Hitler spoke in Innsbruck. "The crowd was so large, there were so many people pushing, I thought I would get crushed," she says. Then she asks, leaning forward, "Why are you so interested in our history?"

I am immediately back in Short Hills, New Jersey. I am thirteen, in junior high school, trying to pass; I am Sandi again, scared to say that I am Jewish. An old fear comes hurtling toward me as I sit at this table with discarded chestnut peelings and empty wine glasses: to admit to a Jew-hater that I am a Jew.

But this time, I know I cannot pretend. Looking first at Margret and then at Arthur, I let out a long breath and give a nod of assent. Arthur then says in German, "*Wir sind Jueden.*"

Now it is Anna's turn to take a breath. She gazes at me and at Arthur, looks down at the table, and is silent. Then slowly looking up, she says quietly, "It is all true. It all happened."

I was prepared for Anna to get up from the table and walk away. I had expected her to defend herself, to say, once again, how hard it was—how she and her husband are not to be blamed. But she does not deny. She does not defend. Instead, she says, "Five years ago, when I was seventy, I tried to read *Mein Kampf* for the first time. I wanted to understand how we were duped. It is all there—the anti-Semitism. But we didn't read it then, and we didn't listen. We only saw what we wanted to see. But tell me," she says, curiously, "I would like to know, what is your religion?"

"Our religion?" I ask, puzzled.

Margret, practically slamming her fork on the table, quickly interprets for us. "Anna is asking what it means to be Jewish. She still thinks Judaism is, well, a race—not a religion."

I sigh. How to explain Judaism to this woman, especially my kind of ambivalent Jewish identity? What would make sense to her? I say, "We are Jewish. That means we observe the Jewish holidays, and sometimes we go to temple. But it is not easy."

I go on, "When I was a child and read about the Holocaust, I became frightened . . . frightened that by being Jewish, I would be persecuted. Later, I was wary of passing this identity on to my children."

"Even in America?" she asks, incredulous.

"Well, yes, there is anti-Semitism in America," I say. But then I realize there is no way to describe the nuances, to explain the ways in which anti-Semitism in a democracy in the United States cannot be likened to the violent, state-sanctioned anti-Semitism she grew up with and witnessed under fascism. I try to retrace my steps, to explain why I did not want to mark my children as different or unworthy in the eyes of the world. "It is very hard," I say slowly, "at least for me, to ask my children to embrace an identity which the world has treated with such contempt."

"But why do you have this interest," she asks, "in our history? Why is our past of concern to you?"

Why would Jews be interested in Austria's past, in the life of a woman who led the Hitler youth? Isn't Anna aware of the impact of all we have been discussing on the Jewish communities that once populated Europe? On people like Arthur and me?

Anna seems not to see her history as having any connection to us. It seems that she has never wondered what her actions might mean to others. It seems that Anna, who at seventy-five is still trying to comprehend this past which marks her life in so many ways, thinks that it is a private affair, as if the rest of the world is not implicated, as if the rest of the world does not have as compelling a desire to understand.

Arthur responds, "These were our people who were murdered here. We feel a connection to them even if we can never meet them or know them. We have come here to try to understand—no matter how hard or impossible that seems."

Margret says, "Cara and Sara, our daughters, are the exact same age, born on the exact same day. Can you imagine what it is like for Sondra and me to imagine . . . ?" Margret's eyes cloud over, her voice tightens, " . . . if we had all been living here sixty years ago?"

At this, Anna looks at me quietly, thoughtfully. She nods, takes a deep breath and lets the air out very slowly.

It is late now; the conversation seems to have gone as far as it can go. Margret tells Cara it is time to go to bed. Before she heads upstairs, Cara walks over to her grandmother and shakes her hand. Then rising from the table, Anna bids us all goodnight, shaking hands with each one of us, emphasizing that she hopes to talk again. I am surprised by the family's formality: handshakes, not hugs or kisses. But I am pleased with Anna's request. As disturbing as some of our talk has been, I, too, would like to continue.

As we clean up, wash the dishes, and put away the remaining food, Gert tells us that it went better than he could have imagined. He is proud of his mother for not getting defensive.

Margret is happiest about Cara. This is the first time she has listened eagerly to such talk. Usually she walks away, showing little interest in the past. I know Margret and I share the same hope: that some day, as she matures, Cara will find her own story embedded in the stories we have told this night. The four of us then say goodnight amid smiles, hugs, and sighs of relief. As Arthur and I head to the guest bedroom on the first floor, I feel sure that each of us is experiencing a private sense of accomplishment. Together, we have surmounted a small hurdle, climbed a foothill, arrived safely at a rest stop.

Undressing, I replay the evening in my mind. Really, I think, it was just six adults and one thirteen-year-old sitting around a dinner table, peeling chestnuts and talking. We did not achieve anything momentous. Nothing has changed. But then I wonder: Why do I not see in Anna and Luis the evil I once associated with Nazis? Who has changed here? Do I no longer see them as Nazis but as two elderly people trying to preserve their dignity? Have I found a way to see beyond my own stereotypes?

As I slip under the covers and let the weight of the fluffy Austrian duvet settle on top of me, I am touched by what has occurred in Margret's home and what these trips to Austria have come to mean to me. I now have a question I could not have imagined asking two short years ago: What does it mean to look, even momentarily, into the eyes of someone I would formerly have seen only as my enemy?

ᴈ♦

The next two days, Saturday and Sunday, are devoted to work with the teachers. People are given time to read their drafts to either a large or a small group. Martina describes the ins and outs of working with two student teachers; Tanja shows us cover letters from the portfolios she has collected. Andrea and Margret describe exciting moments in the writing projects they have conducted with their *Gymnasium* students. Astrid recounts what happened in a writing workshop she did with her *Hauptschule* students; Ingrid brings a transcript of a reading workshop she introduced to hers. Ursula, having recovered from pneumonia and taken a research course with a group of teachers in Vienna, is back and also moving ahead with her research project.

Only two teachers deviate from this path. In February, Hans had said he wanted to conduct a study on the English-language needs for students entering the Austrian business world. I am surprised when he comes empty-handed to our meetings and tells the group that he is currently analyzing responses to a questionnaire he has designed but is not yet ready to present. His lack of preparation disturbs me, and I wonder if it is indicative of unresolved anger from our previous meetings.

Thomas has changed his topic several times since February. To this meeting, he brings a jumbled draft of his latest thinking. As he reads it aloud, I cannot figure out what actually occurs in his class or what story he wants to tell, nor can the rest of the group.

"I guess my barn is just too messy," Thomas jokes.

As we move through these two days of reporting, reading, and responding, people offer comments and suggestions in the spirit of shared inquiry. Rarely does our attention flag. When it does, we break for sweet rolls, dried fruits, chocolate, and nuts contributed by the group, or we stop to nibble on candy corn, a Halloween treat I have brought from New York. Except for Hans, who often appears distracted, hurriedly leaving the room as soon as a break begins, the group seems pleased to be working together again.

This weekend meeting is, in fact, the last time the teachers will formally come together as part of the M.A. program—until graduation at City College in New York. Realizing this, several weeks before I arrive, I send a note asking the teachers to reflect on the program and to write about the impact it has had on them. I ask them to focus on what stands out as important and what they are taking away from it. My plan is to invite everyone to read these reflections aloud as the culminating activity on Sunday. I see this as one way of offering closure to all of our inquiries.

As we approach the end of our last day, I ask for volunteers to read their reflections. Tanja offers to read first, Andrea second. Both describe their growing confidence as teachers. They tell stories of how they taught before the program began and how their practices now differ. Their pieces are professional with momentary touches of humor. I like them. They speak well for the program and the kinds of changes it has enabled the teachers to make. But their words reflect none of the shakiness or soul-searching we engaged in together.

I glance at Margret, sitting opposite me on the other side of the room. In our conversations outside of class, she has told me how disappointed she is in the group. It distresses her that so many separate their personal from their professional lives; it angers her that everyone is eager to ask me for help with the thesis, but no one has asked me what has happened in my life since last February. Sitting now in the classroom, waiting for the next person to volunteer to read, I picture us at her kitchen table and replay our conversation from the previous evening:

"They just don't pay attention to what is on other people's minds," Margret is saying.

"But Margret," I argue, "many of them have written to me. Almost everyone has responded to my paper with a caring and honest letter. When we are all together, the school agenda has to dominate. Really, I think I have asked enough of them."

"But you also have questions," she states emphatically. "Doesn't it anger you that they forget this so quickly?"

"No. I don't get angry. Maybe I should, but . . . " I pause, "asking these questions is hard for me. I often feel as if I am intruding. They didn't ask for this, you know."

Then, groping for what is beginning to dawn on me, I say, "Wait, I do feel something . . . it's as if I am reaching out, across a chasm. When they don't answer, it feels as if I am being ignored. I think . . . more than anything else . . . , I feel rejected—and sad." I sigh, realizing how much this issue actually weighs on me.

"I've told you how much it angers me when they do not take the initiative, when they do not openly ask you about yourself," replies Margaret, "but you must understand something: When they do not answer your questions, there is a different reason. They are silent because they feel so much shame."

Sitting in our classroom with only one hour remaining, I think about the silence. Maybe the teachers are choking on their shame. Should I use the time that remains, I wonder, to share my own reflections, or should I just permit them to complete the course in their own more comfortable way?

Just then, Margret says that she would like to read what she has written. Her voice is quiet at first but gathers force and speed as she continues:

> I entered this program to get rid of my anxieties as a teacher of a language that was then still so alien to me. I got rid of my anxiety of not being good enough, of knowing too little, of being a bad English teacher. I still stammer once in a while, I still search for vocabulary, and I still look up things in grammar books. But all this does not matter any more.
>
> It is Vito Perrone's questions that will stay with me: What is it I want my students to come to understand as a result of their schooling? Are my students "being provided with a basis for active participation in the life of their communities? Do they understand the problems and the need to work toward solutions? Are they, in other words, learning the meaning of social responsibility, of citizenship?"[2]

I so love Perrone. I am glad that Margret has brought him back to us again. It was his statement that teaching is a moral endeavor that initiated this inquiry fifteen months ago. She continues reading:

> If we aren't clear, Perrone says, about such questions, keeping them in mind with everything we do, making them a part of our ongoing discourse, we tend to fill our schools with contradictions—and these contradictions only foster cynicism and limited support, hardly the basis for making schools the centers of inquiry, authority, and change they need to be . . .
>
> I have realized that becoming a kid watcher is a tricky thing: watching without getting involved would reduce my students to objects, would make me withdraw from offering moral guidance, would hardly help provide the basis Perrone is speaking of.
>
> Sondra Perl has come to us with her knowledge and her wisdom, with all the things we have been so eager to take. But she has also come with her anxieties. It was a moment of "catching sense" [everything making sense] when I realized that although I had learned so much about the Holocaust I had never talked to a Jew, I had never tried to find out about them, their culture, their lives, their view of the world today, and I had tried little to REsearch, to REconsider my family's stories, to really become committed as a human being in this world, in my world. The Holocaust and my own country's history had never had a

face, lacked specificity, and I had lacked emotional guidance in coming to grips with my own roots and eventually my standing among my learners.

My God, I think. She is really doing it—naming the issue. I am thankful and scared at the same time.

Sondra has modeled a pedagogy that embraces Perrone's questions. She has gone public with her anxieties and her questions, and has invited us to participate in this REsearching, REconsidering. She has encouraged us to respond to the challenge, evoking new challenges followed by new understandings. She has been teacher and learner the same. She has given a voice to all the words, to all the texts we have studied and welcomed so enthusiastically. She has waited patiently for understanding to happen. She has spoken without pushing, suffered from lack of public response without making us suffer. All this has touched me deeply, me as a teacher here in Austria, me as a human being in this world.

When Margret stops reading, she looks at me. I hold her eyes, not sure what to do or say next. She has placed my personal questions in a context. For this I am grateful. But she has also said that I am suffering. Her strong language embarrasses me. It is painful to have my emotions made so public. Like the teachers, I, too, often prefer to remain hidden.

But once again, words written from Margret's heart have brought the issues out in the open. As we sit, the silence becoming uncomfortable, Christa unobtrusively makes a motion.

"I have prepared something to read," she says in her quiet voice. I nod gratefully at her and she begins, her voice low but sure:

When I read through my reflection of the first course in January 1996, I was embarrassed . . . especially about the shallowness of my thoughts. When I enrolled in the M.A. program, I had expected to improve my language competence through the study of relevant literature in foreign language learning. The articles about whole language and constructivism were not only difficult for me to understand, they also didn't . . . reach out to me—yet. The ideas remained dubious; they didn't fit into my EFL [English as a foreign language] classrooms where true immersion in a foreign language was not possible . . .

The reading and writing workshop with Sondra . . . still lives with me. I experienced the impact reading and writing can have on the community of the classroom. This is what finally made me ready to change my beliefs . . . Constructing meaning for myself in reading and writing was the context that had always been missing for me . . .

It took a lot for some of us to let go of established ideas of what to write about in a thesis . . . Since February 1997 I have often reread *The Tone of Teaching*. It was this book that made me even more aware that putting shame on a child can be so easily done in the rushing school day. I am learning how to become a kid watcher and am learning alongside my pupils now . . .

Doing a bit of ethnographic research in the last course in July 1997 also helped me to become a participant-observer in my own classroom. Writing about where I "caught sense" sharpened my thinking about questions I only now know are feminist—something I will certainly pursue. Cynthia Mitchell was the first African American I had ever met. I liked her liveliness, her good humor, her warmheartedness. Still I don't have the feeling that I know her well. Sondra has told us that Cynthia is sending us some writing. Will she also be telling us about the anger she carries about her people's past? Sondra shared this anguish with us Austrians.

As I learned to hear you, Sondra, and to love you for telling us about this hatred that burned in you, it deemed [*sic*] on me that there still is responsibility for me, for us here in Austria, to go back into history, first of all to inform myself—ourselves. And along with this process of learning about history, to feel empathy with those who suffered, and with those who still share their pain, grief, and anguish, to expose myself to the hatred. It is very late in my life that this has finally been made possible for me . . . I see you, Sondra, as the one who enabled me to make my life less fragmentary . . . And it is indeed an existential and everlasting thankfulness I will have for this.

Deeply moved, I reach over to Christa, who is sitting alongside me, touch her arm gently, and thank her.

Christa has found a way to bring all the learning together, to see herself both as a teacher and a human being, a woman, an active inquirer into what it means to be alive, to teach, to be responsible for the history she has inherited—for what she says about it and for what she has, until now, been unable or unwilling to say. I sit stunned, not so much at how articulate she is, but at the courage she had to muster to read these words to her peers.

As I look out once again at the group, I see Andrea, Ingrid, Martina, and Astrid. Each has written to me and worked hard to come to grips with a past that might have included Nazi forbears. Christa's words now speak of an even larger challenge: to bring empathy to bear on the entire situation, to consider identifying with those who suffered, to consider facing the hatred. Every hair on my body seems to be standing on end.

I generally prefer to save my own reflections until everyone else has had a chance to share, but I realize that as their professor, it is time for me to speak.

Breaking the silence, I say, "I'll read now, if no one else wants to go." I begin:

> . . . A year ago, I could not have envisioned what I am about to write. I could not have envisioned that I would be both committed to and profoundly moved by this desire I have to understand both the Holocaust and what my teaching in Austria means—to me, to you, to other educators, and perhaps to a larger public concerned with issues of history, hate, and hegemony...
>
> And so today, sitting here at home, in New York, Bach playing softly in the background, dogs sleeping on the couch, I feel full—full of all that has already transpired and full of expectation of what is yet to come. I experience the excitement that accompanies the beginning of a new venture. For me, this venture is about teaching and history—where the two have come together in my life and in my classroom—and about bringing history into the present so that we who encounter it can discover our own relationship to it. It is about the ways in which the classroom can become a ground for the exploration of self, set within historical awareness.

I pause for a moment and look up at the group. People seem to be listening. I know they care about teaching, and I hope that they can see the promise of what I am talking about. I take a breath and continue:

> This project, then, is about that dialogue—about a Jewish teacher discovering friends among those she considered her enemies; about the ways in which dialogue allows people to speak and respond; about courage and conviction; about voice and self and location; ultimately, about the power of teaching and what it means to teach.

Once again, I pause and look up. My voice is shaking. I look down and continue:

> I have tried a few times before to say what teaching here in Innsbruck has meant to me. I want to emphasize how much I was caught by surprise. Before I came, I really thought that I was only coming to teach two courses—courses I had designed and have enjoyed teaching for many years. I did not expect to become so personally involved or to find myself so confronted with my own questions.
>
> But now, I welcome these questions. I am grateful to all of you for welcoming me among you and giving me room to ask and explore them. So in some ways, as you complete your theses and send them to me, as you prepare to graduate from this program, your work comes to its natural end. Mine, I think, is only just beginning . . .

When I finish reading, I say, "Margret's response to me has always been crucial. It has enabled me to keep asking questions. I hope it's also clear that Christa's response today is equally important. I am concerned that some of you may think that, because Margret and now Christa have responded so fully, your response doesn't matter. I want you to know that's not true. You have all been on this journey with me, and I welcome what each of you has to say, even if it is different from what Margret or Christa says."

Andrea catches my eye. "I have something I'd like to say." She takes a deep breath before she begins. "You've been honest with us, Sondra, so I want to be honest with you. I realize that I often forget about your questions in pursuing mine. But I also see now—for the first time without any guilt feelings—that these questions are not mine. I see my responsibility in my people's history, but for the time being, I cannot consider it as the core issue. There are other things I have to sort out first. I am grateful for the push or nudge towards facing this issue, but I prefer to go at my own pace here."

Finally, I think to myself, someone is willing to say "Not now. Not for me. Not just yet." While I prefer that people not sidestep these issues, more than anything else, I want them to be able to admit where they stand. I want them to emerge from their silence, even if the only thing they can say is "not yet."

"Andrea, thank you," I say. "Of course, you need to move at your own pace. Of course, this is a legitimate response. What matters to me is that you say it. Then I can acknowledge your response, even if it is to say no to me."

"For the time being," Andrea corrects gently.

"Yes, for the time being," I nod and then go on: "Christa and Andrea have offered us two extremes. Does anyone else have another kind of response, another place to stand?"

Astrid says, "I need more time to think. I will write to you."

Ingrid nods. So does Hilde. Ursula, having missed the February course, looks perplexed.

To the group, I say, "I know these are not comfortable questions. If you feel you need more time to think, please take it and send me your thoughts."

Thomas's face is dark, clouded. "I . . . I can't read . . . I can't write. This is so big . . . I don't know how to think about so much . . . so much pain. My pain . . . the world's pain . . . the pain in my family," Thomas says, tears beginning to slip from his eyes.

We pause. No one knows what to say. I think of all the pain that still lives in this land—the unaddressed pain in so many families, here and elsewhere. Margret, sitting next to Thomas, gently places her hand on his arm.

"Thomas, I know from the letter you sent me that the pain in the world is real to you," I say. "Your words were beautiful and caring and quite profound. I wish everyone could read what you wrote."

"Me too," Thomas says, between sobs. "I almost brought that letter with me. All of this . . . everything we have been talking about . . . it is so hard to understand and so real. So important. The world is still in pain." And then, a deep note of despair in his voice, he sobs, "It is like we never learn."

Thomas, younger than the rest of us, unfocused when it comes to research, floundering when it comes to writing, does not flounder when it comes to revealing how he feels. His tears are cleansing. In some way, I think, he is crying for all of us.

I look out at this group of teachers, sitting respectfully, listening thoughtfully. We have come a long way together, addressed moral issues, participated in a pedagogy that asks hard questions, examined the borders of the private and the professional. It is time to let it rest.

"Yes, Thomas," I respond. "It seems as if we never learn. But together, here, in this group, I see clear evidence of learning. And," I add, smiling gently, "I want to end by thanking all of you for reminding me of something I often forget: When we turn toward such painful issues, tears—or silence—are sometimes more fitting than words."

Before everyone packs up to leave, Hilde announces a surprise. She has brought several bottles of champagne. As she pours a glass for each of us, we mingle. Quiet voices become louder. Timidity in the face of such heart-rending issues turns into a sense of triumph. Toasting their soon-to-be completed theses, we are toasting, I think, more than we can say.

Each teacher comes over say goodbye. Some hug, others shake hands, all promise to mail drafts of their theses to me in Riverdale. Final revisions and corrections await us. Our plan is to meet in eight months, in June, at graduation at The City College in New York.

Left:
Beginning a hike:
Margret, Sondra, Sam,
Josh, Cara, and Sara,
1999

Below:
At the top of the
mountain: Margret,
Sondra, and children,
1999

Gert, Luis, Anna, and Margret Fessler, 1999

Sam, Gert, Sondra, Josh, and Margret, hiking in 2001

Josh and Sam at the top of the Klettersteig, 2001

Sam, Josh, and Gert
ascending the
Klettersteig Nordkette,
2001

Margret and Sondra at a *Gasthof*, 2002

Sondra and Margret in the snow peaks, 2002

Sara and Cara in Manhattan, 2004

Josh and Sam (back row); Margret, Sondra, Sara, Cara, and Gert (front row); Manhattan, November, 2004

9

Uncommon Ground

Saturday, October 11, is Yom Kippur, the Jewish Day of Atonement, the holiest day of the Jewish year. It is the day when Jews fast, attend synagogue, and ask to be forgiven for their sins. It is a day to wash the slate clean, to begin again—a day set aside for repentance and renewal. In the evening, after sundown, people gather to break the fast. In New York, among my friends, the spread will consist of bagels and cream cheese, assorted salads, platters carefully arranged with slices of smoked salmon, whitefish, and sturgeon, pastries for dessert. Many of my friends fast; normally, I do not.

On this day in Innsbruck, Arthur and I are by ourselves. We wake to a quiet house, having returned late the night before from our trip through the Dolomites. Margret will arrive later in the day from a weeklong excursion with her students. Cara is at school, Gert at work. Our plans are to meet up for dinner. Arthur wants to fast and attend synagogue. I want to go along. Having only seen the synagogue from the outside—in February on the walk with Horst—I welcome this chance to enter its sanctuary, to glimpse the reemergence of Jewish life in Innsbruck.

As we walk down the path from Margret's house to town, I look out over the city. The air is crisp, the leaves turning colors, the ground moist with dew. It is impossible not to imagine Jewish life before the *Anschluss*, before the Holocaust. Jews would have walked along similar paths, would have headed to the same place we are heading, would have fasted as Arthur is fasting, would have asked God for forgiveness as he will. Except for the appearance of a few high-rise buildings, Innsbruck would have looked remarkably the same.

And then, one day, Jews like us would no longer be permitted to walk this route; would no longer be free to practice their religion; would no longer be here at all.

Arthur and I walk slowly, holding hands. The mountain path is steep. We are both cautious, afraid of slipping. As much as I am drawn to these mountains, I realize that I also find them frightening. At each bend in the path, I grasp the protective railing, afraid to let go: one misstep and I could sprain my ankle or break my leg. This land feels foreign to me. I find myself wondering whether there is a connection between terrain and the character of a people, whether one can find the same sharpness and forbidding presence of these mountains reflected in the Austrian character. To be born to this place, to these mountains, to grow up learning how to master them, to scamper down their paths and to scale their peaks, how does that shape a people?

As we continue on our way, gingerly taking smaller and smaller steps until the path levels out, I am lost in these thoughts. The longer I remain in Austria, I realize, the more I am faced with unsettling ideas. As uneasy as it makes me, I wonder, again, if the ecology of a land and the ethnicity of a people are in any way related. I shake my head as if to rid myself of such thoughts. They seem so reductive, so rife with judgment and stereotypical thinking, and yet, I seem unwilling to let go of them. In Austria, I find myself compelled again and again to confront the meaning of ethnic identity, of what, specifically, it means to be a Jew.

We are halfway down the mountain. I let out a sigh of relief as we emerge from the woods and pass behind a local church. I know our route will now be studded with churches, some small, others quite grand, all adorned with Christian icons. On my first visit to Innsbruck, I was surprised to see the degree to which Catholicism dominated the landscape. The statues of saints and the figure of Jesus appear everywhere: along the sides of roads, on the tops of mountains, tacked onto trees in the woods, nestled under the door frames of houses. By now I have become so accustomed to them, I barely notice them. But today, on Yom Kippur, I can't not make comparisons. In this staunchly Catholic land, I can't not think about Israel.

My two trips come back to me, the first one with my parents when I was eighteen and the second, after college, when I lived on a kibbutz and worked in the fields, pruning banana trees. Each time, I realize, I felt a connection to the land that I have felt nowhere else.

Yes, I muse, as Arthur and I make our way down the last hill leading to the flat valley of Innsbruck, Israel is also a harsh land, and the Israelis, shaped by the toughness of the desert. Yet I sense differences. Israel's mountains, the Golan Heights, where I spent a week in 1971, Masada, which I climbed one night arriving just in time to watch the sun rise, are gentler, more sloping, more accessible than the mountains here.

The climate, too, the atmosphere itself, is warmer. No, I think, Israelis and perhaps all Jews may be fierce, but we do not embody in ourselves or in our landscape the forbidding harshness I sense in Austria's towering Alps. Nor are we the silent, mountain-dweller type I have come to recognize in Austrians like Gert. The Jews I know, myself included, are anything but silent.

Yet at this moment, I have no desire to talk. Walking quietly with Arthur on the way to synagogue has given me time to reflect. His mood, too, seems contemplative. Our silence is companionable. As we pass in front of a grocery store, I notice a Muslim woman, her head covered in a scarf, duck inside. I know Turks and other immigrants from Eastern Bloc countries now receive the brunt of Austria's anti-foreigner sentiment. But sixty years ago, it would have been the Jews.

Why? I wonder. What sets Jews apart? We have migrated all over the world, have found ways to survive, to thrive even, and to take on local characteristics, and yet we have for centuries managed to embody traits that have marked us as particularly Jewish. What is this ethnicity, I wonder, that is not necessarily derived from religious observance? What is it that makes one Jewish? And why is it that when I stand in certain places I experience my connection to this heritage more deeply than in others? How come the hills of Israel beckon me in a way the cliffs of Austria do not? For a moment, caught in this reverie, I think I understand what calls Jews back to Israel. That land was not only given to us in a covenant with God; it is the ground from which we emerged; it is, in some uncanny way, the soil that suits us.

Arthur and I have reached one of the many bridges that cross the Inn, the river which gives Innsbruck its name. Walking across it, we head in the direction of the Old Town, knowing we can take a short cut through its narrow, winding, cobblestone streets. Once inside, we pass an open-air market, some street vendors, a few tourists taking pictures of the Golden Dome. Soon we emerge onto a main thoroughfare and pass in front of the grand Museum of Art. At the next corner, we turn left onto Sillegasse. Then about half a block in, set back from the street, almost hidden from view, we come upon the synagogue. An armed guard is stationed out front. The door is locked. We ring the bell, and a man in a suit and a prayer shawl cautiously opens the door. He looks us over and beckons us to come in.

Once inside, we hang up our coats, Arthur puts on his *talit*, and we enter a small sanctuary. Everything is new. The marble floor gleams. The recessed lights are bright. The ark with the Torah inside shines. Up front on the *bimah*, a rabbi is chanting in Hebrew.

There are six rows divided by a center aisle. On the left side, I see only three women seated near the front. About twelve men on the right. I judge the total capacity to be about sixty to seventy people. Arthur squeezes my hand, then goes to seat himself with the men. I take a seat on the women's side, alone, in the last row. I sit quietly, drinking in the atmosphere. I comprehend only a few words of the prayers, but it makes no difference. From the time I was a child and my parents sent me to services, I have always responded to the same thing: the mournful tunes, the minor key of Jewish melodies. My eyes fill with tears.

I know that this is the site where the old synagogue once stood— the synagogue that was attacked by Nazis and their sympathizers on *Kristallnacht*, by people eager to burn the sacred books inside, the synagogue that was later destroyed by Allied bombs. Of course, everything now is shiny and new. How could it be otherwise? What's even more remarkable, I say to myself, is that this building stands at all, that there are Jews here who still want to pray, who want to worship again on this site.

I sit and let myself take in what is going on around me. As time passes, more people enter, find seats, pick up prayer books. I ask myself, what is both familiar and strange about this place? There is no threat here. What I see is simple, quiet, observant. Jews are praying, *davening*, heads bowed, bodies rocking, as they have done for centuries.

Jews have been called "the people of the book," a fitting appellation. They are people of the word, who revere texts and devote much of their lives to studying and debating them, writing commentaries, arguing about God and God's purpose, interpreting His word, endlessly interpreting, looking for nuance and meaning.

Living within a Christian world, I hated being marked as different. But today, I realize, my work is not very different from what

Jewish scholars have always done. I read, write, and comment on texts. It strikes me that I have not moved far from my roots at all.

Sitting in the synagogue in Innsbruck, it dawns on me that I am witnessing the replanting of Jewish roots, roots that were pulled and severed more than half a century ago. But I realize that the Judaism practiced here does not resemble what I experience in the synagogues I have attended at home. At home, in Manhattan, Philadelphia, San Diego, in the *shuls* of my childhood and in the services I have attended as an adult, people come and go, children run around, women chat, men chant, babies cry. Observance and prayer go hand in hand with life. It is as if people are so comfortable with the rituals that they don't mind the intrusion of life upon them. It all occurs together: One can pray and gossip too; one can thank God and quiet a baby; one can turn inward without excluding what is outside.

Here all is silent save the voice of the rabbi or of those men he calls forward to read from the Torah. People follow along obediently. They are silent at the silent parts. They listen when it is time to listen. They chant when they are told to chant. It feels constrained, as if no one is quite certain what to do. The ease and comfort I have seen at home are absent here. Again, I ask myself, how could it be otherwise? When practice has been obliterated, when the desire of one's neighbors has been to annihilate all worship, how does the congregation begin anew? Certainly it would take more than a few years. I sigh, feeling the loss, overcome by sadness.

I look around again. There are a handful of boys around the age of twelve or thirteen, Bar Mitzvah age. There is one old man who appears to be about eighty and many middle-aged people. Are they survivors or the children of survivors? I wonder. I notice some young women in their late twenties. Where do they all come from? How did they get here? What is it like today to be a part of the Jewish community in Innsbruck?

After a while, I reach behind me and pick up a prayer book, an English-Hebrew version of the New Year service. I open to a page at random. The words jump off the page:

> *Thou hast set man apart from the beginning and acknowledged him that he should stand before thee.*[1]

I catch my breath. My entire inquiry with the teachers has focused on how we stand in the world. In February, I asked them to consider what it means to stand as teachers. Ever since, I have been challenging them to consider what it means to stand as Austrians. So much of my own personal inquiry in this country has occurred by asking myself how I stand in the world—not only as a teacher but also as a Jew. So much of my journey here, even my thoughts this morning, has focused on how the soil we stand on shapes us. And now, sitting in synagogue, the first words I read ask me to consider how I stand before God. I take the words in. Do I stand here before God? For most of my life, I realize with a start, I have adamantly refused to. I continue reading:

> Yet who shall say unto thee: "What dost thou?" and if he be righteous, what boon is that to thee? Howbeit thou hast given us, O Lord our God, this Day of Atonement to be an end, a forgiving and pardoning of all our iniquities; that so we may stay our hand from violence and return unto thee to perform the statutes of thy will with a perfect heart.[2]

Another dizzying question, one that uncannily causes me to give voice to my own questions. Yes, God, I ask, What do You do? What do You ask of us? Of me? What difference does it make whether I follow Your statutes or not? Why should Jews stay their hands and return to You?

Isn't this what I have always agonized over? Where were You, God? Why did You not rage against our destroyers? Why did You let them torture and murder us? Who, after all, has forsaken whom, God? What do You offer that is worth returning to?

I read on:

> Thou acceptest the repentance of the wicked and delightest not in their death, as it is said: Say unto them, As I live, saith the Lord God, I have no pleasure in the death of the wicked; but that the wicked turn from his way and live . . .[3]

No, I want to scream, this is not possible. You have no delight in the death of the wicked? You do not want to punish them? You accept their repentance? That will not bring back the millions who died. How can such words make any sense after the Holocaust?

I pause and take a breath, looking to calm myself, but my questions continue, insistent, unabated: How can You not want to punish those who committed atrocities? How can You want them to live? Are You really so forgiving?

The cantor begins a song familiar to me, "*Osay Shalom.*" His voice is strong and deep. It fills the room. Soon a few people join in, then everyone. I picture my children at home, surrounded by family, and I recall the many times we have sung this song together, "May He who brings peace bring peace to us, to Israel . . . "

I see the whitewashed walls of Jerusalem blazing in the sun, the dark, rich soil north of Tel Aviv, the stinging, salt-drenched water of the Dead Sea, and I yearn for peace to descend on that war-torn country. I wish for peace, for the tantalizing promise that all children may one day live in peace. But here, in the midst of this service, I realize, I am in turmoil. My head is beginning to throb, my heart to ache.

When he has concluded the song, the rabbi returns to his prayers. Restless, I turn to a new page in my prayer book and continue reading in English:

> Thou art acquainted with our sins both of presumption and of ignorance, whether of will or by compulsion, both the revealed and the secret. Before thee, they are revealed and known. What are we? What is our life? What our piety? What our righteousness? What our salvation? What our strength? What our might? What shall we say before thee, O Lord our God and God of our fathers? Are not the mighty ones as naught before thee, and men of fame as though they were not, wise men as if they were without knowledge, and men of understanding as if they were void of discretion? For the multitude of their works is emptiness, and the days of their life are vanity before thee; and the pre-eminence of man over beast is naught: for all is vanity.[4]

Is that so? I ask myself. Is all the searching and striving, questioning and grappling—all the yearning of the human race—for naught? Is it really all vanity? What do we say in the face of the one and a half million children who died in the Holocaust? How do they stand before Thee, and what do You say to them? Can You say anything, utter even one word, to atone for their deaths? Or is it wiser, finally, to turn from You?

I can no longer sit still. These words do not comfort me. I put the book back where I found it and get up. I am angry—angry that God did not bring his wrath upon the perpetrators, that he did not protect his people from their enemies, that Jews, observant and unobservant alike, were turned to ashes in the crematoria. What kind of all-powerful, all-knowing God would allow such destruction? And if he is unable to act on behalf of his people, how powerful is he? To whom are we singing praises?

I am acquainted with the standard answers to such questions. The Holocaust could only occur in a country where men elevated themselves to godlike stature and took upon themselves the determination of who was fit to live or die. God is not responsible for man's inhumanity; man is. The worst result of the Holocaust would be to deny Judaism after we have survived. To do so, would, in the most ironic of twists, hand Hitler his victory. But such words seem hollow to me.

I get up, find my coat, and go outside. The sun is shining, the air cool. I am incapable of grasping these prayers. When they are recited by one who believes, perhaps they make a certain kind of sense. But when one has lost one's faith or has never known faith, what then? Can they mean anything at all?

I walk down the block slowly reconsidering the passage I have just read. I know the writer has a point. Much of what we do in life is vain, driven by a desire for fame, wealth, or power. Human beings are often deceitful and dishonest, acting on impure impulses. I can see this. And yes, I admit, the questions are valuable: What does anybody know for certain? Should I not be more humble? Who presumes to have the final answer?

But as I walk along the street, aimlessly looking in shop windows, I am also distracted, pursued by doubt, by rage, by pain and shame. I know these streets that surround the synagogue were the streets where Jews once lived. I know they—we—were not welcomed, that the Church perpetuated what has been called "the teaching of contempt"—the doctrine that Jews were responsible for the death of Christ. I know that for centuries the refusal of Jews to accept Jesus as the messiah has led to pogroms and inquisitions, to spilled blood and bitterness.

I pass a café and consider stopping for a coffee, but I feel as though I cannot swallow. I am choking on sadness and rage. I know I can return to Margret's house, but I don't feel ready to socialize. Instead, I find myself drawn back to the synagogue, to the one place I know Jews are welcome. I retrace my steps, reenter the building, and return to my seat in the back row.

The room is more crowded now. Maybe twenty women and twenty-five men. I reach behind me and pick up a different volume entitled *Sabbath and Festival Prayer Book*. I scan the table of contents and find a supplemental reading called "I am a Jew." Curious, I turn to page 304 and read:

> I will continue to hold my banner aloft. I find myself born—aye, born—into a people and a religion. The preservation of my people must be for a purpose, for God does nothing without a purpose. His reasons are unfathomable to me, but on my own reason I place little dependence; test it where I will, it fails me. The simple, the ultimate in every direction is sealed to me. It is as difficult to understand matter as mind. The courses of the planets are no harder to explain than the growth of a blade of grass. Therefore I am willing to remain a link in the great chain. What has been preserved for 4,000 years was not saved that I should overthrow it. My people have survived the prehistoric paganism, the Babylonian polytheism, the aesthetic Hellenism, the sagacious Romanism; and it will survive the modern dilettantism and the current materialism, holding aloft the traditional Jewish ideals inflexibly until the world shall become capable of recognizing their worth.[5]

Perhaps any excerpt I turn to this morning will be meaningful. Perhaps any passage will bring solace to my bruised heart. I cannot be sure. But I am aware that working and walking in Innsbruck have altered my sense of self, that the world's hatred of the Jews, embodied most vehemently in the policies of the Nazis, has finally, fundamentally, shaken me to the core, and that I must face my own fear up close.

I am a Jew. I cannot deny it. I cannot pretend otherwise. I did not want to be marked or hated. For most of my life, I have done everything in my power to blend in with what I considered to be a more pristine and privileged Christian culture. But had I been born here I would not have been given the choice. So why do I assume there is one now? Judaism calls me as much as anything else in the world. I may not embrace it easily, but embrace it I must.

Sitting in the synagogue in Innsbruck, I feel as if I have read the words I need to read. My recent study of Judaism has already convinced me that there is an intellectual tradition worth preserving here. But these words I have chanced upon, reprinted in this prayer book, these words that have found their way into my hands, have also found their way into my heart. I have repeated them silently to myself. They have taken hold.

Sitting here, in the synagogue, I acknowledge that I, too, have found myself born into a people, into a religion, I can no longer turn my back on. I can no longer pretend that Judaism is not my heritage or that my questions this morning, spoken from a despairing heart, are not also the beginning of my own silent dialogue with a God I have wanted to deny. I can stop hiding and stop running. I can stand in the world and claim my place as a Jewish woman. I can now leave this synagogue in peace, more whole than when I entered it. *Osay Shalom.*

❧

At 6:00 P.M., we are reunited. Margret, Gert, Cara, and I meet Arthur and Horst Schreiber and his teenage son in town. I had hoped Horst could take us on the same walking tour he conducted for the group in February. But it is later than we had planned, and the weather is turning cold. We have time for only one stop. Horst decides to take us to a monument that was recently erected to commemorate the deaths of four Jewish men who were murdered in Innsbruck on the night of November 9, 1938.

As we walk toward a plaza not far from the imposing French-designed war monument that Horst showed the group in February, he explains a recent change. "*Kristallnacht,*" Horst says, "is the name the Nazis used. We reject that term now. It is too poetic. Today we use the word *Pogromnacht,* the Night of the Pogrom. It is clearer, then, what we are really meaning."

We nod as we stand facing this new monument. It is modest in scale: a short, round column about five feet high with seven metal candlesticks rising out of it, reaching for the sky. Protruding from the inside of the column are shards of glass. Etched on the outside of the rounded column are the names of the four murdered men, Josef Adler, Wilhelm Bauer, Richard Berger, and Richard Graubart. The given names, unmistakably German; the surnames, unmistakably Jewish.

I like the monument. The murdered Jews are identified by name. The broken glass atop the column serves as a visible reminder not only of shattered storefront windows but also of shattered Jewish lives. But as Horst tells us the story behind the memorial, I realize that for Austrians like him and Margret this monument is a sham.

According to Horst, a group of students who were working as government interns in Innsbruck lobbied the local ministry of education to commemorate the Holocaust. The ministry responded by deciding to hold a contest. The school that came up with the best design for a memorial would have it erected on this spot. The only problem, Horst tells us, is that no funds were offered, and almost no planning went into the announcement. Many schools did not know about it, heard about it too late, or ignored it.

"How many designs came in?" I ask, as we stand together looking at the monument.

"About twenty—out of all of Austria—which is really disgraceful. But what is worse, many were embarrassing—full of Christian imagery. Crosses. Yet, how can you blame the students? When they think of suffering, they think of Christ."

We all sigh, drawing closer as the wind picks up.

"Yes," I respond, "but at least you now have public recognition of four men who lived here and were murdered here on *Kristallnacht*—on *Pogromnacht*. That says something, don't you think?"

"Yes, it says the acknowledgment is too little, too late, and not sincere. Yes, four men were murdered here. But I worry about the future. What about the murders that number into the thousands, into the millions? What does commemorating four people say about that? It's as if the only thing that happened here was these four deaths," Horst says in disgust.

"It's something," I say hesitatingly, glad that the lives of even four men are being commemorated.

"It's not enough," Horst answers flatly.

ঽ▲

At dinner, Margret tries to explain why she and Horst are so despairing. "Perhaps," she speculates, her fork poised in the air, "we want you to express our anger for us. We don't want you to be satisfied with tokens. But maybe it is our job to say that. We are the ones who are angry at our own people for their silence—for their lack of caring."

I look into Margret's eyes and can sense the anger that fuels her. She is outraged when Austrians refuse to look at the past, when they want to cover it up or, even worse, to defend it. I know she feels their willed blindness places a larger burden on her, and she fears it will ultimately affect her daughter. I, on the other hand, am grateful when even a small gesture is made. But, I think to myself, half-listening to the conversation, our paths are different here. I do not live with the perpetrators, nor do I have to answer for them. I live with a kind of emptiness, a sense of a loss, and with the childhood fear that it could happen again. When faced with the enormity of the loss to Jewish life and culture, I can summon anger, but more often than not, I am overcome with grief.

As I turn my attention back to the conversation, Horst is explaining to Arthur what he does at the Institute for Contemporary History. "We are collecting documents, looking to write biographies of every Jewish person who once lived in Innsbruck, attempting to trace what happened to each one. It is hard work. It is not so hard to identify the names of former Nazis. There are lists. Even lists that show which stores were to be patronized and which had to be avoided."

"What will you do with these documents?" I ask, "once you have collected them?"

"Preserve them so that no one can ever say it did not happen here."

I nod, thinking that Horst is involved in a worthy endeavor. But his work cannot bring back the lost lives nor will it help Austrian students understand why Christian iconography is inappropriate for conveying Jewish suffering. So much work, I realize, still needs to be done. So much remains unaddressed. No wonder Margret and Horst feel so alone.

But it turns out that they are not the only ones. Gert describes a talk he had with his mother while we were all away: "I told her I was proud of her for not denying the past. Do you know what she answered? She feels alone in her thoughts. If her friends heard her speak, they would call her a traitor. To them, her thoughts are what you would call . . . "—he searches for the English word—"treason."

"So few people here are willing to admit what went on. They prefer to ignore it, to cover it up, not to say anything at all," adds Horst.

"Just like in our course," Margret comments.

I nod. I am coming to understand how the whole issue is fraught with complexities, how burdened each side feels. The enormity of what happened is overwhelming. Anyone who tries to speak for it or about it begins on shaky ground. There are no models here, no well-worn paths to follow, no handrails at the tricky turns. Only one's own heart.

"But Margret," I respond, "have you ever heard Anna say she feels so alone? Can you imagine a generation of people unable to say what is in their hearts? Unable to express remorse, to ask to be forgiven—even for what is ultimately unforgivable?"

"No," she says slowly, "I have not heard that from her before. This is new. But still . . . " she sighs, her heart still heavy.

We are at Kapeller, the restaurant where Margret and I dined together in February. In such an elegant setting, with such exquisite food, it is difficult to keep talking in such a serious vein. Besides, we are eager to recount stories of the trips we have just completed. Arthur and I describe our hike in southern Tyrol. Margret tells of her excursion to Carinthia and her students' antics. Then the talk turns to movies. The teenagers perk up. *Men in Black*, it turns out, is as big a hit in Innsbruck as it is in New York.

Our sojourn in Innsbruck is coming to an end. In a few days, Arthur and I will return home. Sitting comfortably in Restaurant Kappeller, across from my husband, next to my dear friend, I am grateful that I accepted the invitation to teach in Austria.

I do not have answers for Margret's anger or Horst's disgust; I do not have answers for Anna or Luis, for my own sadness, for all the loss of innocent life and all the loss to Jewish culture. I do not have answers for anyone. But I do know that born into different histories, raised on very different soil, this group of friends and I have found common ground. This, in my mind, is undeniable. Where it will lead is unknown to me.

As we order dessert, I realize that it is still Yom Kippur. My day began many hours ago with my walk into town with Arthur, with my sitting in the synagogue. The words I read in the prayer book suddenly return to me: Jewish ideals are worth preserving; one day the world may recognize their worth. As Margret, Horst, Gert, and the teenagers lapse into German, I am caught up in my own reverie. For centuries, the Jews have held inflexibly to a particular vision of the world, a vision that claims the world is perfectible. Now I wonder whether *tikkun olam*, the perfecting of the world, does not begin with the central theme of Yom Kippur, with *teshuva*—returning to what calls us, to land, to spirit, to goodness, to friendship—so that we can begin anew. On Yom Kippur, Jews are asked to repent. Might repairing the world, I muse, first require that we repair ourselves?

๛

On Monday, October 13, we prepare to leave. Our flight is scheduled for early the next day. At lunch, Gert informs us that Anna has invited us for drinks at her house. Would we stop by before we drive into town for dinner? He will be at work, but the rest of us can go.

I was never sure if Anna would follow through on her desire to keep talking. But it seems as if we will have at least a brief moment to meet again, this time, at her invitation. I wonder what is on her mind and whether this visit will be more than social.

At 6:00 P.M., Margret, Cara, Arthur, and I walk over to Anna and Luis's front door. Their flat is adjacent to Margret and Gert's. While the house was divided into separate living spaces several years ago, every level looks out at the same extraordinary view, the towering mountains, their peaks already covered with snow.

We knock, enter, and greet one another again. I take in their living quarters: the small rooms, the traditional heavy wooden furniture, the china knickknacks, everything neat and in its place, orderly, clean. Is the room cramped, I wonder, or is this cramped feeling something inside me? It calms me to look out the large glass windows at the mountains beyond.

Luis motions us to sit down at the small dining table. It is covered by a white cloth and placed so that one side runs along the *Kachlofen*, a green-tiled oven that warms both the room and our backs as we lean against it. Their wooden furniture—the hutch, the backs of the chairs, even Anna's desk against the wall—each piece, Anna proudly explains, was designed and carved by Luis who prefers an elaborate, antique style.

Five tiny cordial glasses sit on a tray in the middle of the dining table. We sit quietly as Luis takes out a bottle and fills our glasses with homemade schnapps. He tells us it is pine schnapps, made by a friend of his, a specialty, since the pine needles are collected at the timber line. I find it warming and bitter at the same time. Margret claims it tastes like medicine.

Clearly, no one is sure how to begin the conversation. Small talk is easier. Anna asks us about our hiking trip in the Dolomites and our travel plans for the next day. I answer, but Arthur then turns the conversation to the past. He mentions that his father was an officer in the Navy during World War II and although he died many years ago, Arthur feels that his father would be pleased that his son is here now, in his place, talking with an Austrian veteran.

"Very few American veterans of my generation have had a chance to sit down with the Vietnamese," he says, "but somehow this talking is important—at least to me," Arthur adds.

"And what about the Indians in America?" asks Luis, his eyebrows raised ever so slightly. "Do you talk with them about the past?"

Margret's eyes narrow. She has heard this refrain from Luis too many times and has warned me that this is one of his favorite ways of attacking America. His comment irks me.

But Arthur responds, not yet willing to give up on Luis. "Well," he says, "many Americans work hard to help improve the living conditions of Native Americans. But it is also true that not one of our leaders has been willing to admit publicly that our treatment of Native Americans is a black spot on our history."

I smile, sip my schnapps, and hope that Arthur's hidden message is sinking in.

Then Arthur makes one more attempt to engage Luis in conversation. "For a man like me, Herr Fessler, talking is very important. It is also this way for the people who come to work with me. When they talk, they feel better."

"For me," Luis answers sharply, "it is the opposite. For me, not talking is better."

Margret straightens her back, tightens her lips. I know she is ready to leave. I feel torn, wishing there were some way to reach this man and sensing that no amount of prodding will release the words we want to hear.

Arthur makes one more stab in Luis's direction. "Yes, I understand," he comments. "Some people ask, 'Why suffer twice? It is best to forget.' But maybe that is not possible either."

"My friends cannot forget. They cling to the past. I try to see the future," Luis answers, but his comment does not invite further questions, at least none that I can imagine.

Just then, Anna gets up and rummages among the papers on her desk. She brings back a book catalogue in German. She says, "Since last week, I have been thinking about our conversation. I would like to read, to learn about Jewish knowledge, Jewish wisdom. Would you look over these listings," she asks Arthur and me, "and tell me if you know of any of these authors? Would you recommend a book or two for me?"

Margret, Arthur, and I glance at each other in surprise. What does she want to know? I wonder. The list includes books on Jewish mysticism and spirituality. I take her interest in good faith, ready to accept that her motives are sincere. She seems to be saying that for the first time, she realizes how woefully ignorant she is and how inadequate her understanding of those she was taught to hate. She seems intrigued by these issues in a way her husband is not.

I cannot translate the titles but I recognize a few of the names and read them out loud. Wiesel. Buber. Stories from the *Kabbalah*, the chasidic movement, the mystical teachings. Margret asks Anna if she would prefer to start with something simpler, something more historical. "No," Anna answers flatly. "I want to read about the wisdom tradition."

Arthur talks about a few of the authors as I underline the specific titles. Anna seems pleased. Then she looks at both of us very closely and says in a very quiet voice, "Anti-Semitism was all around us. It was very common. But, you must believe me," she says, her voice faltering, "I did not know—not until later."

I look at Margret and Arthur. They look back at me and at one another. It is late. Gert is waiting for us in town.

It is a moment for eyes, not words, and a different kind of silence. My doubts are still there, but so is my heart. I have been touched by this seventy-five-year-old woman who is trying to reach beyond what is safe and known.

Margret breaks the silence by reminding us that we must leave for dinner. As we stand up and make our goodbyes, Anna asks us when we are planning to return.

"In two years," I respond, "in the summer when we hope to bring our children."

"Perhaps," she suggests clutching her catalogue, "we can discuss these ideas."

"And then," motioning out the window to the snow-covered peaks in the distance, Luis adds, "we will invite you and your children to hike with us."

I hear in Luis's offer his own attempt to reach out to us. The mountains may be the only part of life he revered as a child that has not left him disillusioned. They are what he still knows and, as an old man, loves intimately. But his offer strikes me as bizarre. Perhaps the schnapps is making me giddy, but all I can hear is the incredulous voice of my mother: *"You are planning to go on a hike with Nazis—and to take the kids along?"* Or the skeptical voices of my more cynical friends: *"Hiking with Nazis? Be sure you don't get too close to the edge."*

Arthur, however, is either unaffected by schnapps or able to keep a stronger hold on his thoughts. He speaks for both of us when he says, "Herr Fessler, perhaps talking is not so important when you have such a wise woman at your side. Maybe your friends cling to the past because they did not marry someone who thinks like Anna."

As Anna shakes my hand, she holds it just a moment longer than necessary. Much remains unsaid. Much may never be said. But, for now, it seems a fitting way to end.

10

The Question of Forgiveness

"You met the Nazis? How could you?"

"They were nice people? Nuremberg interviewers will tell you that there was no one more charming than a Nazi in his cell."

"What do you mean they claimed not to know? Everyone knew. Watch Lanzmann's Shoah. *Ordinary people knew what was going on."*

"Their acts were criminal. The Nazis were accomplices in the most horrific moral outrage of the twentieth century. None of them should ever be forgiven."

These are the responses my friends and family throw in my face whenever I tell the story of meeting Margret's in-laws. "They are all evil." "It could happen again." "They hated us then, and they still hate us now." My friends are convinced they are right. I am the fool.

When I listen to them, I recognize their wrath. My friends, Jews and non-Jews alike, want only their versions of the story. Yet their responses make me question myself: Have I now become a Nazi apologist?

But then I ask myself: Who is so righteous as to decide who is entitled to a hearing? Isn't the capacity for hatred a human trait? Isn't the Nazi descent into bestiality something of which every human being is capable? Isn't it really all too easy, all too ordinary, to take the first and then the subsequent steps into hatred, prejudice, and then atrocity?

Some say such questions are gratuitous. Having never committed an atrocity, one is not compelled to subject oneself to such scrutiny. The only ones to be judged here are those who acted in the interests of the Third Reich. Within the realm of world events, of action and complicity, the questions are not speculative. Acts of atrocity cry out for judgment, and those who commit them deserve to be punished.

But for me the moral dilemma takes on a different cast. I have looked into the eyes of a woman who at sixteen became an ardent Nazi. This same woman at seventy-five asked me to believe that she did not realize the full implications of her actions. To me, conversations aimed at understanding are different in nature from conversations that seek to condemn; to me, a dining table is not a courtroom.

I want to suggest that the specifics of what Anna and I said to one another are less important than the fact that we sat face-to-face, broke bread, and talked together. I want to argue that what is most important here is that our dialogue was witnessed by a grandchild, a member of the third generation. For in this encounter lies the beginning of a new story.

When I looked into Anna's face, I realized that I could no longer condemn all Germans and Austrians. My trips to Austria have shown me that I can no longer identify only with the victims. I now ask in what ways I am linked to the perpetrators. I wonder about the ways I choose not to see. When, I ask, have I closed myself off? When have I dismissed the other? Rather than proclaiming my differences from Anna, I now want to consider our similarities.

ε&

This transformation in my sense of self and of my view of Austrians took place slowly, over many months. But I recall distinctly the moment it began. In February 1997, curled up in a blanket in my bedroom at Tanja's, reading Margret's journal, I am startled when I come across the following words:

I ask you to forgive me.

Forgive you for what? I ask silently. You did not commit atrocities. You are not responsible. For what are you asking to be forgiven?

And even if you feel compelled to ask, who am I to grant your request or to deny it?

I smile at myself. These are such rational questions—questions that assume we can separate who we are from the history we carry within us, from the land in which we live; questions that assume history has no hold, soil no shaping power.

Margret, I think, has nothing to be forgiven for; my granting forgiveness will be, at best, an empty gesture. But as I read her request, it is as if I am seeing myself for the first time. For what I see is a woman who has always found it impossible to forgive; a young girl grown into an adult who has taken pride in condemning the Germans and has happily maintained that they are all Nazis, making it impossible to see anything else about them; a person so sure of her stand, so confident in her righteousness, she has been blind to any other view.

Margret's request reverberates for months. In March, I write back, telling her that I don't understand the concept of forgiveness; that to me, it has always seemed a Christian virtue. I tell her that from the time I was a child, my mother impressed upon me that as Jews, we can never forgive, that we can never let the Germans "off the hook"; that we must, I write, "hold onto our pain, preserve it, never let it go." In April, I write that such fierceness has "the harshness of the desert in it, the hard-edged voice of a vengeful God." From this point of view, I realize, there is no room for forgiveness.

But as the weather in New York becomes warmer, and daffodils and then tulips begin to bloom, I keep thinking about Margret's request. *I ask you to forgive me.* I consider how I now want to "stand in the world." And I start to see aspects of myself in a new light.

It occurs to me that from the time I was a young girl, I experienced the Holocaust as a betrayal so huge and hurtful that I stopped trusting. I turned, quite consciously and deliberately, away from God, saying, in effect, "If You can let this happen, then I want no part of You," finding validation in Eli Wiesel's oft-quoted phrase, "God died at Auschwitz."[1] And while I felt justified in taking this stand, I was unaware how, from that moment on, I effectively closed myself off from any sense of awe in the face of the Ultimate.

I also see, looking back, that from the moment I turned my back on God, I also, subtly, turned my back on humankind. I lived within a self-made protective shell. Carefully camouflaged, I nonetheless stood in the world as a woman who bore the burden of betrayal.

And so, all through the spring, I struggle: Do I forgive Margret, or do I not? Even if I do, I am not convinced that anything I say can lessen her pain or absolve her of the collective guilt she is experiencing. But, on the other hand, how can I know what will come from forgiving her if I refuse to do so? I care deeply for her; I have been close enough to her anguish to know its depth. Can I willingly deny my friend the solace my words might bring?

In May, I write to Margret and tell her, simply, that I forgive her. I don't expect any great change to occur. And to Margret, nothing life-altering happens. It is in my life that these words reverberate.

I notice that the act of granting forgiveness carries great resonance. Words of forgiveness are not mere words spoken into a void. They are performative: speaking them alters me. For once I do, the grip of hatred and righteousness begins to loosen. I begin to feel as though I have shed a layer of my skin, a covering that has encased me and kept me closed. Suddenly, I am free to see my past differently, to reinterpret it, and to extend compassion to the young girl who could not accept the world's betrayal of her people. I notice, much to my great surprise, that I stand in the world with a new sense of freedom, no longer so burdened, not quite so suspicious.

Soon I notice something else: It is a relief not to stand in the world as someone who is, has been, and expects to be betrayed. I feel as if my step is lighter, as if my blood flows more freely. It feels new, as if there are untapped possibilities here—possibilities I could never have imagined had I not forgiven Margret.

I feel compassion for Margret. I see my own struggles reflected in her anger and shame. And it is natural for me to want to reach out and respond. It is harder for me to see myself in her mother-in-law. And yet this is precisely where this inquiry has taken me—to Anna's face, to her deeds, to her humanity. She was shaped by the land in which she lived, by her parents and her culture. Must I now condemn her? Must I turn my back because she did not see, refused to see, turned away? Isn't her turning away all too human?

Anna's turning away from the implications of her actions serves as a mirror for me. In her blindness I see my own. I see, in fact, the blindness of all people, of all races and nationalities, whenever we look at others but refuse to see them, when we allow inherited hatreds to close us off from compassion and understanding.

The act of forgiving Margret leads me to reflect on larger issues. It teaches me that forgiveness radically affects the life of the one who forgives. It shows me that words spoken in certain contexts can change one's relationship to the past even if they cannot alter the past itself. But most of all it teaches me a human lesson, one that moves me beyond my own private pain and personal story.

I consider the countless ways human beings blind themselves. We turn away from those we have been taught to fear or to hate; we allow pettiness to turn to scorn; we become caught up in self-protection; and often unthinkingly, we teach our children to do the same: to carry on and to live out the stories that justify our inherited hatreds and acts of wrongdoing. It is this all-too-human failing, the blindness we perpetuate from generation to generation, that calls out most of all for forgiveness.

To take such a stand is not to proclaim that the wrongs of the Holocaust can be righted. The loss can never be restored. What remains is a huge emptiness. Those who brought it about will carry the knowledge of what they did to their graves. But what, then, remains beyond the emptiness? What do those of us who live in its aftermath inherit? What are we to do? How are we to act?

I have feared that raising such questions risks denigrating the memory of the millions who entered the gas chambers or lost their lives in ghettoes or in hastily dug, unmarked graves. What was taken from them—their lives, their loved ones, the continuity of family— is not forgivable. They remain victims of genocide.

But working in Austria and coming to know a small group of Austrians and their families has allowed me to see the agony of those who carry this legacy from the other side. It has allowed me to see that each side has inherited its own mix of horror and pain, sadness and loss, confusion and misunderstanding. And I now see how the silence and shame carried by many children and grandchildren of the perpetrators have their own unbearable weight.

I no longer think that these burdens must remain the only legacy of the Holocaust. Unspeakable loathing and inexpressible regret are not, I am convinced, the only responses. I now see an alternative. For if standing on Austrian soil has taught me anything, it is that new tasks fall to new generations. And these tasks begin by turning toward those we cast as our enemies, asking for their stories, and listening to them in the spirit of dialogue.

Not to do so is to remain blind—at great cost. For if we continue to reject the other, if we keep turning away, if we continue to stand only on ground we consider safe and familiar, we perpetuate the ignorance, the silence, the one-sidedness, and the hatred.

The twenty-first century must begin with the courage to reach across ethnic divisions and inherited hatreds with a human gesture. In *The Sunflower*, when faced with the request to forgive a young Nazi soldier who was about to die, Simon Wiesenthal writes that he walked away.[2] But sixty years later, do we still walk away? This is the task that falls to the next generation: finding places to stand as witnesses and as friends, allowing the earth's tortured, blood-soaked soil to give rise to new stories.

Margret and I began to live a new story the moment we faced each other, spoke honestly about our fears, and made requests we each felt were "asking too much." The letters, the e-mails, the hours of talking and writing and asking and apologizing took us inside each other's minds and hearts. None of this happened easily. At each step, we struggled to create the stories that would now represent us—the stories we would want to pass on to our children. The story took a new turn when Margret asked me to forgive her. Its shape shifted again, when, at the end of my trip in October, I asked Margret to accompany me to a Nazi concentration camp.

11

When the Wind Whispers

On Friday, July 10, 1998, two years after we first met, Margret and I meet again, this time with an explicit agenda: to visit the Mauthausen Concentration Camp in upper Austria, on the outskirts of Linz, the town where Hitler was born. If you asked us why, we might say many things. We are teachers. We see it as our task to make this history our own, to take it in deeply, so that we can return to our classrooms and teach. But we are also friends now, an Austrian and an American, a Christian and a Jew. We want to stand together on this ground.

We are staying at Margret's mother's flat in Linz. Her mom is away visiting relatives. Margret drove here from her home in Innsbruck. I took the train from Vienna. She met me at the station late at night.

In the morning when I awake, I look out the window. The sky is overcast. For summer, it is surprisingly chilly. Margret gets up and makes coffee as I set out the plates for breakfast. We eat, chatting aimlessly. We are both edgy.

"Did you sleep well?" she asks.

"Not really," I answer. "What time do you think we'll get back?"

"I don't know," she muses. "We have all day."

The milk is sour. Margret rummages in the pantry until she finds some packaged non-dairy creamer. Within an hour, we are on the road. Margret avoids the highway, preferring the local route. As we approach the town of Mauthausen, she slows down. "There is the town," she says, her voice unusually flat. It resembles many small towns I've seen in Austria: attractive, quaint, innocuous with its flowers, its brown wooden houses, its town square.

We look innocuous, too: two women out for a drive. But this gray summer morning, we are quiet. We don't chat, as we usually do, about our daughters or our students. We know our outing is anything but innocuous. We are making a pilgrimage to a site of death.

I look out the side window. This land, I think, must have looked much the same for centuries: the same immense sky, the same fields, neatly plowed, the same trees with their silver-tipped leaves growing ever taller. It has a timeless quality, the countryside reminiscent of a Brueghel landscape. Already my heart feels heavy, weighed down by the knowledge of what else happened here. I glance at Margret. She is intent on driving, her hands tightly gripping the wheel, her mouth firm.

We are driving up a winding road that ascends gently into the hills. We pass a grove of pine trees, a barn or two. The houses are further apart now. One has a swing set and an overturned bike out front. As we come around a bend, I gasp. Out of nowhere looms a massive stone wall with a guard tower on top. The wall is so long, I can't see where it ends. It appears to stretch on forever. My first thought: It's a fortress.

Margret, who has been here before with her students, turns into the small visitors' lot, parks the car, and sighs heavily. As I get out of the car, I shiver and pull my jacket tighter around me. It is still early. Not many tourists, only a few other cars. We walk ahead without talking.

Two blackbirds whirl overhead, swooping down low in the dark sky. We pass underneath the guard tower and walk through the entrance gate. We enter the garage yard, the first gathering place. I know the numbers. Close to 200,000 prisoners passed through this yard; more than half died in Mauthausen, the largest Nazi concentration camp in Austria, or in one of its more than sixty subcamps. But it is not facts I am after today. I want to stand here and let this place speak to me. I want to hear the massive wooden doors slam shut; the dogs bark ferociously as they strain on their leashes; the Nazis scream commands. I listen to the stillness. What do I hear? Only the beating of my heart.

My throat tightens. Tears sting my eyes. I am trying to absorb the nightmare eyes can no longer see. I glance again at Margret. She looks back. Quickly we both look away and move on. We climb some stairs, pass the SS headquarters, pay the entrance fee, and enter the main camp.

Each building is neatly labeled. There are rows of barracks. We pass the *Appelplatz*, where roll call occurred every day, at first three times daily, later on only twice a day, where emaciated inmates stood for hours, where the band played at hangings. The kitchen. The infirmary. We walk around not yet prepared to enter. Wordlessly, we move closer to the perimeter, search the sky beyond the barbed wire, read the plaques on the stone walls. There is a quote in German from Brecht. Margret translates: "Those who did not give in were slain; those who were slain never gave in."

The plaques are from Italy, Germany, Slovenia, America, Israel, Russia, and the list goes on. Honored are prisoners of war, Jews, gypsies, homosexuals, resistance fighters. Of course, it hits me: This place is a huge graveyard with plaques to commemorate the dead. I inhale deeply, but feel as if I still cannot breathe.

A chill wind blows. I have goose bumps. We walk inside one of the buildings. What once served as the kitchen has been transformed into a museum with newsreel footage, photographs, and newspaper articles that document Hitler's rise to power. The story is not new to me. But I stand transfixed nonetheless as the newsreels play over and over: March 1938, the *Anschluss*, Hitler in the Heldenplatz, the Viennese crowds delirious with joy.

"Mass psychosis," I mutter, as I try to imagine what it must have been like to stand there, cheering, waving, caught in the spell of that horrid voice. Margret and I have discussed this many times. Her parents, her in-laws, the parents and grandparents of people in our generation, were young then. The majority adored Hitler, yearned for Austria to return to its former greatness, and contributed, knowingly or not, to the destruction of the Jews. My mouth tightens in disgust. I brace myself for what lies ahead.

We pause at the photographs of women, gypsies, and schoolchildren. Margret calls my attention to one picture in the corner of a display case. In it, children stand at their desks, posing politely for the photographer. Someone has cut out the faces of those who were Jewish. Over half stand there as bodies without heads.

We stare at the propaganda posters of Hitler youth with their shapely bodies, their bulging muscles, their clean faces; of young, blond women blooming with health; of mothers who receive ribbons for making babies for Hitler. We recoil from the posters of fat Jews with hooked noses and dark coats, of money-grubbing Jews, their pockets overflowing with schillings, of salacious Jews, leering at children. We shake our heads in disgust, wishing to rid ourselves of such images, as if through denial we can push away the pain. Soon we've had enough and go outside.

We cross the *Appelplatz* and stand in front of one of the barracks. The green paint is peeling. A sign informs us that each building was built to accommodate 200 but usually contained between 300 and 500 prisoners. The showers were used for punishment. Inmates were forced to stand naked under freezing water. Most did not survive such treatment.

Inside the floors creak. The rooms are empty except for a bunk bed or two. It all looks so harmless. It could be a defunct summer camp in the Adirondacks, except for a photograph of inmates with large eyes and starving bodies staring at me silently over a divide of more than fifty years.

We cross the square again. It is starting to rain. We enter a building called "the prison." *As if the entire place were not a prison,* I think. But this building is markedly different. There are bars on the windows and small cells inside. The air is stale. I know people were beaten here, thrown against the cell walls, tortured.

Between 1939 and 1945, a sign informs us, 4,600 men and women were prisoners in this jail. Of those, 4,200 were killed by gas, shooting, or hanging. We follow the arrows on the floor and come upon a crematorium. This one, we are told, operated from May 5, 1940, through May 3, 1945. Hitler, I know, had already committed suicide at the end of April. But the murders continued nonetheless, the machinery of death mindless, unabated.

Next to the crematorium is the dressing room. It is here that gold teeth were removed from corpses. I touch the cold, stone table; imagine the mouths pried open, the gold extracted, then turned into bullion and sent by the Reichsbank to Switzerland and Portugal.

We have entered this building from the wrong end. We are tracing the history of destruction backwards, moving from the final process to the beginning. Now we come to a room labeled *Leichenraum,* cold storage. A place to store the corpses prior to dissection and cremation. I shudder.

We walk into a room with gallows, a crossbeam, metal hooks on the wall. Once again, my throat closes. I feel as if I am about to gag. In this room, we read, one corner was set up for neck shots. A sign explains that here we can see a special measuring gadget, a

Galgenrichtstatte, a device which enabled the executioner to measure the victim's height accurately, allowing one clean shot through the throat. I cannot swallow.

We turn around and come upon *die Gaskammer*. The gas chamber. It is tiny, maybe ten feet by ten feet, lined with white tiles, the ceiling fit with shower heads, a peep hole in its massive door, a miniature version of what remains today at Auschwitz, of what once existed at Treblinka, Sobibor, and Majdanek. I know that Mauthausen was planned as a slave labor camp, not an extermination camp. But clearly, labor camps were also places of extermination. I stand here attempting to grasp the meaning of such a place. The air in this room is musty. Margret has tears in her eyes. I suppress the urge to run.

In an adjacent room, we discover another crematorium. This one has two separate chambers for bodies. This room is twice the size of the one we saw earlier and is filled with memorials. On the walls, the floor, the metal stretcher that once held the corpses, we see candles, chocolate, pictures, wreaths, drumsticks, books—worldly reminders of those who were ripped from the world. A *yahrzeit* candle burns at the base of the crematorium. It is lit daily in memory of the dead. There are plaques on the walls in Italian, Dutch, Greek, English, Hebrew, German, French, Russian, and some languages I do not recognize.

Slowly we leave this place. We make our way upstairs to what appears to be an exhibit. There are pictures on the walls, this time of the camp itself, pictures of bodies lying naked in the snow, skin hanging off half-alive skeletons, genitals limp and exposed, of corpses thrown against electrified fences, of starving children.

I walk over to a scale model of the camp. If I didn't know better, I could mistake it for a backdrop for a set of Lionel trains, the kind my brothers loved to play with as boys.

On a nearby sign I read that the ratio of inmates to guards was fifteen to one. It is impossible not to have the next thought: What would have been the chances? Had they only realized—a useless thought, an impossible dream.

In this exhibit, the explanatory texts are written only in German. I no longer have the energy to work at translating. I see lists of countries with names, ages, dates. More pictures of children. A case filled with instruments of torture: whips, sticks, a bench, a syringe six inches long. I feel myself going numb.

But I am drawn to one other case. The objects fashioned secretly by inmates: chess pieces carved surreptitiously, drawings made on scraps of paper, poems in tiny handwriting. My heart swells with pride, pity, longing. Even here, I nod to myself, even here: the human need to create, to make beauty, the human need to record.

Margret and I are walking at different paces, each alone now. We meet up at the end of the exhibit. She looks pale, drawn. Is that the way I look to her? Gently, we touch each other's arms, search each other's faces: Have you had enough? Can you take any more? Our eyes transmit unspoken messages. Can we, even here, still find solace in each other's presence?

I can see by her face that it makes no difference whether this is one's first visit or one's tenth. To open oneself to atrocity is to be shocked, pained, altered. We don't yet know what will come of this, but we agree to keep going, to move on. We persevere.

It is almost 2:00 P.M. A film about Mauthausen is about to be shown. We take seats. It is a documentary that consists primarily of interviews with eyewitnesses: a priest who admits knowing that evil was being committed; a woman whose mother hid some escaped Russian prisoners; a local man who laughs nervously; an American GI who weeps. Worst of all are the images in which no one speaks: the footage of dead bodies being thrown onto wooden wagons, eyes open, mouths drawn back, teeth jutting out, flies swarming.

We walk outside together. We are speechless. For the past two years we have talked endlessly. Now we have nothing to say. Margret suppresses a sob. I wipe my eyes. Silently, we walk toward an open area, once the site of barracks, now a cemetery, with trees, grass, gravestones. We walk to the center. The wind blows. It warms us. I can almost hear it whispering. We look at one another and allow the tears to come.

"It is so hard to look into your eyes," Margret says softly. I know it shames her that these events happened here, in her country.

I am no stranger to shame. Shame is what I felt at thirteen when I realized that I, too, could have been stripped naked and sent to the gas chamber. Even worse was imagining my mother, standing naked and defenseless, and my father, powerless to protect us.

I am a descendant of the victims; Margret, of the victimizers. We have come to explore this legacy, to face our shame and horror together. We believe that being here together will teach us something coming here alone cannot, that from this journey something new might be born, a new tale might be told.

Standing with Margret in the middle of a graveyard at Maut-hausen, I think that if we listen to the wind, we will hear its message. If we listen to our hearts, we will hear more than separate heartbeats.

ॐ

We have one more site to visit: the quarry. It is here that thousands of prisoners were put to work, hauling stones. Here, thousands perished, crushed under the weight of the rocks or shot by the guards. We read that the Nazis dubbed this area the Parachutists' Cliff because the SS made a sport of throwing entire transports of Jews onto the boulders below.

To reach the quarry, we must leave the main camp and walk along a dusty path. The sun is attempting to break through the clouds. It warms us as we pass by the monuments and memorials that spring up from the earth, symbols of remembrance from eighteen different countries, each one different in design, all strangely disquieting in their silence.

I pause at one: the Hungarian Memorial to the Holocaust. Massive stone figures stand on a block of stone, legs apart, arms raised, fists clenched. This sculpture speaks to me, conveying anguish, resistance, struggle—and ultimately, suvival. Tears spring to my eyes. Hatred has not won. Margret and I stand in silence, then move on.

When we arrive at the top of the quarry, we know without speaking that we will descend to the bottom. I have read about the "death steps," all 186 of them, of unequal height, used by prisoners to haul blocks of stone on their shoulders, day after day, only to return and haul some more. Later, as we climb up, I silently count them. I do not pause to catch my breath and arrive at the top panting, sweating, nearly exhausted; I, in good health, after one trip, carrying only a purse.

When we reach the quarry pit, we sit on the ground and look around. It is peaceful. The sun shines brightly now. A bee buzzes, a cricket chirps. A heavy-set man passes by with three children. From their accent, Margret can tell they are locals.

"I'm glad," she says, "that ordinary people bring their kids here." I nod.

We talk of other massacres: Wounded Knee, Rwanda, Bosnia. We resist the urge to make comparisons. We know that there are other atrocities to face; we know that suffering is not limited to this event. But it is this event we choose to take on together. Given who we are, it is the Holocaust that calls us.

I am spent. My eyes sting; my throat hurts. I feel indescribably sad. Conflicting impulses come and go. The desire to scream, to rage, to decry the injustice competes with the wish to withdraw, to hide, to ignore so much loss and pain. Any attempt at understanding is impossible.

I look at Margret. We are sitting among the rocks, both quiet. What brought me to see my pain reflected in her eyes or her pain answered in mine? What brought us here together and to what end? I breathe in, let the air reach down into my lungs, my body, then slowly exhale. I notice my throat is not quite so tight. Where is the constriction? I wonder. Slowly, it dawns on me: I have come to a place I had never wanted to know, stood on ground I have feared since I was a child, and I did so by the side of a woman whose mother tongue I had long equated with everything evil in the world. Suddenly, it strikes me, the fear that has gripped me for so long has lost its hold.

With a new breath comes a sense of relief. It was right to come here. I am glad I finally did it, glad I finally turned toward the agony rather than away. The story of coming to Mauthausen is not the only story I have to tell or even the most important. But without it, I realize, the others would have seemed strangely incomplete.

Sitting in the pit of the quarry, letting myself be warmed by the sun and my friendship with Margret, I realize that I will never have answers. Standing on Austrian soil will always be unsettling for me; this history is too vast, the losses too great, to be put to rest.

But I do know that what began as a classroom inquiry has become a life-altering event. What began as a simple invitation to teach has become a lifelong calling to learn. And I know this: If you listen to the wind, you can hear it whisper.

ह

A warm wind caresses my cheeks,
Blows gently,
Lifting my hair.
Stand still, it whispers.
And listen.

Leaves rustle.
The branches sway.
And I remain motionless,
Wishing to obey.
Straining my ears to hear.

I sense them; I do.
Their presence descends
Upon me
Like angels from on high.
And then I hear it:

The voice in the wind
That commands me.
Take your friend's hand,
Hold her arm,
And walk from this place.

Take your children
Sing them songs of love.
And let the legacy
Of hatred
Remain here.

As the grass grows greener
As the slender trees
Widen with age,
Tell your story.

Let it be a balm
To the pain
Lodged in this land.

From where, I wonder,
Do such words come?

For rising within and around me,
I hear words,
Prayerful words,
Words I have never heard
Before.

May those who strangled
On this soil
Find their rest.

May stories
That instill such hatred
Cease.
And may new stories
Be borne
In their place.

May we all find
The enemy within
And the beloved
Among the enemy.

May this hated and hateful land
Give birth to a new tale
May the tale speak
For what has not been spoken.

May it breathe new life
Into a silenced land
A shameful past,
The most hardened heart.

Osay Shalom.

Epilogue: On American Soil

t is one of those perfect June days in New York. The sky is a clear blue, the air crisp, the clouds white and puffy— perfect for an outdoor graduation. At The City College of The City University of New York at Convent Avenue and West 138th Street, all is ready: chairs for the spectators, a podium for the speakers, arcs of multi-colored balloons in pinks, purples, oranges, and whites under which faculty in formal academic attire and then graduates will march.

The Austrian teachers arrive early. Some come by subway; others take taxis. With spouses, children, and parents in tow, they make their way through the maze of barricades erected to keep order among what will soon become an unruly crowd of cheering families. Dr. Susan Weil, the coordinator of the M.A. program, ushers them inside to hand them caps and gowns and to help them get dressed. I remain outside to help the families find seats.

All of the Austrian teachers have come to New York for graduation, even Thomas who has not yet finished his thesis. He still wants to celebrate, he tells me, whether or not he completes the program. No one at City College objects. It is exciting to welcome all of the teachers to New York, especially to City College, in the heart of Harlem.

Everyone has received a leave from work to spend graduation week in New York. Most are staying in hotels in Manhattan. Margret, Gert, and Cara are staying with me in Riverdale. Trips to the Museum of Modern Art, the Metropolitan Museum, the Statue of Liberty, the World Trade Center, Chinatown—even a boat ride around Manhattan on the Circle Line—have been planned. Months before,

I reserved seats to the Broadway production of *The Lion King* for Margret's family and mine. Following graduation, I am hosting a graduation party, American style, for the teachers and their families: a barbecue with hot dogs, hamburgers, corn on the cob, French fries, soda and, for them, beer and *Apfelsaft gespritzt*.

Packed in among the parents, grandparents, children, and grandchildren of City College's thousands of graduates, surrounded by African American parents carrying bouquets, Dominican girls in taffeta dresses, Haitian boys in blue suits, sari-clad grandmothers pushing strollers, wide-eyed toddlers sticky with cotton candy, the wind blowing and the band playing, the families and friends of the Austrian teachers are caught up in the moment. They raise their voices loud, clapping and cheering, as Andrea, Astrid, Christa, Hans, Hilde, Ingrid, Margret, Martina, Tanja, and Ursula walk down the aisle to receive their degrees.

Back at my house, the faculty toasts the teachers, and the teachers toast us. Gathering in small groups, in the living room, on the deck, in view of the Hudson River, we chat.

"I've never seen so many people at a graduation," says Hilde.

"And they were so . . . lively," comments Ingrid.

Recalling the crowd and the poster board signs with "Congratulations, Tanisha" and "You did it, Mom!" waving in the air, I ask, "It's not like that at Austrian graduations?"

Everyone laughs.

"Our graduations are formal events," explains Hans, "people would never be so loud. There is decorum."

"And no babies," remarks Andrea.

"Yes, and tedium," laughs Margret.

"Oh, but it was wonderful," says Christa. "It was touching to see how happy the families were. You could feel the pride."

"And the band? It was spectacular. All those horns blaring—and the big, bass drum. I loved it," says Thomas.

We all loved it. Having worked so long and so hard, we are thrilled to be celebrating together, drinking, laughing, watching the barges travel upstream. Together, we have raised hard questions and have found common ground. And today I have opened my home— and my heart—to Austrians.

ଅ

In the ensuing years, much happens to the Austrian teachers—and to me.

Andrea, upon returning to Innsbruck, asks me to help her arrange a partnership with a Jewish high school in New York. For one term, her Austrian students and a group of Orthodox Jews from a day school on Long Island read the same book, Livia Bitton-Jackson's *I Have Lived A Thousand Years*, and then exchange weekly e-mails, sharing reactions and responses to this survivor's story. Andrea then goes on to pursue a doctoral degree at the University of Innsbruck, becoming an authority on portfolio assessment. Her work leads to the acceptance of portfolios as an official alternative to the standard written tests in Austrian high schools.

Ingrid begins corresponding with me about books. She takes her students on field trips to Holocaust sites and to the Jewish Museum near her home, a place she comes to know well. She becomes an expert on survivor testimonies and takes an increasing interest in Jewish-Austrian relations.

Christa, too, becomes an avid reader of Holocaust testimonies. Now Holocaust stories written for young adults are among the books her students can choose to read in their reading and writing club. Isabella Leitner's *The Big Lie: A True Story* becomes a cherished book for her fourteen-year-old girls. Christa also starts working with teachers, demonstrating student-centered approaches to language learning, and serves on a committee that designs the Austrian version of the European Language Portfolio.

Although he gives it several more tries, meeting with me when I return to teach other groups in Austria, Thomas never finds a topic for his thesis. Eventually, he stops trying.

Tanja resigns from her permanent job at the university and opens a consulting firm, conducting workshops on English language and literacy for businesses and schools. In 2003, her institute is ranked sixth in Austria by a respected business monthly, and the *Oesterreichischer Bundesverlag*, the Austrian national textbook publisher, invites her to develop a new four-volume English textbook series for Austrian schools. In 1997, she falls in love with an Austrian; several years later she marries him.

After several more years teaching, Hilde retires. Martina becomes a teacher trainer at a local pedagogical institute. Hans develops a university program in English-language skills for business students and creates a job center modeled on career service programs in American universities. And Astrid, much to my surprise, stays in touch by e-mail. Every four months, like clockwork, she sends a note, asking about my family, commenting on world events, or letting me know when the Vienna Philharmonic will be playing at Carnegie Hall.

Margret and I continue to live parallel lives. In addition to teaching history and English at her high school, Margret begins teaching university courses on writing pedagogy for prospective teachers. I, too, add another focus to my life at school: I design and teach courses on the Holocaust, focusing in part on the roots of hatred, on the ways ethnic and religious groups are taught to cast others as their enemies.

The inquiry Margret and I began also continues to resonate in our personal lives. In April of 2001, Margret comes to New York to celebrate Passover with my family. She accompanies us to a Seder, a modern version of the gathering I was reminded of in 1996 when I first walked along the Inn River. In 2001, my father's extended family numbers 110. This time, we gather not in the basement of a *shul* but in a private room in a restaurant in Livingston, New Jersey, and this time, I am among the adults reading from the prayer book while my children and their younger cousins refuse to sit still.

On one of her trips to New York, Margret meets my mother. On one of my trips to Innsbruck, I meet hers. I also plan to talk again with Anna. But by the time I return to Innsbruck, Anna has been diagnosed with cancer. Several rounds of chemotherapy have left her thin and worn, a pale replica of the woman I spoke to several years before. This time, when I go to see her, I hold her hand.

Between 1999 and 2002, I continue to travel to Austria to teach other groups of teachers enrolled in the M.A. program. Whenever I ask participants to read Vito Perrone and to consider if teaching is a moral as well as an intellectual act, I face the same response I faced in Innsbruck: surprise mixed with shock. Some things, it seems, do not change. But some things do.

After twenty-two years of marriage, Arthur and I divorce. He no longer travels with me to Austria, but Sara, Josh, and Sam often do. In winter, they go tobogganing with Margret; in summer, rock climbing with Gert. Together, we hike the glaciers and snowcapped peaks of the Austrian Alps and sleep in the massive, three-story stone inns, called *Huetten*, built high above the timber line in the early 1900s by a German hiking society.

In Innsbruck, Sara, Josh, and Sam, teenagers now, party late into the night with Cara and her friends; they learn to like *Spinatknoedel* and to joke in German. And they learn a lesson I hadn't known I wanted to teach them when I first traveled to Austria: in the land one's mother once hated, it is possible to make lifelong friends.

Acknowledgments

Austria—a country I never wanted to visit. Innsbruck—stunningly beautiful, breathtaking, awe-inspiring. Teaching—my life's work.

Everyone I thank here has heard this story, probably far too often. Each has, in his or her own way, helped me see the story in a new light; helped me fashion it so that it became clearer; listened to me, over drinks or dinner, nibbling on sushi or samosas, walking in the park or talking on the phone, so that I heard it freshly and understood better what I next needed to do.

It's been a long process, several years at least. Talking about Nazis and Jews, belief and nonbelief, the purpose of teaching, classroom research, dialogue, redemption, the meaning of God. These themes are woven throughout this book. And the traces of many people, whose ideas both challenged and supported mine, are present in these pages.

I thank you all:

Goldie Alfasi and John Siffert, who, over dinner, first saw the promise.

The rabbis who taught me about Judaism: Steven Greenberg, James Hyman, Dianne Esses, Irving Greenberg, and Avi Weiss.

Dear friends and members of my Jewish Study Group: Meredith Feinman and Eric Seiff, Judy Hochman and Richard Fuchs, and Ronnie Scharfman and Joe Youngerman.

Neighbors who listened: Sybil Wailand and Barry Willner, Manon and Ian Slome, Martha Olson and Bill Bernstein, Ellen Blye and Elliot Arons, June Bingham and Robert Birge, Blu Greenberg, Carla Glasser, Hilary Baum, Betty Diamond and Bruce Volpe.

Holocaust survivors, dear friends, whose lives inspired me to make peace with my own demons: Livia Bitton-Jackson and Irving Roth. Holocaust scholars and dear friends who counseled me when the road became rough: Eva Fleischner, Mark Goldberg, and Ruth Zerner.

Professional colleagues: Susan Weil and Alfred S. Posamentier of The City College, The City University of New York, Ingrid Farthofer and Elisabeth Nabor-Kock of the Austrian-American Educational Cooperation Association in Vienna, Horst Schreiber of the Institute for Contemporary History in Innsbruck, Judith Block, Fran Keneston, and Priscilla Ross at State University of New York Press, my friends and colleagues at the New York City Writing Project and in the English departments at Lehman College and the CUNY Graduate Center, too numerous to name.

Current and former graduate students, particularly Tim McCormack, Mark McBeth, and Emily Schnee, who while working on their own projects always asked about mine.

My Austrian students from Innsbruck, from Feldkirch, and from Vienna—in particular, Tanja Westfall, and the nine other teachers who, though represented here pseudonymously, hold a very real place in my life and my heart.

Those who commented critically on drafts: Mimi Schwartz, Nancy Sommers, Joe Trimmer, Judith Rodgers, Maureen Stanton, and Scotia MacRae and, at the eleventh hour, Barbara Hurd and my Cape May writing group.

Those who kept me company, calling or sending e-mail, during the tumultuous last year: Diane Burkhardt, Ed Hack, Ralph Blum, Kathie Packer, Fred Vogel, Naomi and Bill Zitin, Daniel Zitin, Linda Hirsch, Betsy Sargeant, and Charles Schuster.

Those who kept the faith, cheering me on no matter what: Franny and Denny Dennison, Susan Eisenstat and Henry Siegman, Alison Fisch, Shawn Reischmann, and Gene Gendlin.

My trusted friend Nancy Wilson whose unerring ear and love of language made editing a pleasure, and her husband Peter Wilson for welcoming me and my project into their lives.

My loving family: Ruth Perl Fox, Sheri Perl and Jerry Migdol, Richard Perl and Susan Fried Perl, and Bob and Judy Perl.

The Fessler family: Cara, Gert, Anna, Luis, and Margret, my soul sister.

My ex-husband Arthur Egendorf, who lived this story with me, and my children, Sara, Josh, and Sam, who carry it on.

Notes

Chapter 1. A Simple Invitation

1. Vito Perrone, A Letter to Teachers: Reflections on Schooling and the Art of Teaching (San Francisco: Jossey-Bass, 1991), 4.

2. Ibid., 9.

3. Ibid., 1.

4. Louise Rosenblatt, *Literature as Exploration* (New York: Modern Language Association, 1938/1995), 16.

5. Ibid., 124.

Chapter 4. A Second Course, a Second Inquiry

1. Glenda Bissex, *Partial Truths: A Memoir and Essays on Reading, Writing, and Researching* (Portsmouth, N.H.: Heinemann, 1996), 10.

2. Ibid.

3. Ibid., 181.

4. Ibid., 170–171.

5. Ibid., 90.

6. Ibid.

7. Ibid., 14.

8. Max van Manen, *Researching Lived Experience: Human Science for an Action Sensitive Pedagogy* (Albany: State University of New York Press, 1990), 1.

9. Ibid., 5.

10. Ibid., 4.

11. Ibid., 18.

12. Ibid., 7.

13. Ibid., 12.

14. Ibid., 6.

15. Christine Cziko, "Dialogue Journals: Passing Notes the Academic Way," in *Cityscapes: Eight Views from the Urban Classroom* (Berkeley: National Writing Project, 1996), 101.

16. Howard Banford, "The Blooming of Maricar: Writing Workshop and the Phantom Student," in *Cityscapes*, 3.

17. Marcie Resnick, "Making Connections Between Families and Schools," in *Cityscapes*, 115.

18. Douglas Barnes, James Britton, and Mike Torbe, *Language, the Learner, and the School* (Portsmouth, N.H.: Boynton/Cook-Heinemann, 1969/1990), 106–107.

19. Ibid., 157.

20. Ibid., 125.

21. Bissex, *Partial Truths*, 183.

Chapter 5. Whipped by the Wind

1. Bissex, *Partial Truths*, 184.

2. Max van Manen, *The Tone of Teaching* (Portsmouth, N.H.: Heinemann, 1986), 50.

3. Ibid., 15.

4. Ibid., 42–43.

5. van Manen, *Researching Lived Experience*, 7.

6. Zora Neale Hurston, *Their Eyes Were Watching God* (Chicago: University of Illinois Press, 1937/1978), 17.

7. Hannah Arendt, *The Life of the Mind: Thinking* (New York: Harcourt Brace Jovanovich, 1971/78), 4, 13.

Chapter 7. A Dialogue in Letters

1. Charlotte Delbo, *Auschwitz and After* (New Haven, CT: Yale University Press, 1995), 12.

Chapter 8. Unexpected Lessons

1. Thomas Lux, "The Voice You Hear When You Read Silently," *The New Yorker*, July 14, 1997.

2. Perrone, *A Letter to Teachers*, 6.

Chapter 9. Uncommon Ground

1. *Synagogue Service—New Year and Atonement* (Jersey City, NJ: KTAV Publishing House, n.d.), 251.

2. Ibid.

3. Ibid.

4. Ibid., 234.

5. *Sabbath and Festival Prayer Book with a New Translation, Supplementary Readings and Notes* (New York: Rabbinical Assembly of America, United Synagogue of America, 1988), 304.

Chapter 10. The Question of Forgiveness

1. Although attributed to Elie Weisel, this exact phrase does not appear in any of his work. The closest statement can be found on page 32 of *Night*, where he implies that the God of his childhood died at Auschwitz, not that God no longer exists.

2. Simon Wiesenthal, *The Sunflower* (New York: Schocken, 1976), 97.

Bibliography

Arendt, Hannah. *The Life of the Mind: Thinking*. New York: Harcourt Brace Jovanovich, 1971/78.

Barnes, Douglas, James Britton, and Mike Torbe. *Language, the Learner and the School*. Portsmouth, New Hampshire: Heinemann-Boynton/Cook, 1969/1990.

Bissex, Glenda. *Partial Truths: A Memoir and Essays on Reading, Writing, and Researching*. Portsmouth, New Hampshire: Heinemann, 1996.

Blume, Judy. *Then Again, Maybe I Won't*. New York: Yearling, 1986.

Borowski, Tadeusz. *This Way for the Gas, Ladies and Gentlemen*. New York: Penguin, 1967.

Cityscapes: Eight Views from the Urban Classroom. Berkeley: National Writing Project, 1996.

Cleary, Beverly. *Socks*. New York: Morrow, 1973.

Dahl, Roald. *Matilda*. New York: Puffin, 1990.

Dawidowicz, Lucy. *The War Against the Jews 1933–1945*. New York: Bantam, 1975.

Delbo, Charlotte. *Auschwitz and After*. New Haven: Yale University Press, 1995.

Des Pres, Terrence. Introduction to *Treblinka*, by Jean-Francois Steiner. New York, Penguin, 1994.

Egendorf, Arthur. *Healing from the War: Trauma and Transformation after Vietnam*. Boston: Houghton Mifflin, 1986.

Friedlander, Saul. *Nazi Germany and the Jews*. New York: HarperCollins, 1997.

Gilbert, Martin. *The Holocaust: A History of the Jews of Europe during the Second World War*. New York: Holt, 1985.

Goldhagen, Daniel. *Hitler's Willing Executioners: Ordinary Germans and the Holocaust*. New York: Random House, 1996.

Hegi, Ursula. *Stones from the River*. New York: Scribner, 1994.

Hilberg, Raul: *Perpetrators Victims Bystanders The Jewish Catastrophe, 1933–1945*. New York: HarperCollins, 1992.

Hinton, S. E. *The Outsiders*. New York: Prentice Hall, 1967/1997.

Hurston, Zora Neale. *Their Eyes Were Watching God*. Chicago: University of Illinois Press, 1937/1978.

Krondorfer, Bjorn. *Remembrance and Reconciliation: Encounters between Young Jews and Germans*. New Haven: Yale University Press, 1995.

Levi, Primo. *Survival in Auschwitz*. New York: Simon and Schuster, 1993.

Levin, Meyer. *Eva*. New York: Simon and Schuster, 1959.

Lux, Thomas. "The Voice You Hear When You Read Silently" in *The New Yorker*. July 14, 1997.

Morrison, Toni. *Sula*. New York: Penguin, 1973.

Perrone, Vito. *A Letter to Teachers: Reflections on Schooling and the Art of Teaching*. San Francisco: Jossey-Bass, 1991.

Roiphe, Anne. *A Season for Healing*. New York: Summit, 1988.

Rosenblatt, Louise. *Literature as Exploration*. New York: Modern Language Association, 1938/1995.

Sabbath and Festival Prayer Book with a New Translation, Supplementary Readings and Notes. New York: Rabbinical Assembly of America, United Synagogue of America, 1988.

Semprun, Jorge. *Literature or Life*. New York: Penguin, 1997.

Synagogue Service—New Year and Atonement. Jersey City: KTAV Publishing House, n.d.

van Manen, Max. *The Tone of Teaching*. Portsmouth, New Hampshire: Heinemann, 1986.

———. *Researching Lived Experience: Human Science for an Action Sensitive Pedagogy*. Albany: State University of New York Press, 1990.

Wiesel, Elie. *Night*. New York: Bantam, 1982.

Wiesenthal, Simon. *The Sunflower*. New York: Schocken, 1976.